MANIFEST DESTINY

CHRIS DINGESS — WRITER

MATTHEW ROBERTS — PENCILLER & INKER PAGES 90, 104, 106, 118

TONY AKINS — INKER

OWEN GIENI — COLORIST

PAT BROSSEAU — LETTERER

ARIELLE BASICH — ASSOCIATE EDITOR

SEAN MACKIEWICZ — EDITOR

MATTHEW ROBERTS & OWEN GIENI
COVER ART

IMAGE COMICS, INC.
Robert Kirkman—Chief Operating Officer
Erik Larsen—Chief Financial Officer
Todd McFarlane—President
Marc Silvestri—Chief Executive Officer
Jim Valentino—Vice President
Eric Stephenson—Publisher / Chief Creative Officer
Corey Hart—Director of Sales
Jeff Boison—Director of Publishing Planning & Book Trade Sales
Chris Ross—Director of Digital Sales
Jeff Stang—Director of Specialty Sales
Kat Salazar—Director of PR & Marketing
Drew Gill—Art Director
Heather Doornink—Production Director
Nicole Lapalme—Controller
IMAGECOMICS.COM

For SKYBOUND ENTERTAINMENT
Robert Kirkman - Chairman
David Alpert - CEO
Sean Mackiewicz - SVP, Editor-in-Chief
Shawn Kirkham - SVP, Business Development
Brian Huntington - VP, Online Content
June Alian - Publicity Director
Andres Juarez - Art Director
Jon Moisan - Editor
Arielle Basich - Associate Editor
Carina Taylor - Production Artist
Paul Shin - Business Development Coordinator
Johnny O'Dell - Social Media Manager
Sally Jacka - Skybound Retailer Relations
Dan Petersen - Director of Operations & Events
International inquiries: ag@gcagcneinlrights.com
Licensing inquiries: contact@skybound.com
www.skybound.com

MANIFEST DESTINY
CREATED BY
CHRIS DINGESS

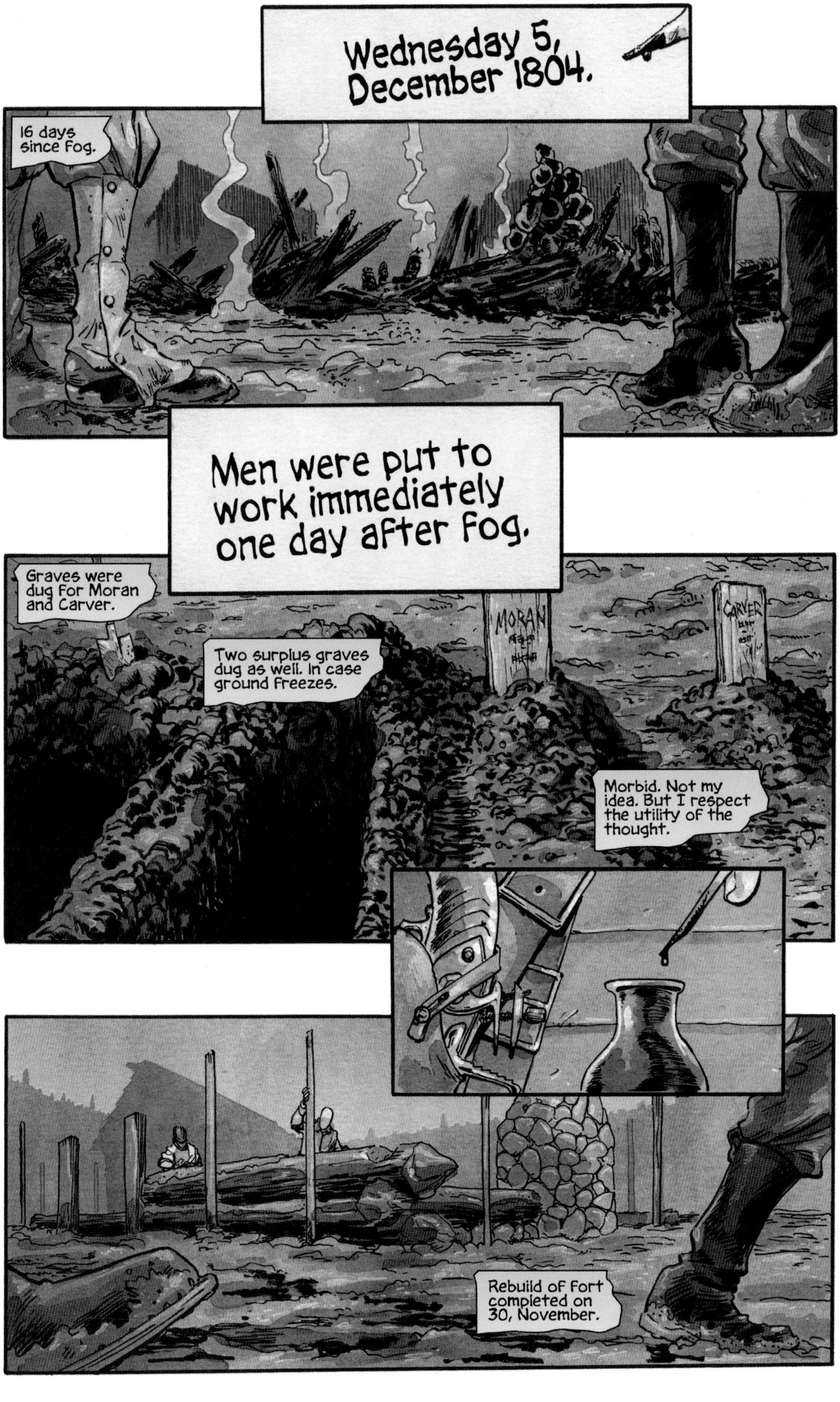
Wednesday 5, December 1804.
16 days since fog.
Men were put to work immediately one day after fog.
Graves were dug for Moran and Carver.
Two surplus graves dug as well. In case ground freezes.
MORAN
CARVER
Morbid. Not my idea. But I respect the utility of the thought.
Rebuild of Fort completed on 30, November.

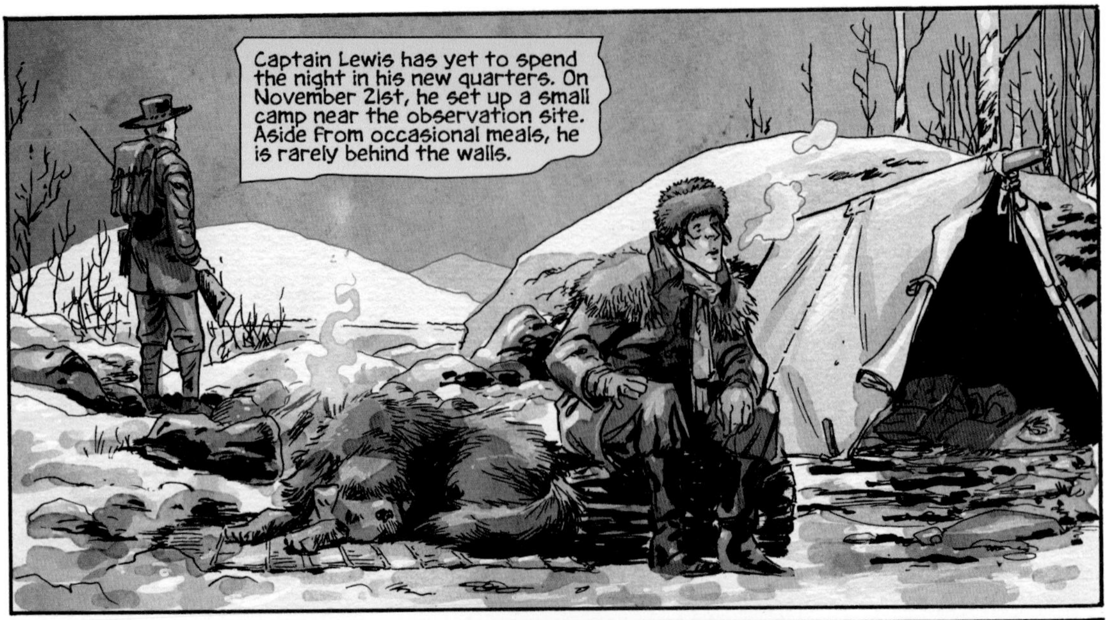
Captain Lewis has yet to spend the night in his new quarters. On November 21st, he set up a small camp near the observation site. Aside from occasional meals, he is rarely behind the walls.

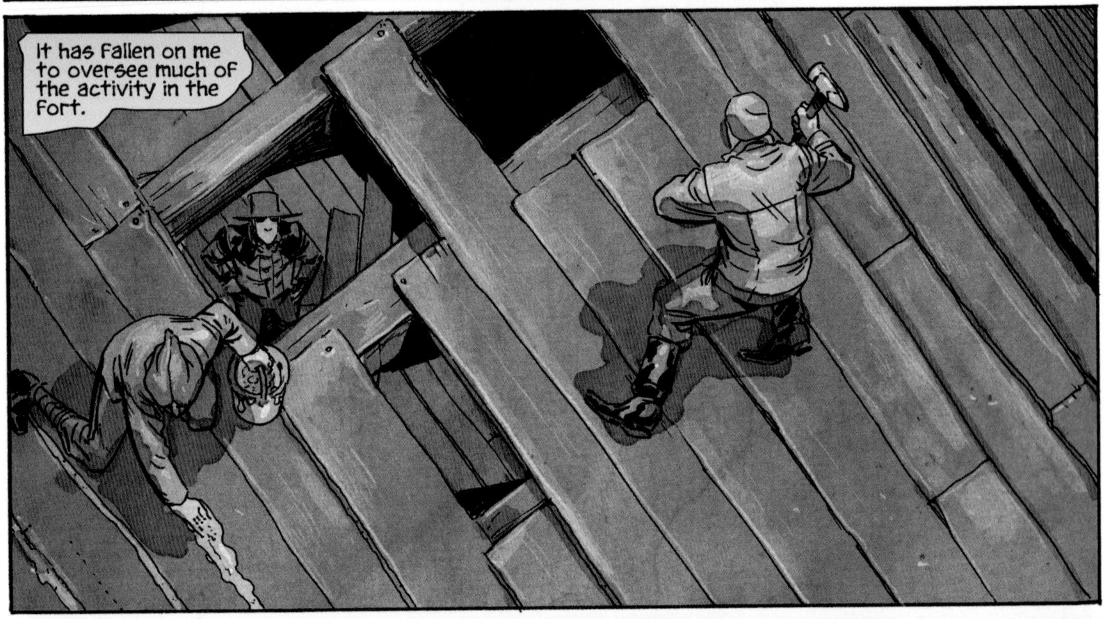
It has fallen on me to oversee much of the activity in the fort.

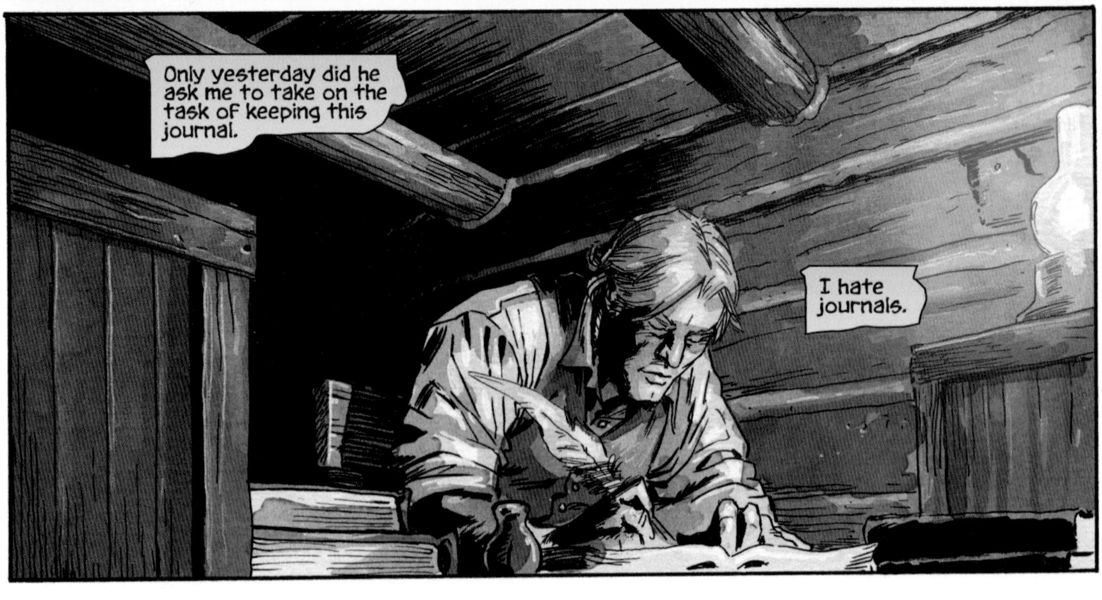
Only yesterday did he ask me to take on the task of keeping this journal.
I hate journals.

Lewis insists on focusing his attention on the arch. And so I write, bringing events up to date.

I hate writing.

I admire Lewis's determination. It must be hard to study something you cannot see.

Guards are posted at the site day and night. Miserable assignment. They do not complain as far as I know.

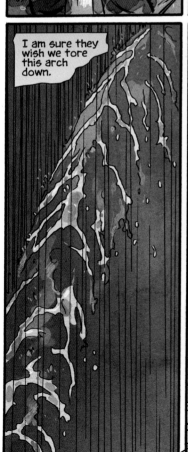

I am sure they wish we tore this arch down.

As long as it is here, so is the fear it brings.

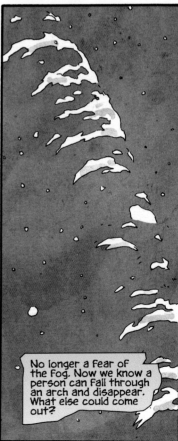

No longer a fear of the fog. Now we know a person can fall through an arch and disappear. What else could come out?

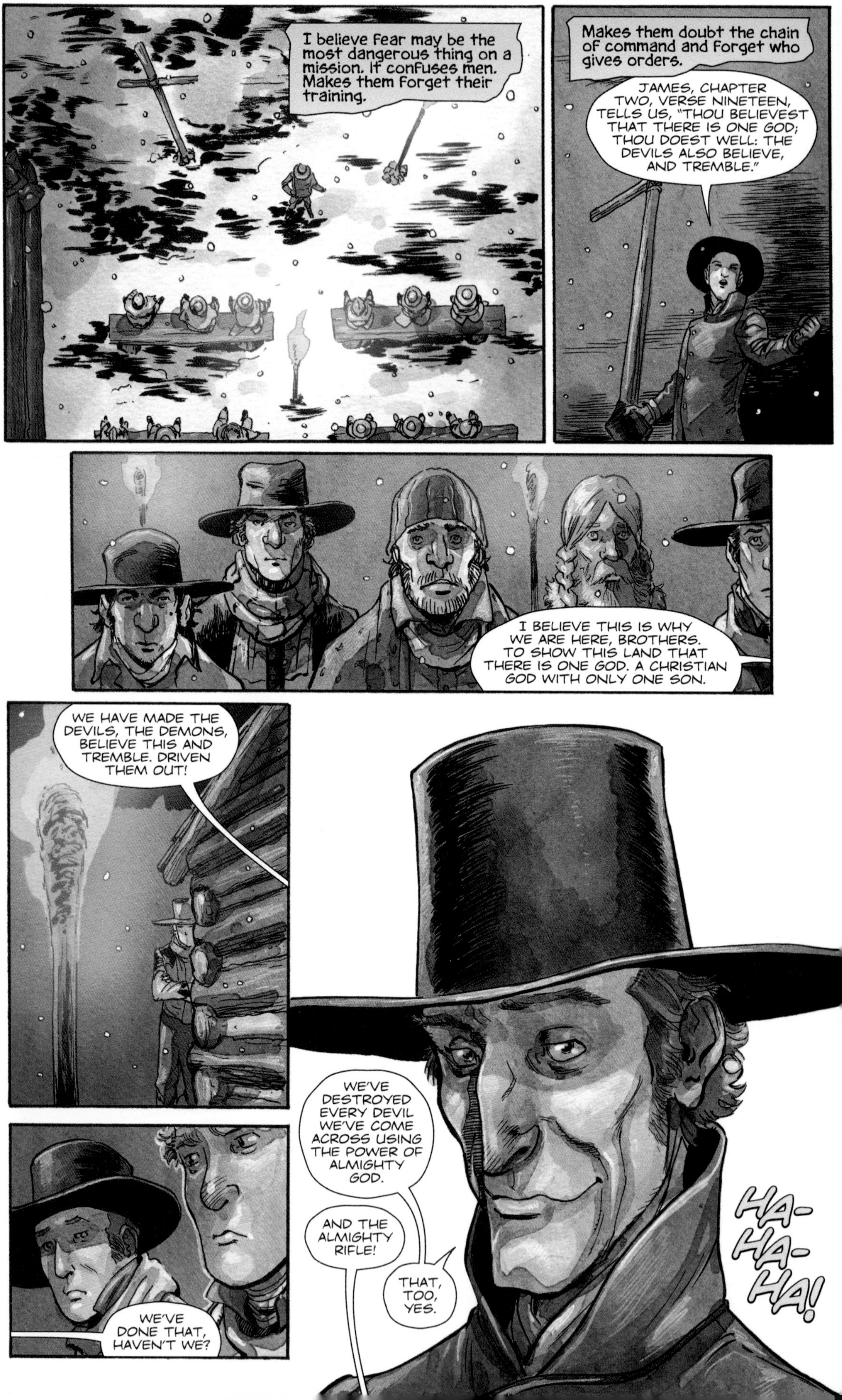
I believe fear may be the most dangerous thing on a mission. It confuses men. Makes them forget their training.
Makes them doubt the chain of command and forget who gives orders.
JAMES, CHAPTER TWO, VERSE NINETEEN, TELLS US, "THOU BELIEVEST THAT THERE IS ONE GOD; THOU DOEST WELL: THE DEVILS ALSO BELIEVE, AND TREMBLE."
I BELIEVE THIS IS WHY WE ARE HERE, BROTHERS. TO SHOW THIS LAND THAT THERE IS ONE GOD. A CHRISTIAN GOD WITH ONLY ONE SON.
WE HAVE MADE THE DEVILS, THE DEMONS, BELIEVE THIS AND TREMBLE. DRIVEN THEM OUT!
WE'VE DESTROYED EVERY DEVIL WE'VE COME ACROSS USING THE POWER OF ALMIGHTY GOD.
WE'VE DONE THAT, HAVEN'T WE?
AND THE ALMIGHTY RIFLE!
THAT, TOO, YES.
HA-HA-HA!

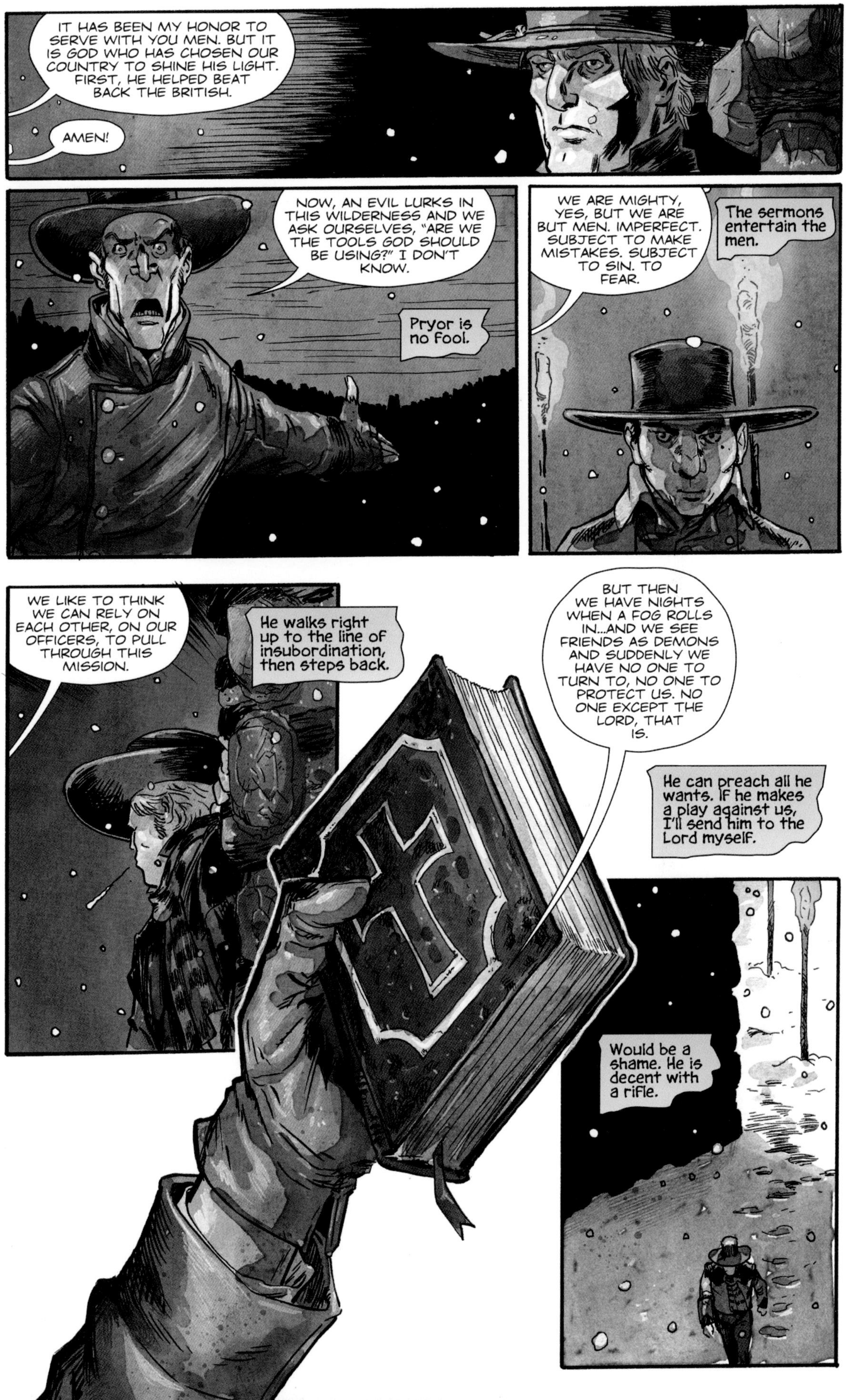
IT HAS BEEN MY HONOR TO SERVE WITH YOU MEN. BUT IT IS GOD WHO HAS CHOSEN OUR COUNTRY TO SHINE HIS LIGHT. FIRST, HE HELPED BEAT BACK THE BRITISH.
AMEN!
NOW, AN EVIL LURKS IN THIS WILDERNESS AND WE ASK OURSELVES, "ARE WE THE TOOLS GOD SHOULD BE USING?" I DON'T KNOW.
Pryor is no fool.
WE ARE MIGHTY, YES, BUT WE ARE BUT MEN. IMPERFECT. SUBJECT TO MAKE MISTAKES. SUBJECT TO SIN. TO FEAR.
The sermons entertain the men.
WE LIKE TO THINK WE CAN RELY ON EACH OTHER, ON OUR OFFICERS, TO PULL THROUGH THIS MISSION.
He walks right up to the line of insubordination, then steps back.
BUT THEN WE HAVE NIGHTS WHEN A FOG ROLLS IN...AND WE SEE FRIENDS AS DEMONS AND SUDDENLY WE HAVE NO ONE TO TURN TO, NO ONE TO PROTECT US. NO ONE EXCEPT THE LORD, THAT IS.
He can preach all he wants. If he makes a play against us, I'll send him to the Lord myself.
Would be a shame. He is decent with a rifle.

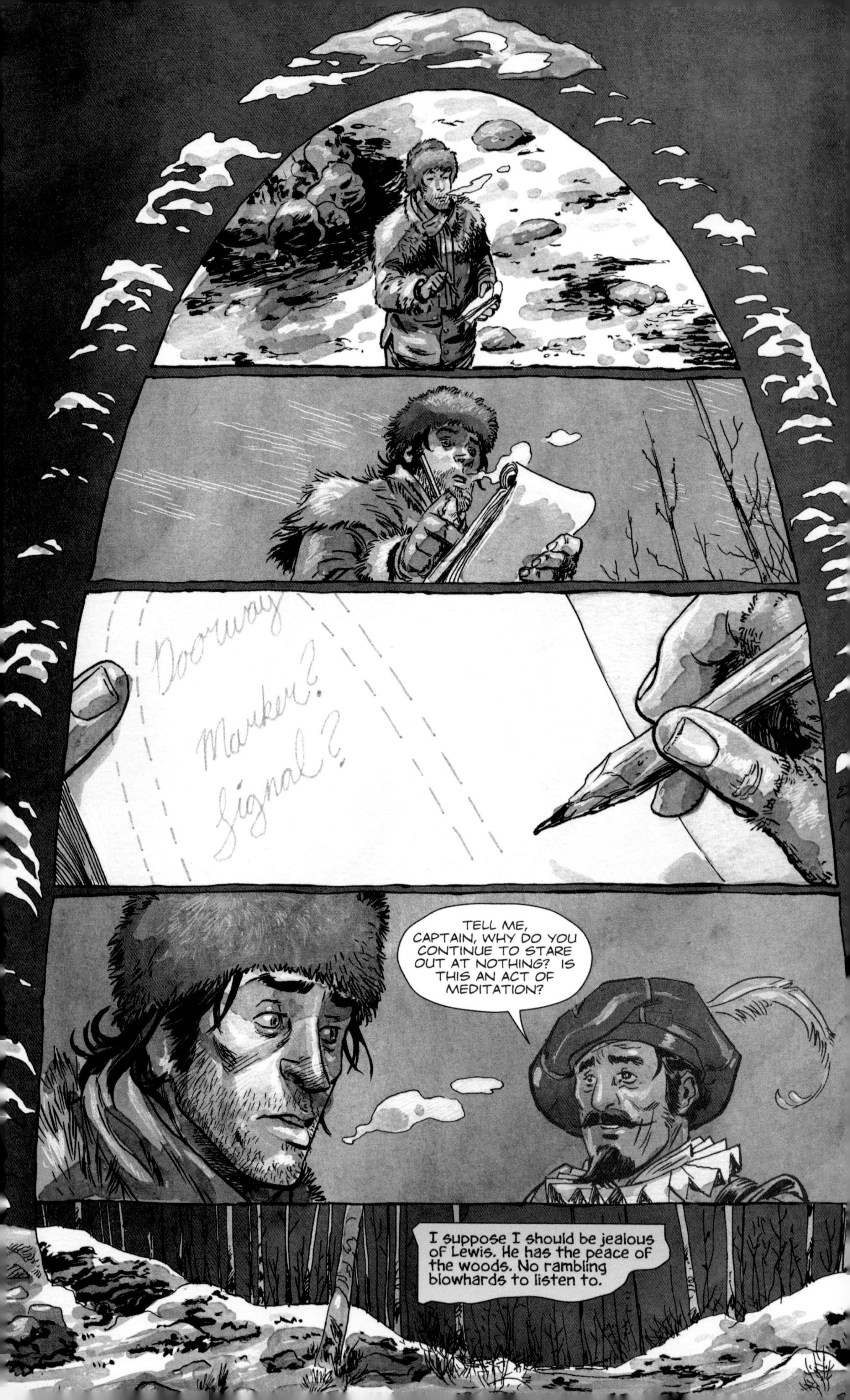
Doorway
Marker?
Signal?
TELL ME, CAPTAIN, WHY DO YOU CONTINUE TO STARE OUT AT NOTHING? IS THIS AN ACT OF MEDITATION?
I suppose I should be jealous of Lewis. He has the peace of the woods. No rambling blowhards to listen to.

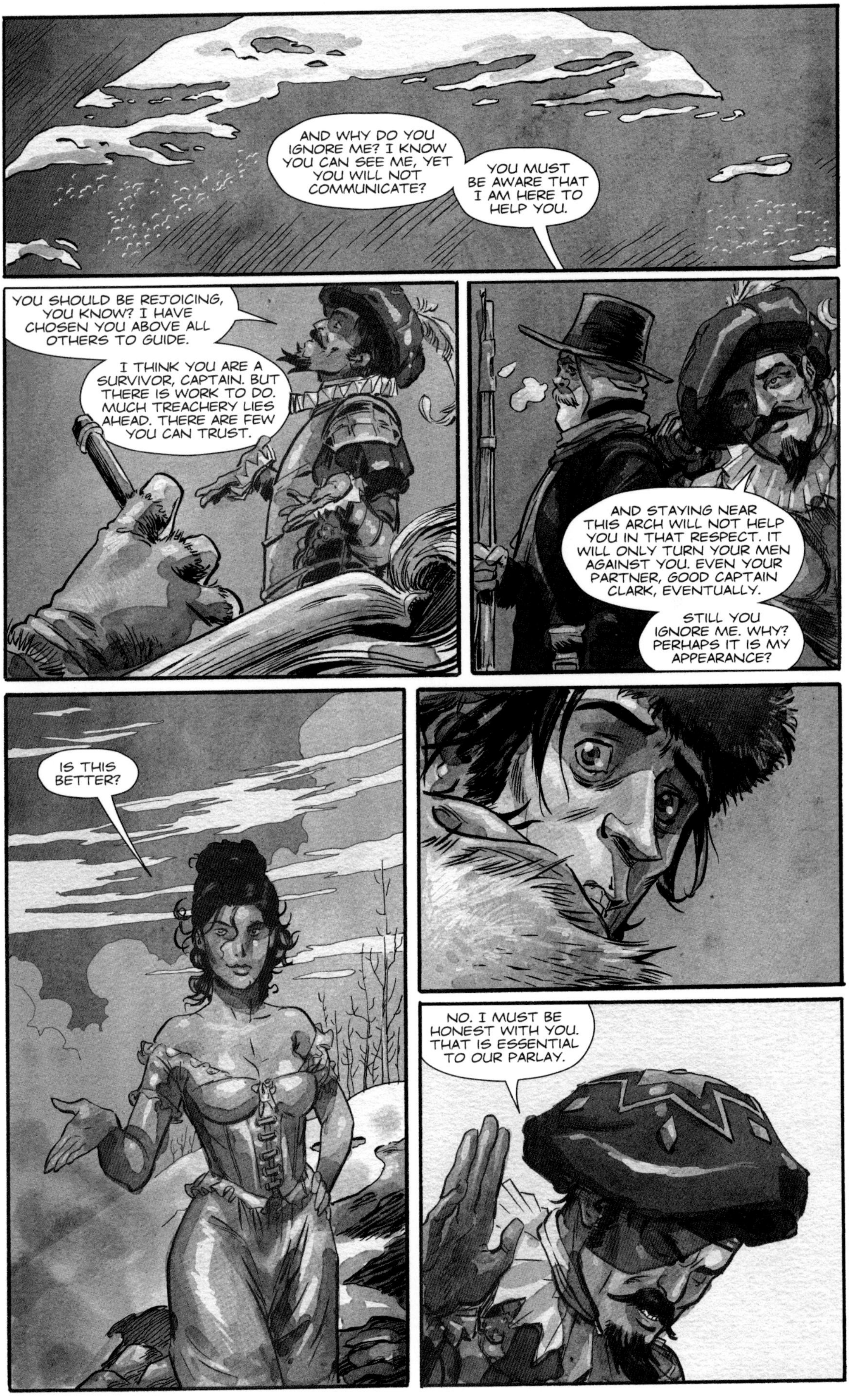
AND WHY DO YOU IGNORE ME? I KNOW YOU CAN SEE ME, YET YOU WILL NOT COMMUNICATE?
YOU MUST BE AWARE THAT I AM HERE TO HELP YOU.
YOU SHOULD BE REJOICING, YOU KNOW? I HAVE CHOSEN YOU ABOVE ALL OTHERS TO GUIDE.
I THINK YOU ARE A SURVIVOR, CAPTAIN. BUT THERE IS WORK TO DO. MUCH TREACHERY LIES AHEAD. THERE ARE FEW YOU CAN TRUST.
AND STAYING NEAR THIS ARCH WILL NOT HELP YOU IN THAT RESPECT. IT WILL ONLY TURN YOUR MEN AGAINST YOU. EVEN YOUR PARTNER, GOOD CAPTAIN CLARK, EVENTUALLY.
STILL YOU IGNORE ME. WHY? PERHAPS IT IS MY APPEARANCE?
IS THIS BETTER?
NO. I MUST BE HONEST WITH YOU. THAT IS ESSENTIAL TO OUR PARLAY.

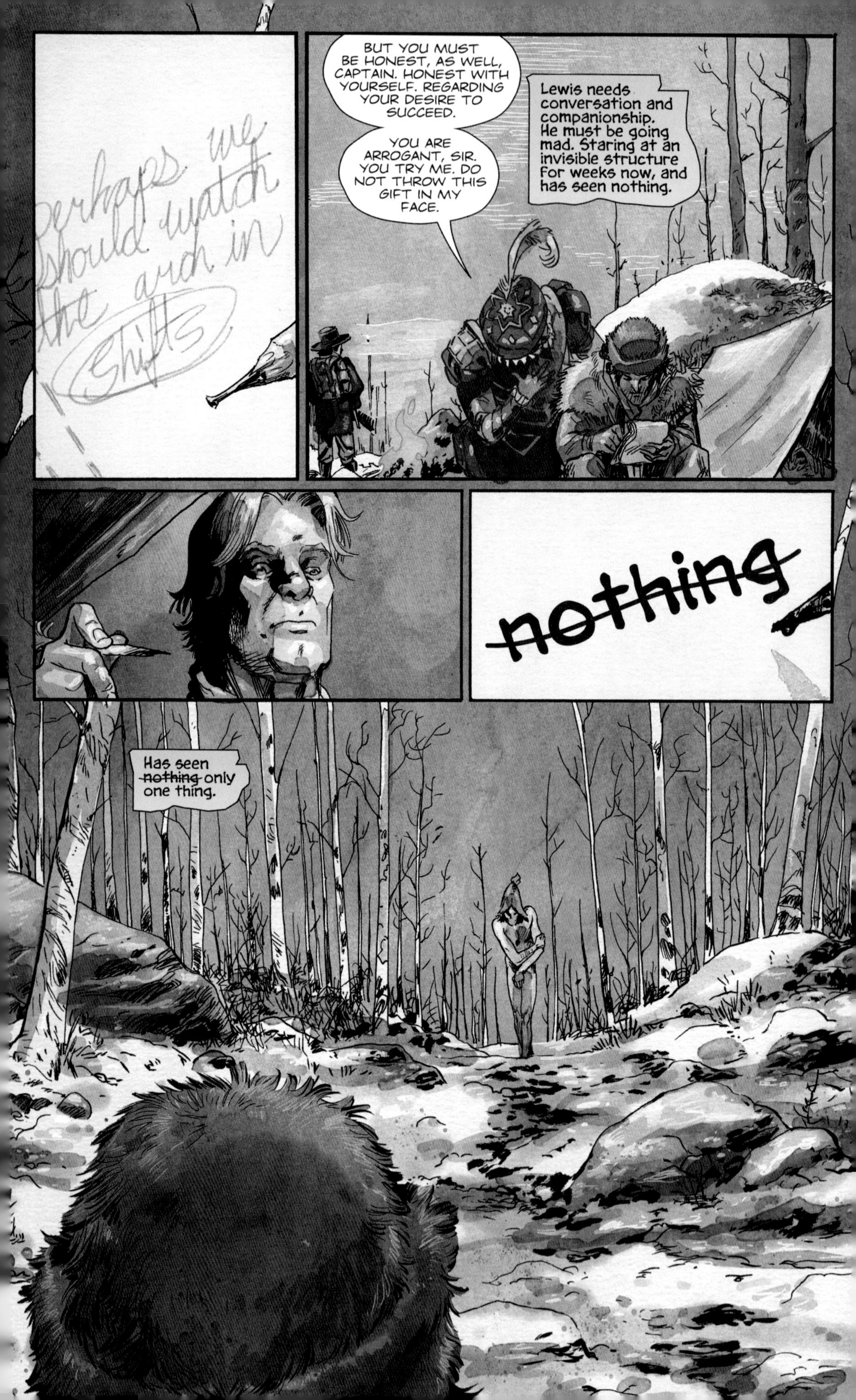
Perhaps we should watch the arch in Shifts
BUT YOU MUST BE HONEST, AS WELL, CAPTAIN. HONEST WITH YOURSELF. REGARDING YOUR DESIRE TO SUCCEED.
YOU ARE ARROGANT, SIR. YOU TRY ME. DO NOT THROW THIS GIFT IN MY FACE.
Lewis needs conversation and companionship. He must be going mad. Staring at an invisible structure for weeks now, and has seen nothing.
~~nothing~~
Has seen ~~nothing~~ only one thing.

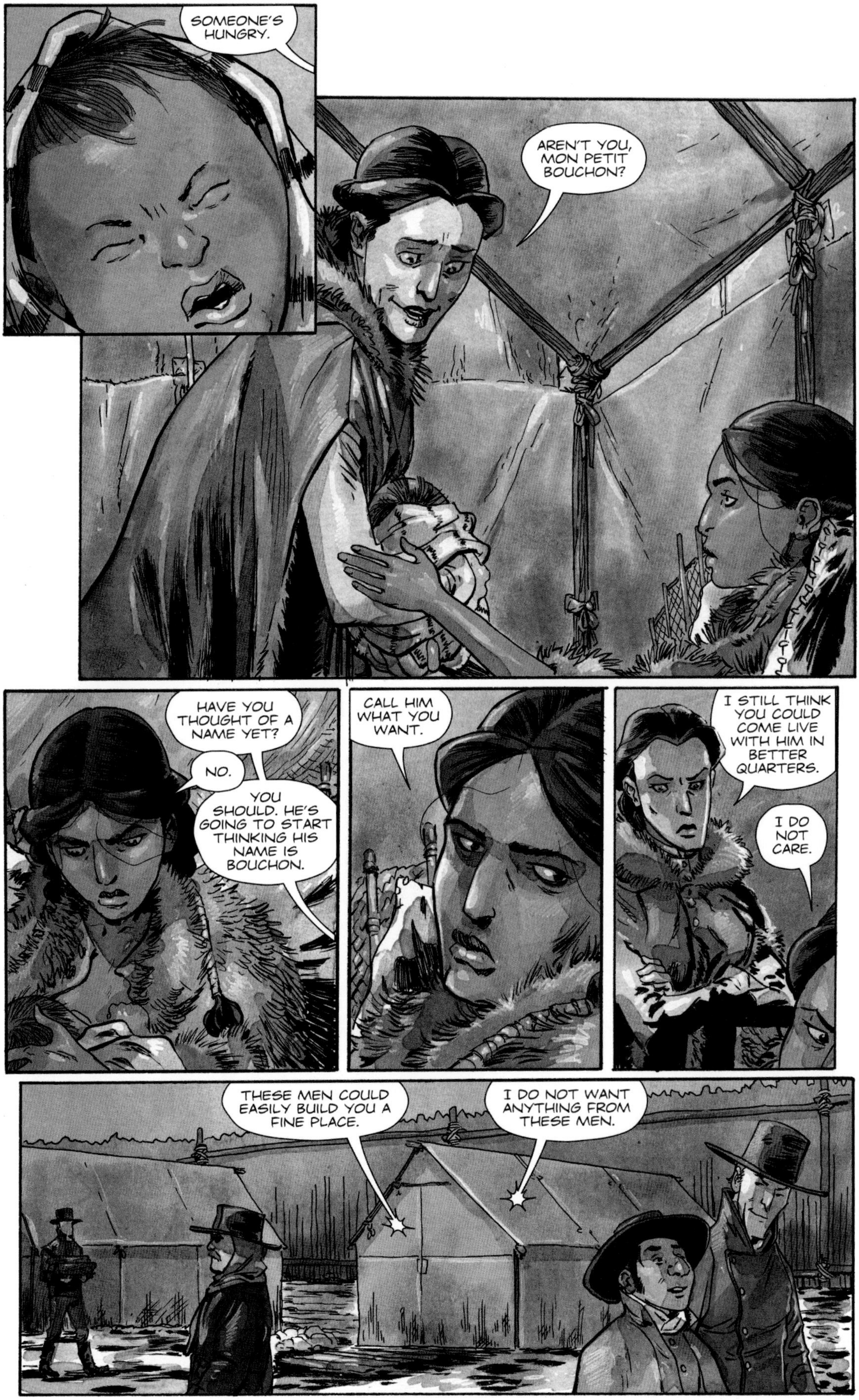
SOMEONE'S HUNGRY.
AREN'T YOU, MON PETIT BOUCHON?
HAVE YOU THOUGHT OF A NAME YET?
NO.
YOU SHOULD. HE'S GOING TO START THINKING HIS NAME IS BOUCHON.
CALL HIM WHAT YOU WANT.
I STILL THINK YOU COULD COME LIVE WITH HIM IN BETTER QUARTERS.
I DO NOT CARE.
THESE MEN COULD EASILY BUILD YOU A FINE PLACE.
I DO NOT WANT ANYTHING FROM THESE MEN.

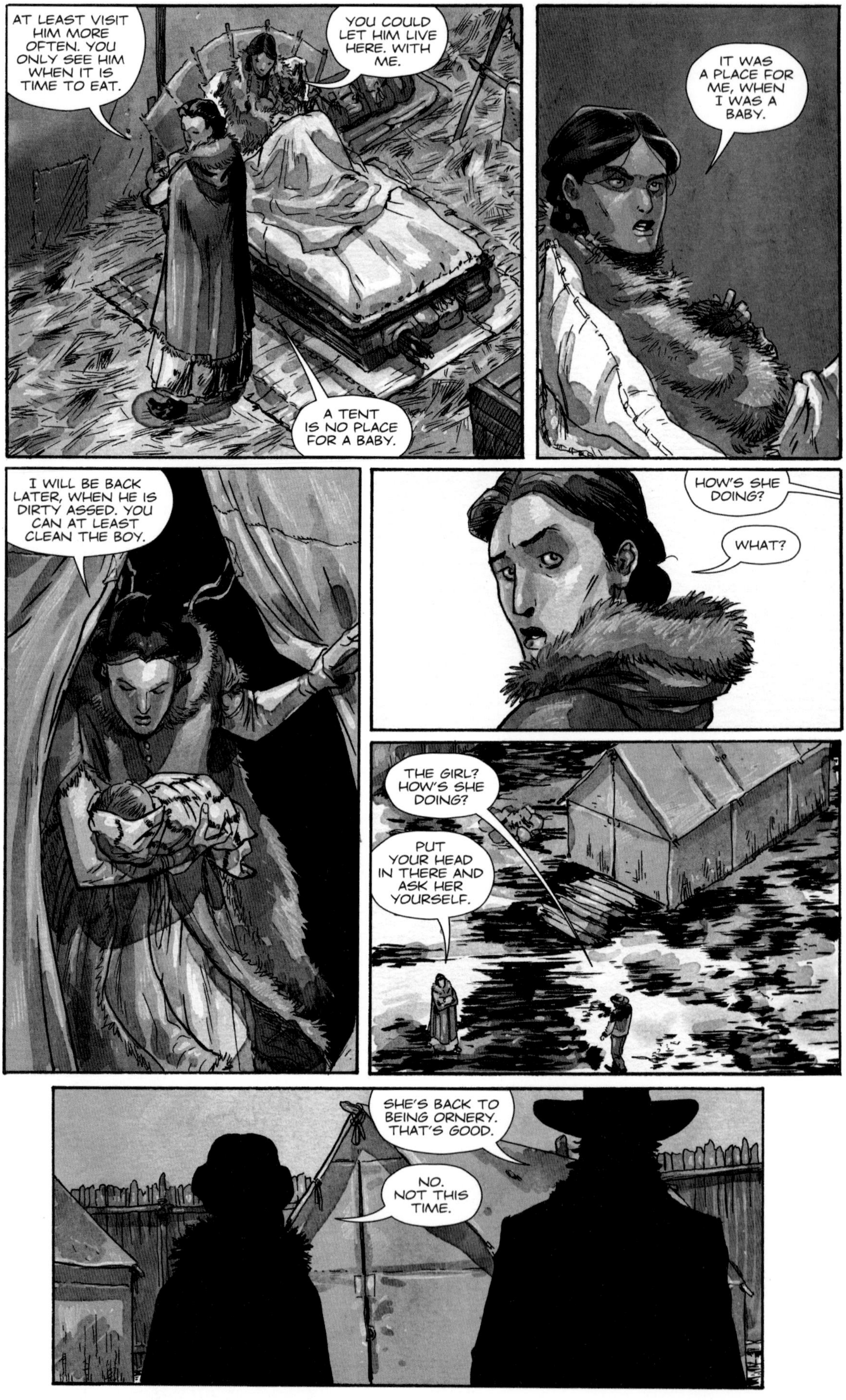
AT LEAST VISIT HIM MORE OFTEN. YOU ONLY SEE HIM WHEN IT IS TIME TO EAT.
YOU COULD LET HIM LIVE HERE. WITH ME.
A TENT IS NO PLACE FOR A BABY.
IT WAS A PLACE FOR ME, WHEN I WAS A BABY.
I WILL BE BACK LATER, WHEN HE IS DIRTY ASSED. YOU CAN AT LEAST CLEAN THE BOY.
HOW'S SHE DOING?
WHAT?
THE GIRL? HOW'S SHE DOING?
PUT YOUR HEAD IN THERE AND ASK HER YOURSELF.
SHE'S BACK TO BEING ORNERY. THAT'S GOOD.
NO. NOT THIS TIME.

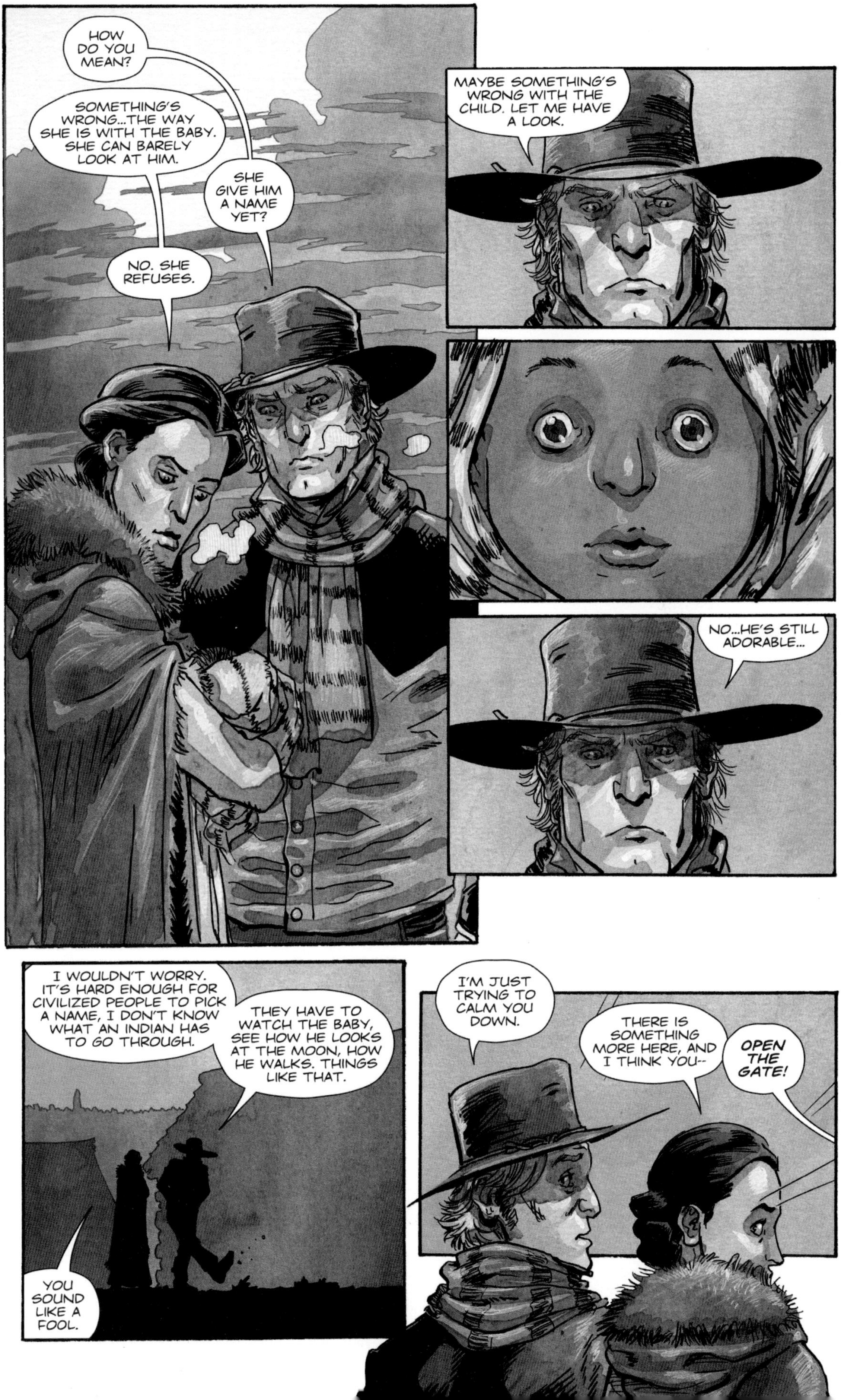
HOW DO YOU MEAN?
SOMETHING'S WRONG...THE WAY SHE IS WITH THE BABY. SHE CAN BARELY LOOK AT HIM.
SHE GIVE HIM A NAME YET?
NO. SHE REFUSES.
MAYBE SOMETHING'S WRONG WITH THE CHILD. LET ME HAVE A LOOK.
NO...HE'S STILL ADORABLE...
I WOULDN'T WORRY. IT'S HARD ENOUGH FOR CIVILIZED PEOPLE TO PICK A NAME, I DON'T KNOW WHAT AN INDIAN HAS TO GO THROUGH.
THEY HAVE TO WATCH THE BABY, SEE HOW HE LOOKS AT THE MOON, HOW HE WALKS. THINGS LIKE THAT.
YOU SOUND LIKE A FOOL.
I'M JUST TRYING TO CALM YOU DOWN.
THERE IS SOMETHING MORE HERE, AND I THINK YOU--
OPEN THE GATE!

28, November. Charbonneau wandered out of wilderness. Brought back to camp.

He was half-mad from the fog, as well as weather and starvation.

This man is like an alley cat. Shows up at just the right time.

Right when the fire is stoked. When the soup is hot.

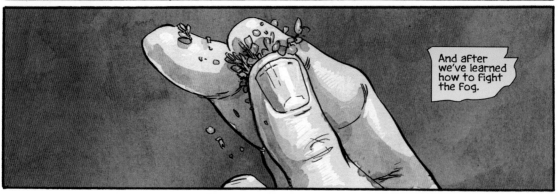

And after we've learned how to fight the fog.

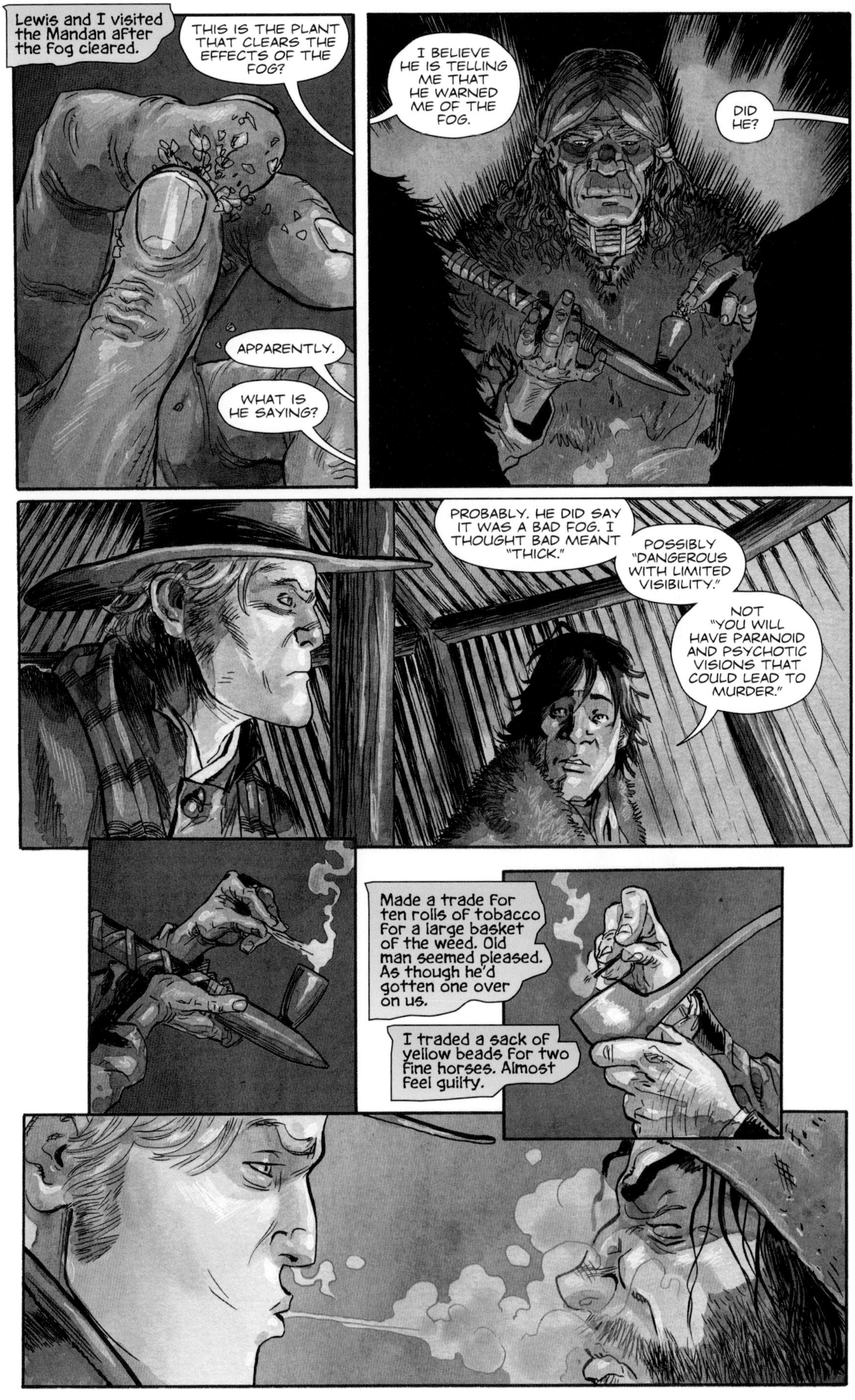
Lewis and I visited the Mandan after the fog cleared.
THIS IS THE PLANT THAT CLEARS THE EFFECTS OF THE FOG?
APPARENTLY.
WHAT IS HE SAYING?
I BELIEVE HE IS TELLING ME THAT HE WARNED ME OF THE FOG.
DID HE?
PROBABLY. HE DID SAY IT WAS A BAD FOG. I THOUGHT BAD MEANT "THICK."
POSSIBLY "DANGEROUS WITH LIMITED VISIBILITY."
NOT "YOU WILL HAVE PARANOID AND PSYCHOTIC VISIONS THAT COULD LEAD TO MURDER."
Made a trade for ten rolls of tobacco for a large basket of the weed. Old man seemed pleased. As though he'd gotten one over on us.
I traded a sack of yellow beads for two fine horses. Almost feel guilty.

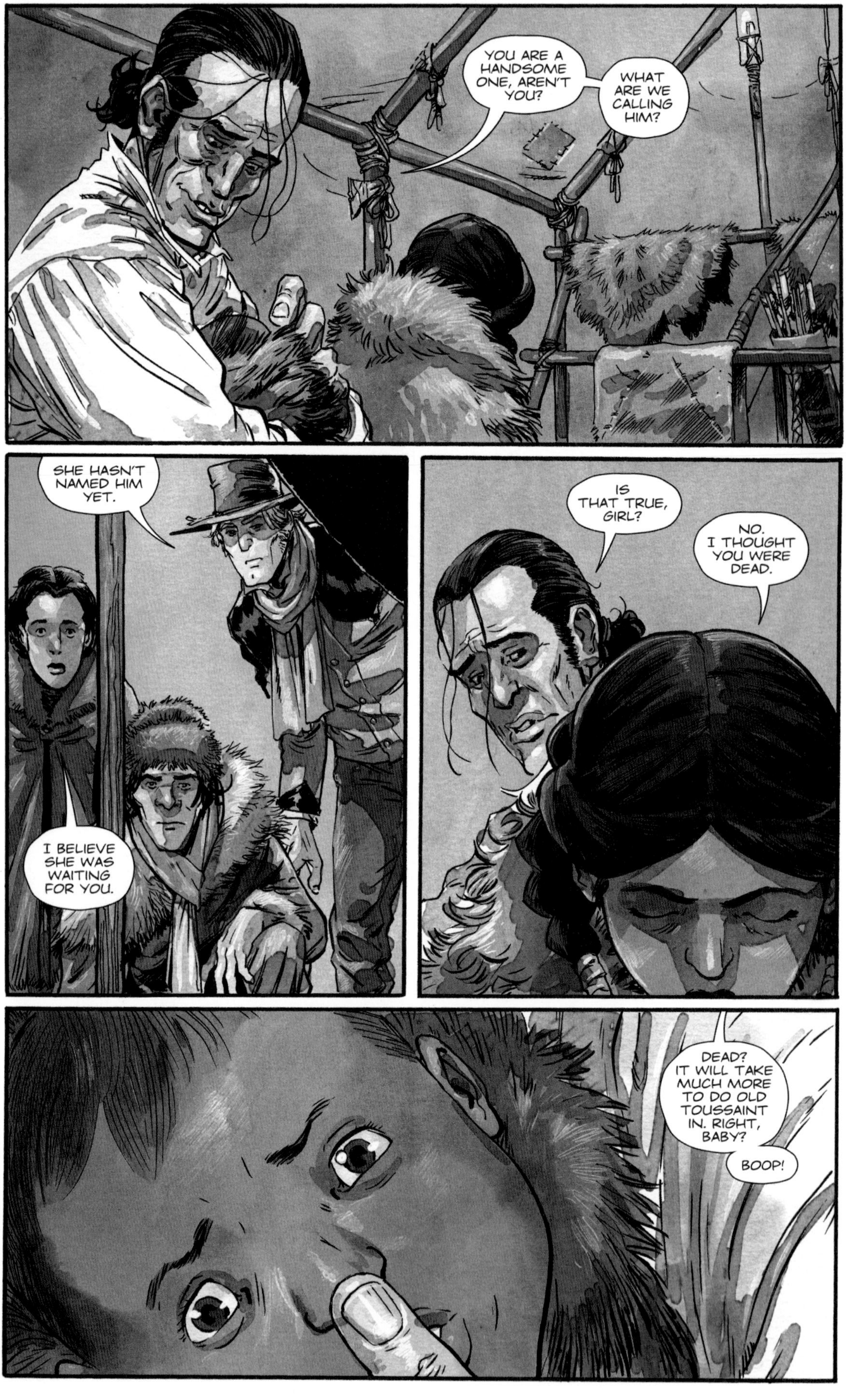

YOU ARE A HANDSOME ONE, AREN'T YOU?
WHAT ARE WE CALLING HIM?
SHE HASN'T NAMED HIM YET.
I BELIEVE SHE WAS WAITING FOR YOU.
IS THAT TRUE, GIRL?
NO. I THOUGHT YOU WERE DEAD.
DEAD? IT WILL TAKE MUCH MORE TO DO OLD TOUSSAINT IN. RIGHT, BABY?
BOOP!

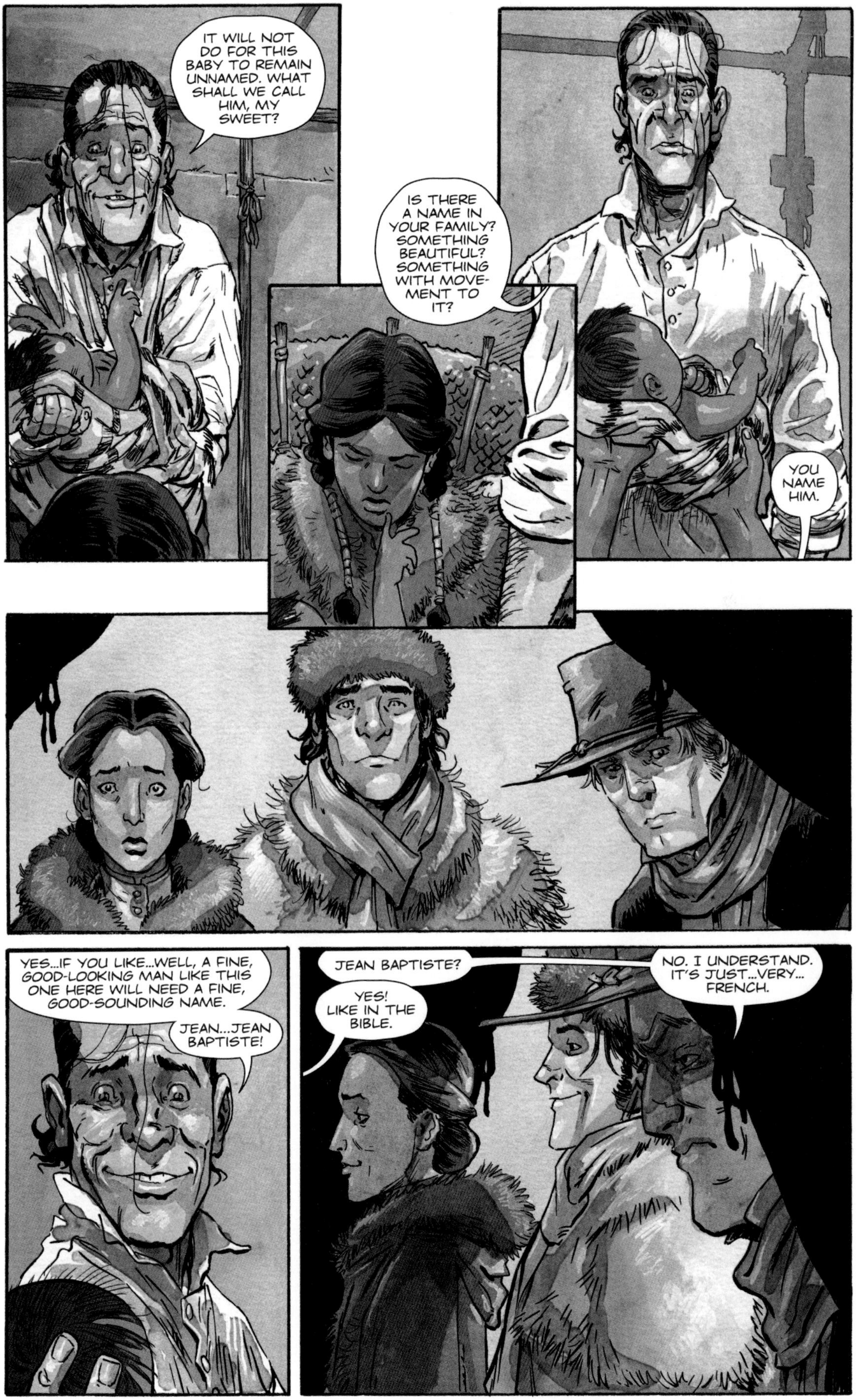
IT WILL NOT DO FOR THIS BABY TO REMAIN UNNAMED. WHAT SHALL WE CALL HIM, MY SWEET?
IS THERE A NAME IN YOUR FAMILY? SOMETHING BEAUTIFUL? SOMETHING WITH MOVE-MENT TO IT?
YOU NAME HIM.
YES...IF YOU LIKE...WELL, A FINE, GOOD-LOOKING MAN LIKE THIS ONE HERE WILL NEED A FINE, GOOD-SOUNDING NAME.
JEAN...JEAN BAPTISTE!
JEAN BAPTISTE?
YES! LIKE IN THE BIBLE.
NO. I UNDERSTAND. IT'S JUST...VERY... FRENCH.

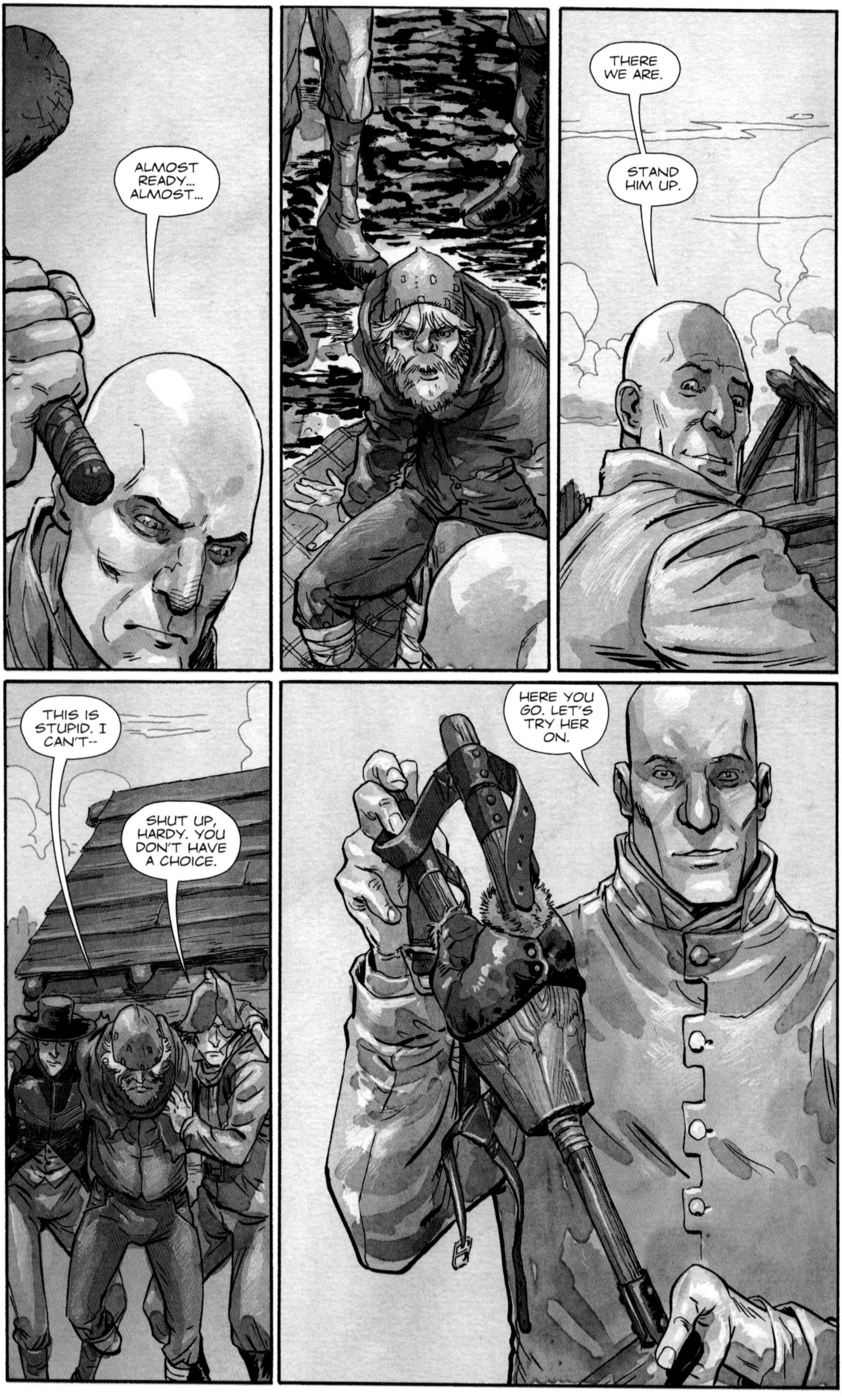
ALMOST READY... ALMOST...
THERE WE ARE.
STAND HIM UP.
THIS IS STUPID. I CAN'T--
SHUT UP, HARDY. YOU DON'T HAVE A CHOICE.
HERE YOU GO. LET'S TRY HER ON.

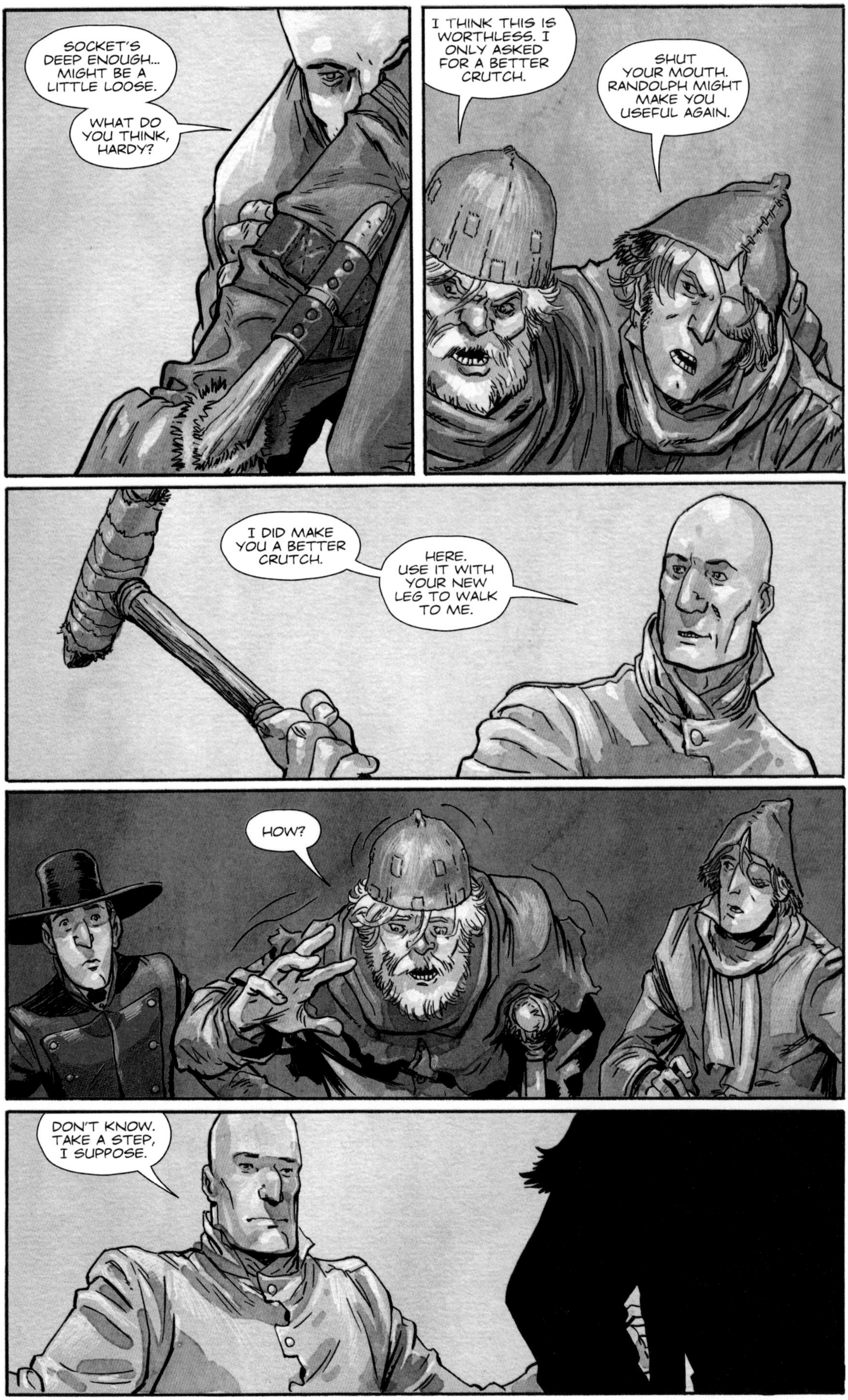
SOCKET'S DEEP ENOUGH... MIGHT BE A LITTLE LOOSE.
WHAT DO YOU THINK, HARDY?
I THINK THIS IS WORTHLESS. I ONLY ASKED FOR A BETTER CRUTCH.
SHUT YOUR MOUTH. RANDOLPH MIGHT MAKE YOU USEFUL AGAIN.
I DID MAKE YOU A BETTER CRUTCH.
HERE. USE IT WITH YOUR NEW LEG TO WALK TO ME.
HOW?
DON'T KNOW. TAKE A STEP, I SUPPOSE.

COME ON, SOLDIER.

USE THE CRUTCH. PUT YOUR WEIGHT ON IT AND BRING THE LEG AROUND.

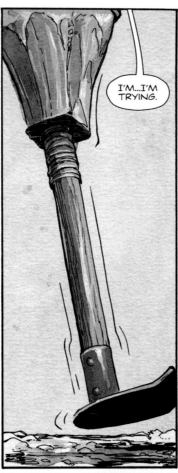

I'M...I'M TRYING.

THERE IT IS, BOY. KEEP AT IT.

IT WORKS. IT WORKS!

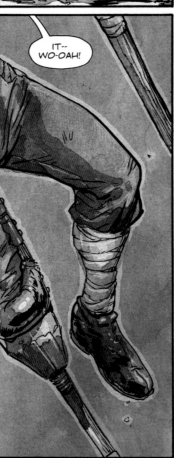

IT-- WO-OAH!

YOU ALRIGHT?

CAN WE TRY THIS AGAIN?

The men are finding ways to distract themselves from their fear. Religion and other projects, like helping each other. Even those who don't deserve it.

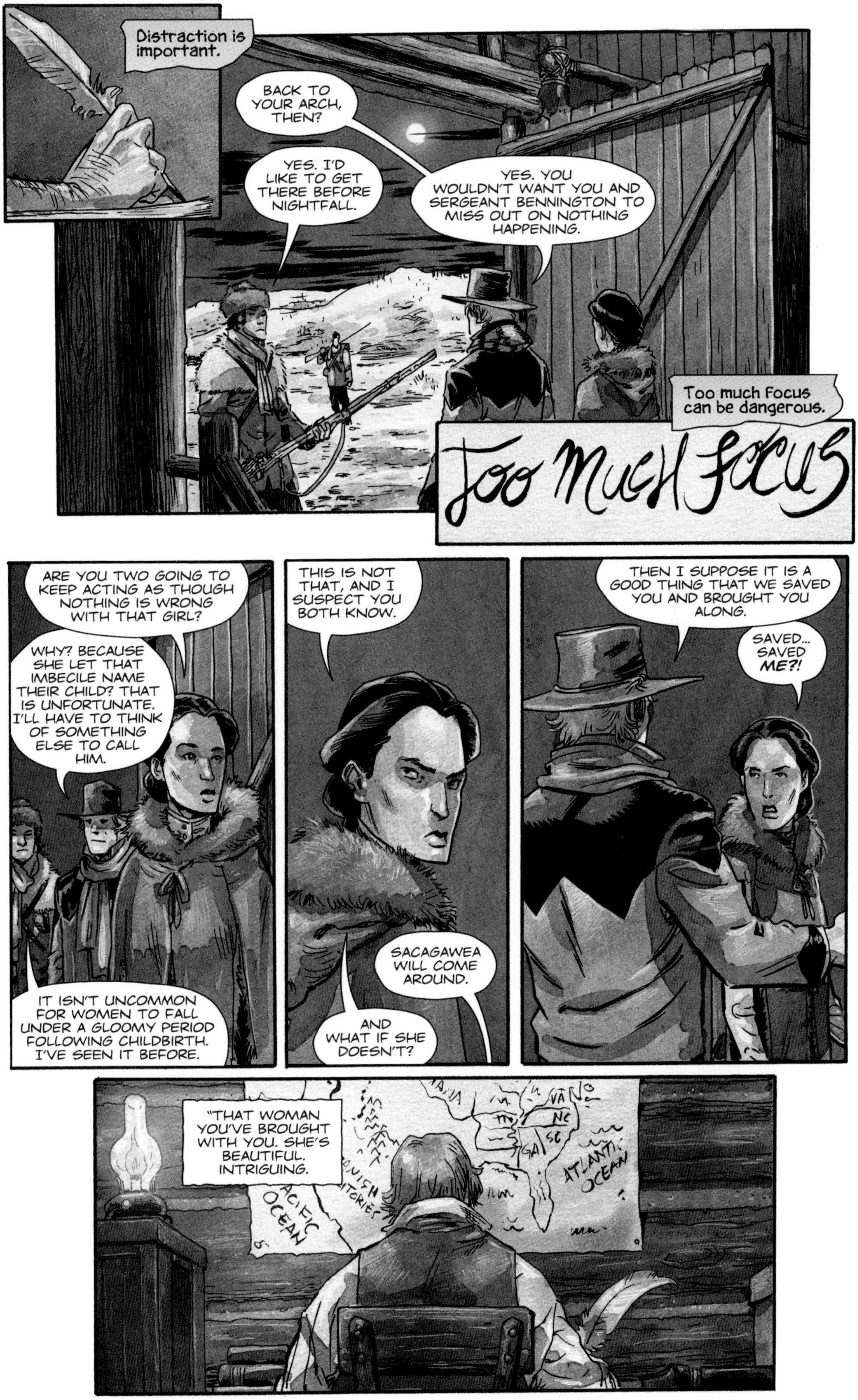
Distraction is important.
BACK TO YOUR ARCH, THEN?
YES. I'D LIKE TO GET THERE BEFORE NIGHTFALL.
YES. YOU WOULDN'T WANT YOU AND SERGEANT BENNINGTON TO MISS OUT ON NOTHING HAPPENING.
Too much focus can be dangerous.
Too Much Focus
ARE YOU TWO GOING TO KEEP ACTING AS THOUGH NOTHING IS WRONG WITH THAT GIRL?
WHY? BECAUSE SHE LET THAT IMBECILE NAME THEIR CHILD? THAT IS UNFORTUNATE. I'LL HAVE TO THINK OF SOMETHING ELSE TO CALL HIM.
IT ISN'T UNCOMMON FOR WOMEN TO FALL UNDER A GLOOMY PERIOD FOLLOWING CHILDBIRTH. I'VE SEEN IT BEFORE.
THIS IS NOT THAT, AND I SUSPECT YOU BOTH KNOW.
SACAGAWEA WILL COME AROUND.
AND WHAT IF SHE DOESN'T?
THEN I SUPPOSE IT IS A GOOD THING THAT WE SAVED YOU AND BROUGHT YOU ALONG.
SAVED... SAVED ME?!
"THAT WOMAN YOU'VE BROUGHT WITH YOU. SHE'S BEAUTIFUL. INTRIGUING.
VA
NC
SC
GA
ATLANTIC OCEAN

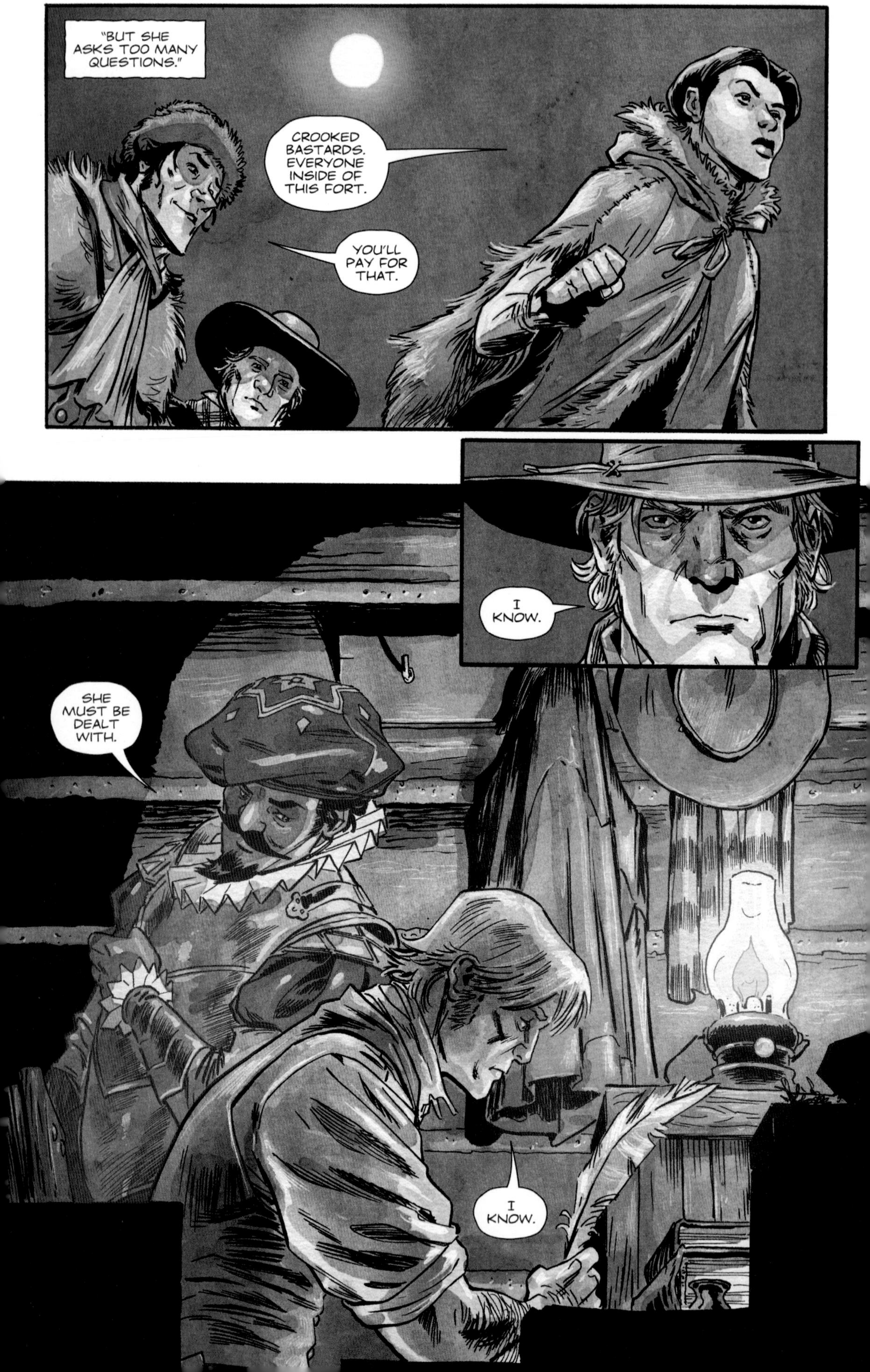
"BUT SHE ASKS TOO MANY QUESTIONS."
CROOKED BASTARDS. EVERYONE INSIDE OF THIS FORT.
YOU'LL PAY FOR THAT.
I KNOW.
SHE MUST BE DEALT WITH.
I KNOW.

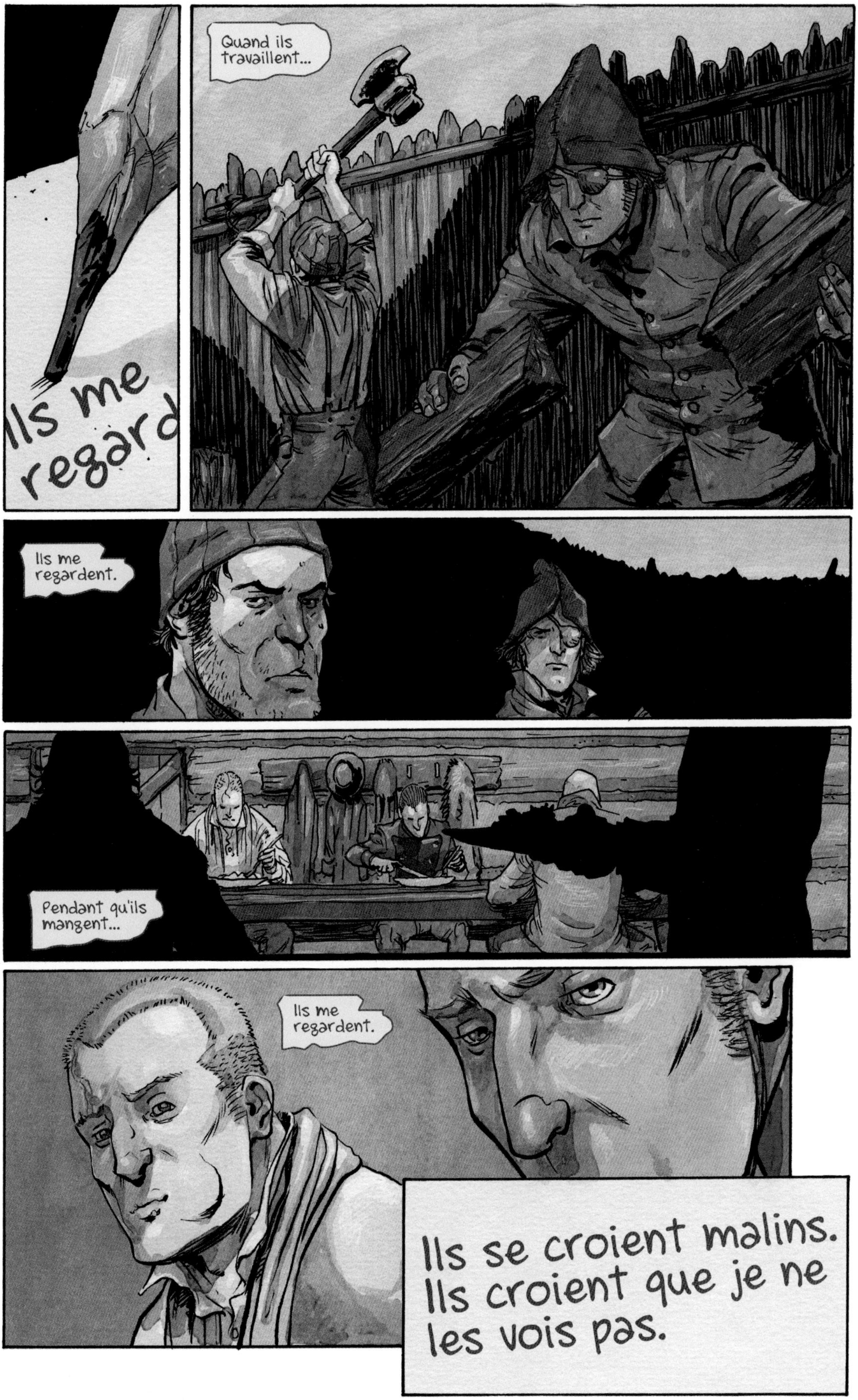
Ils me regard
Quand ils travaillent...
Ils me regardent.
Pendant qu'ils mangent...
Ils me regardent.
Ils se croient malins. Ils croient que je ne les vois pas.

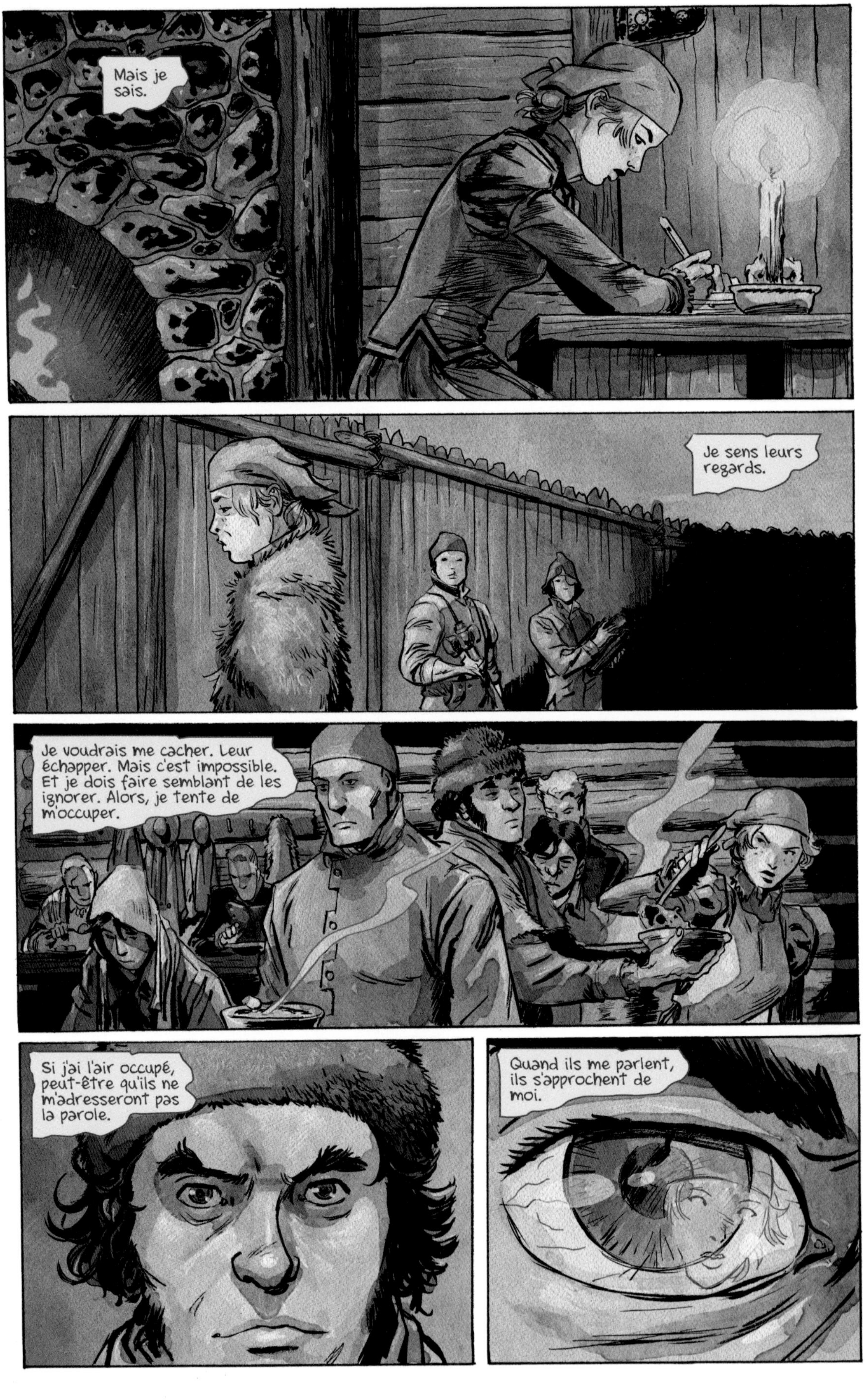
Mais je sais.
Je sens leurs regards.
Je voudrais me cacher. Leur échapper. Mais c'est impossible. Et je dois faire semblant de les ignorer. Alors, je tente de m'occuper.
Si j'ai l'air occupé, peut-être qu'ils ne m'adresseront pas la parole.
Quand ils me parlent, ils s'approchent de moi.

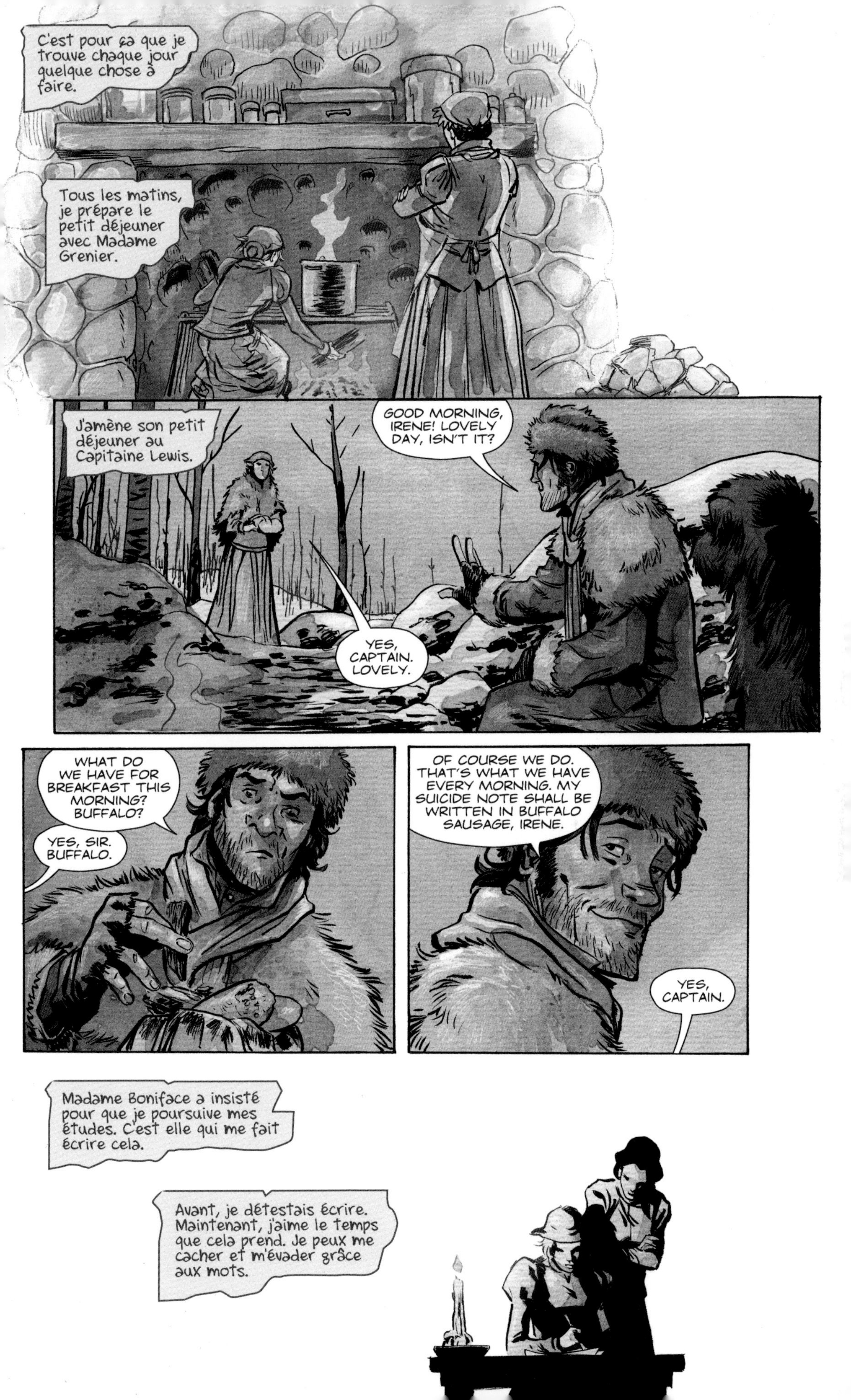
C'est pour ça que je trouve chaque jour quelque chose à faire.
Tous les matins, je prépare le petit déjeuner avec Madame Grenier.
J'amène son petit déjeuner au Capitaine Lewis.
GOOD MORNING, IRENE! LOVELY DAY, ISN'T IT?
YES, CAPTAIN. LOVELY.
WHAT DO WE HAVE FOR BREAKFAST THIS MORNING? BUFFALO?
YES, SIR. BUFFALO.
OF COURSE WE DO. THAT'S WHAT WE HAVE EVERY MORNING. MY SUICIDE NOTE SHALL BE WRITTEN IN BUFFALO SAUSAGE, IRENE.
YES, CAPTAIN.
Madame Boniface a insisté pour que je poursuive mes études. C'est elle qui me fait écrire cela.
Avant, je détestais écrire. Maintenant, j'aime le temps que cela prend. Je peux me cacher et m'évader grâce aux mots.

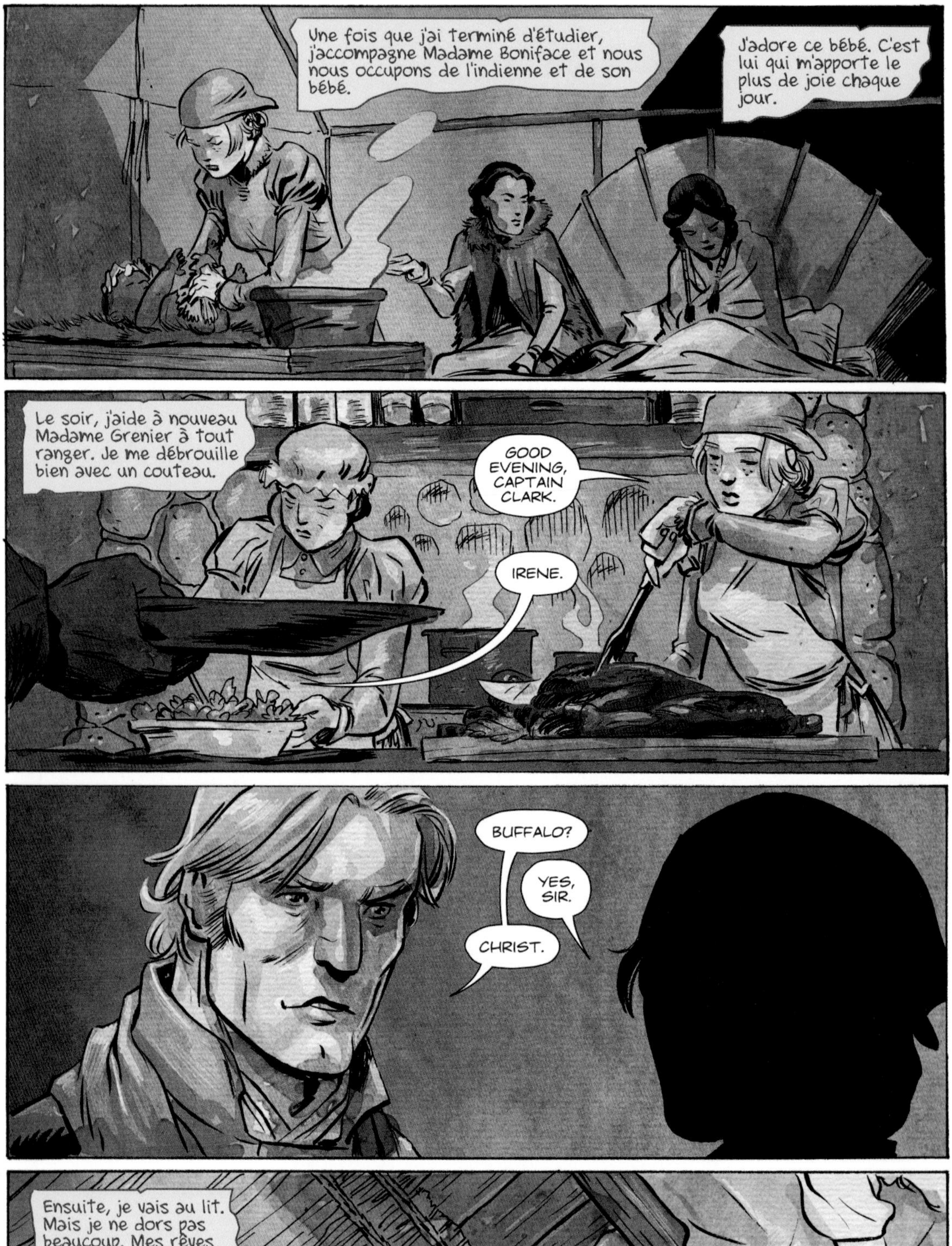
Une fois que j'ai terminé d'étudier, j'accompagne Madame Boniface et nous nous occupons de l'indienne et de son bébé.
J'adore ce bébé. C'est lui qui m'apporte le plus de joie chaque jour.
Le soir, j'aide à nouveau Madame Grenier à tout ranger. Je me débrouille bien avec un couteau.
GOOD EVENING, CAPTAIN CLARK.
IRENE.
BUFFALO?
YES, SIR.
CHRIST.
Ensuite, je vais au lit. Mais je ne dors pas beaucoup. Mes rêves sont pleins de choses terrifiantes.
Pour un temps, j'ai été capable de garder toutes ces horreurs tapies au fond de moi, pendant que je dormais.

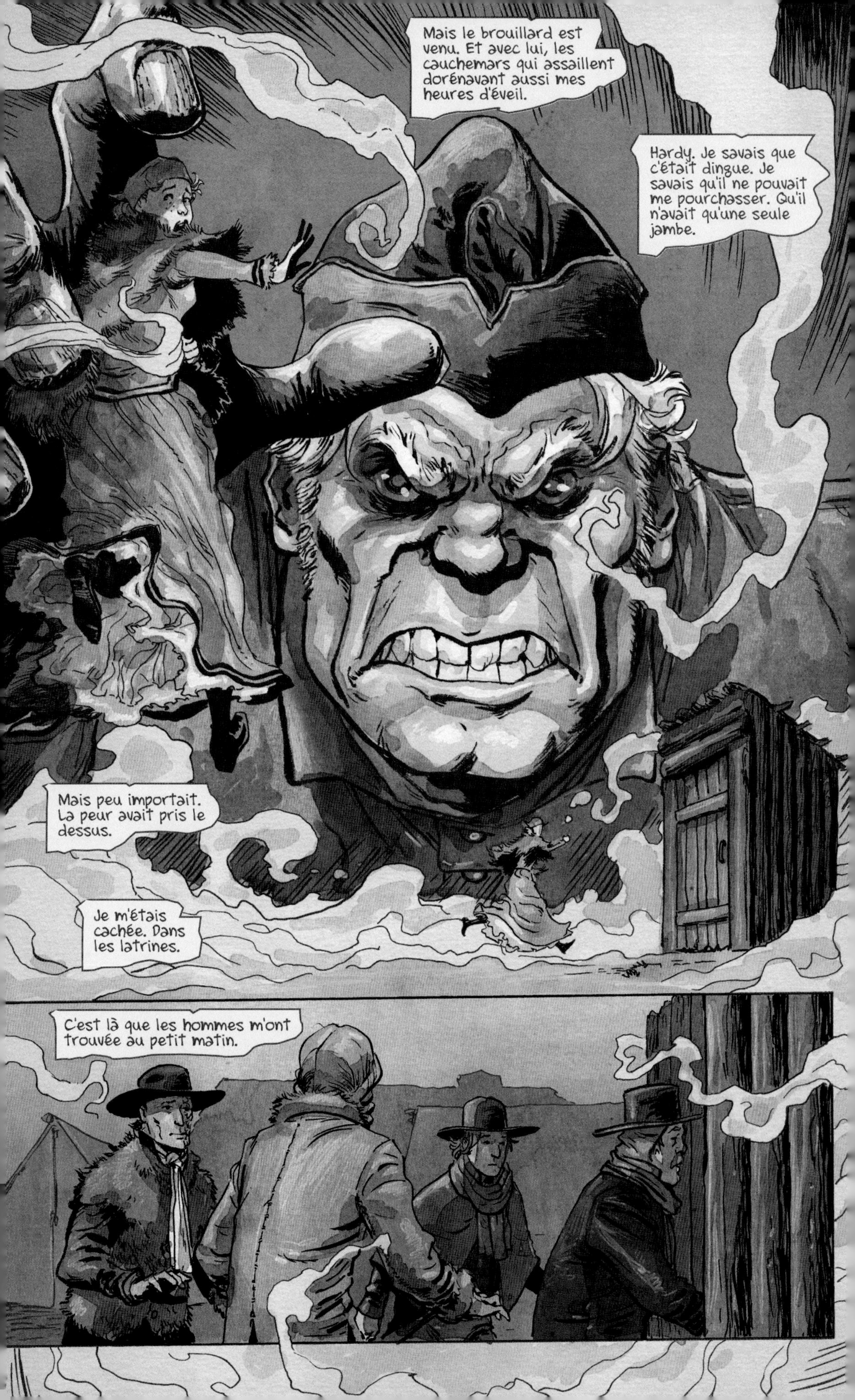
Mais le brouillard est venu. Et avec lui, les cauchemars qui assaillent dorénavant aussi mes heures d'éveil.
Hardy. Je savais que c'était dingue. Je savais qu'il ne pouvait me pourchasser. Qu'il n'avait qu'une seule jambe.
Mais peu importait. La peur avait pris le dessus.
Je m'étais cachée. Dans les latrines.
C'est là que les hommes m'ont trouvée au petit matin.

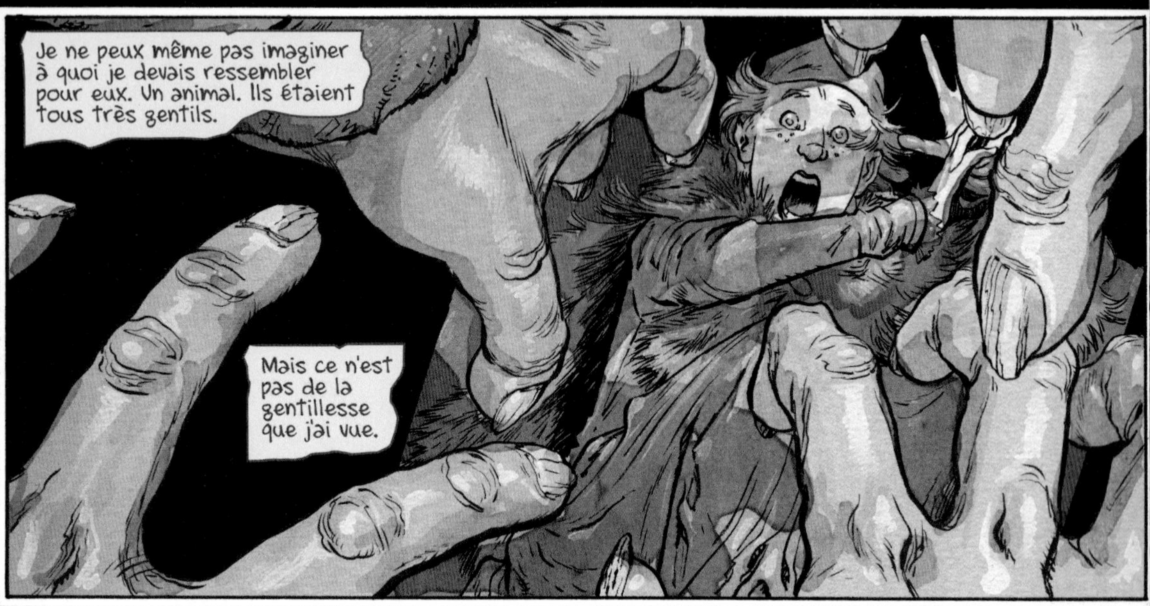
Je ne peux même pas imaginer à quoi je devais ressembler pour eux. Un animal. Ils étaient tous très gentils.
Mais ce n'est pas de la gentillesse que j'ai vue.
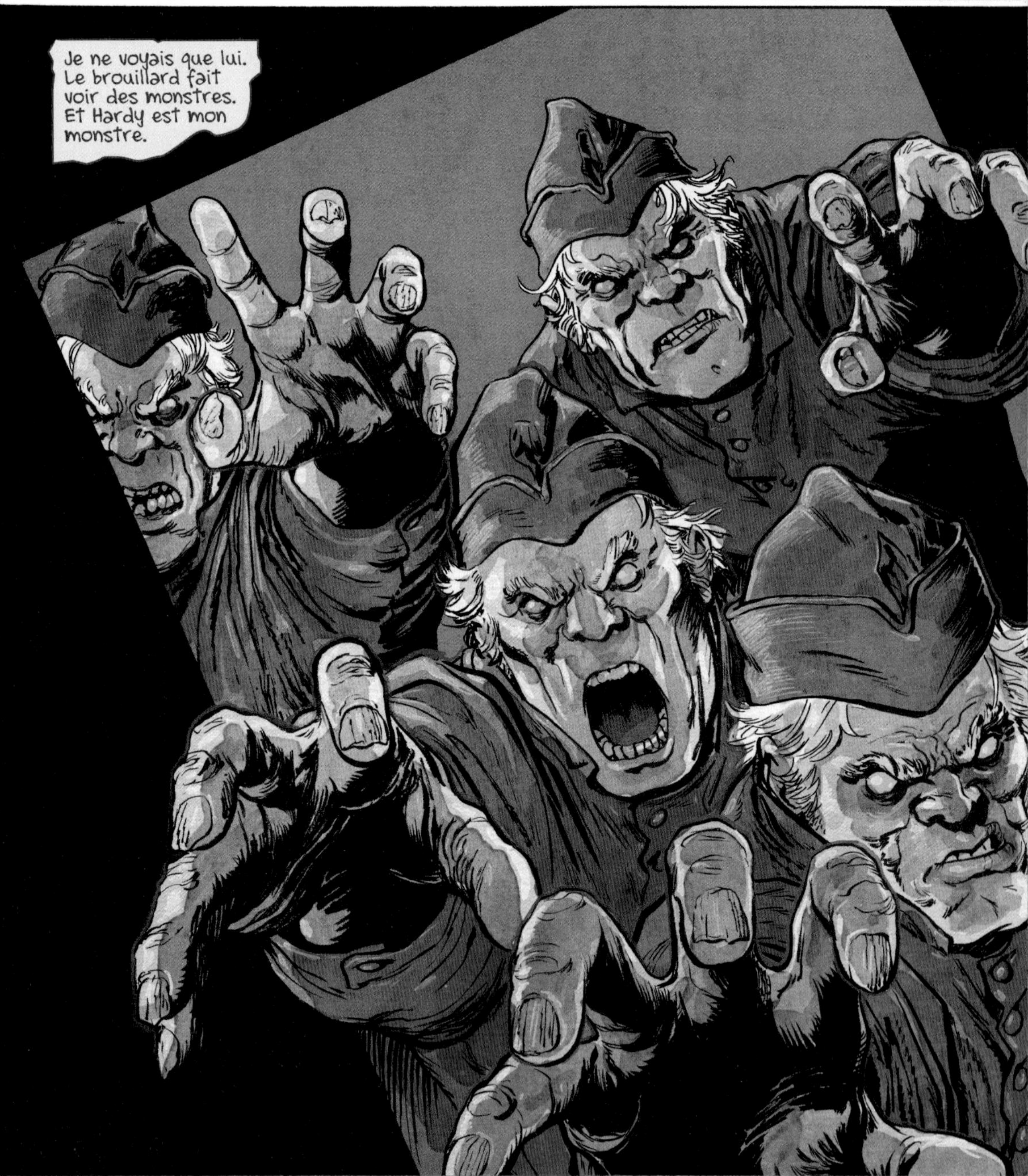
Je ne voyais que lui. Le brouillard fait voir des monstres. Et Hardy est mon monstre.

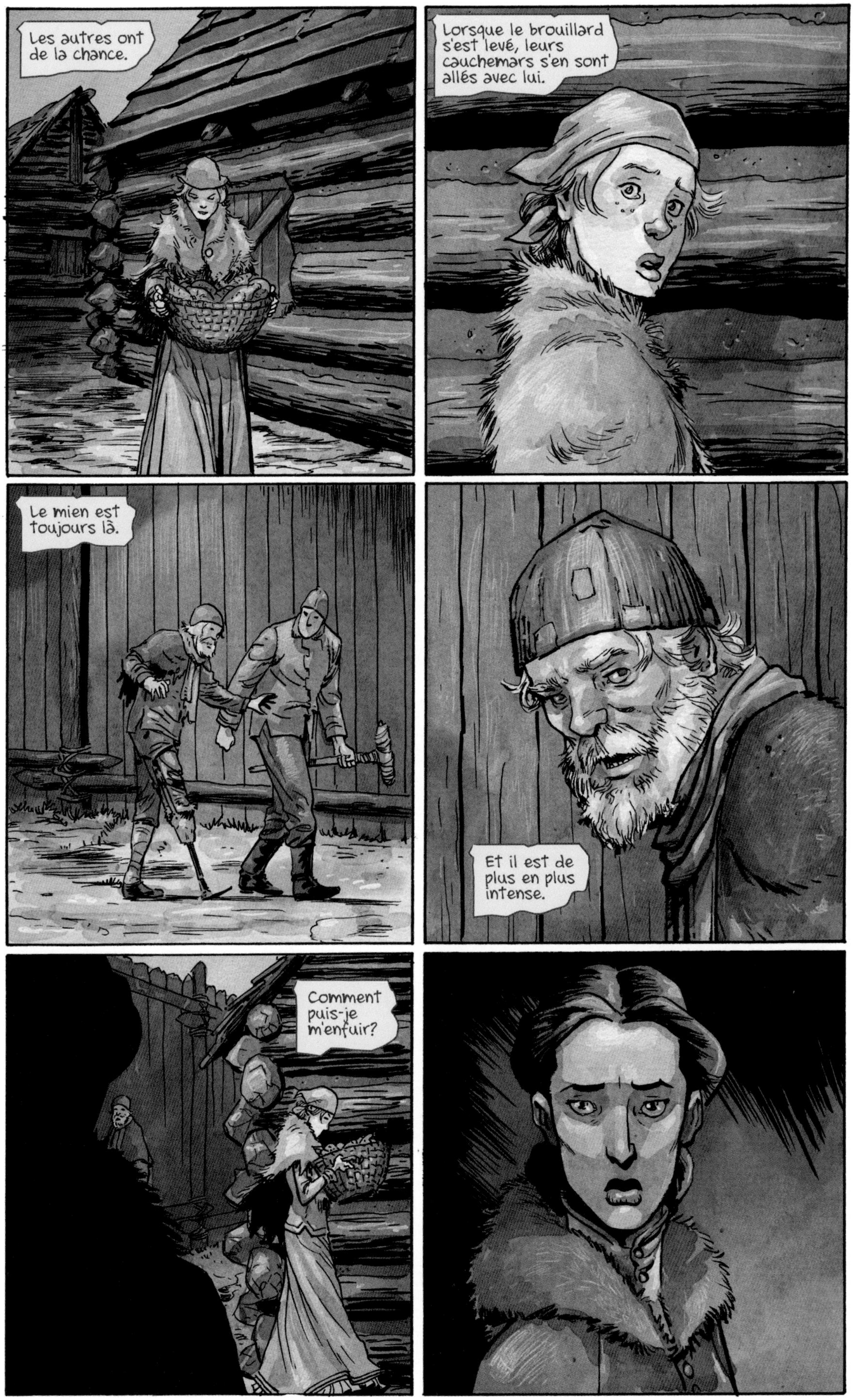
Les autres ont de la chance.
Lorsque le brouillard s'est levé, leurs cauchemars s'en sont allés avec lui.
Le mien est toujours là.
Et il est de plus en plus intense.
Comment puis-je m'enfuir?

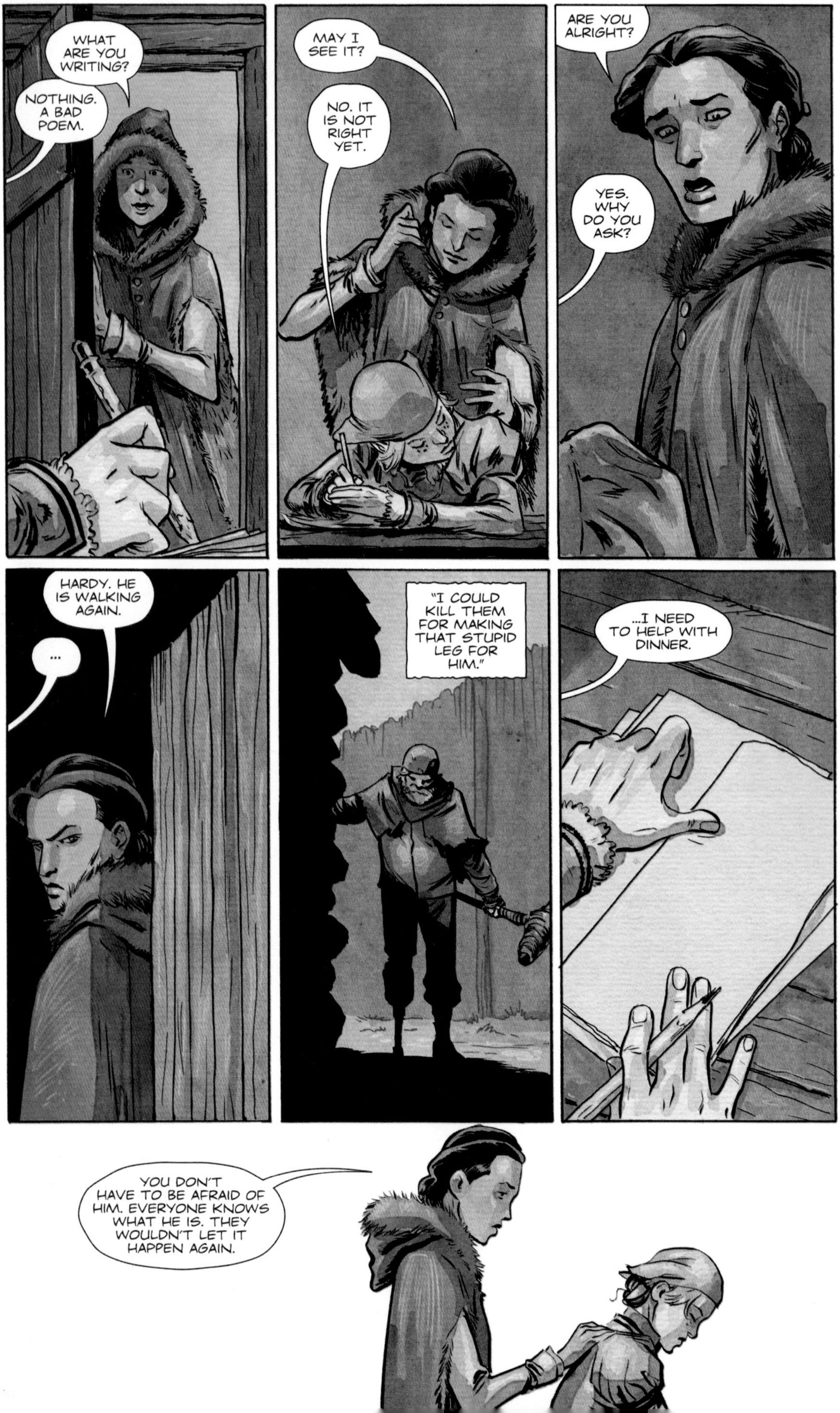
WHAT ARE YOU WRITING?
NOTHING. A BAD POEM.
MAY I SEE IT?
NO. IT IS NOT RIGHT YET.
ARE YOU ALRIGHT?
YES. WHY DO YOU ASK?
HARDY. HE IS WALKING AGAIN.
...
"I COULD KILL THEM FOR MAKING THAT STUPID LEG FOR HIM."
...I NEED TO HELP WITH DINNER.
YOU DON'T HAVE TO BE AFRAID OF HIM. EVERYONE KNOWS WHAT HE IS. THEY WOULDN'T LET IT HAPPEN AGAIN.

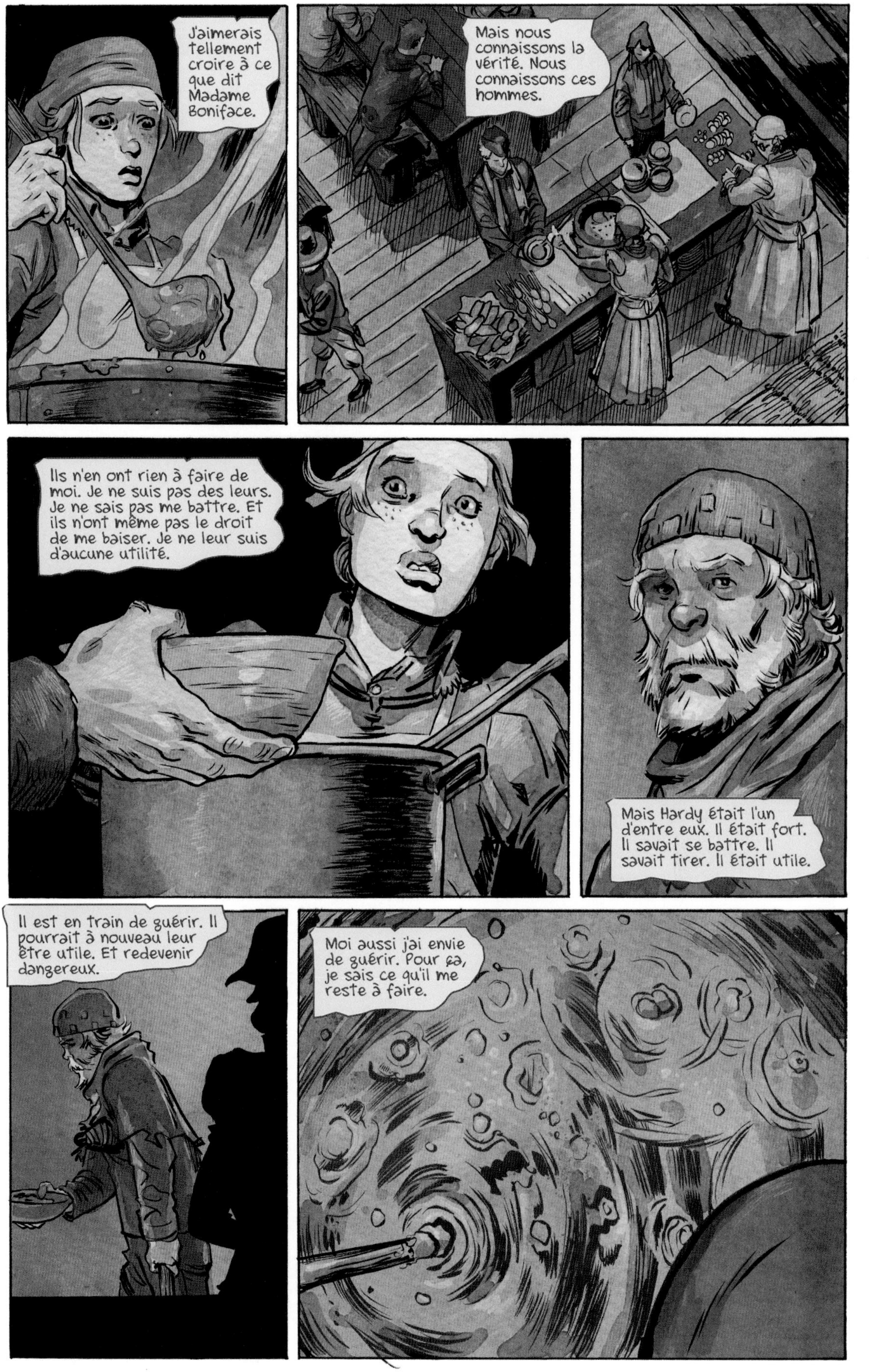
J'aimerais tellement croire à ce que dit Madame Boniface.
Mais nous connaissons la vérité. Nous connaissons ces hommes.
Ils n'en ont rien à faire de moi. Je ne suis pas des leurs. Je ne sais pas me battre. Et ils n'ont même pas le droit de me baiser. Je ne leur suis d'aucune utilité.
Mais Hardy était l'un d'entre eux. Il était fort. Il savait se battre. Il savait tirer. Il était utile.
Il est en train de guérir. Il pourrait à nouveau leur être utile. Et redevenir dangereux.
Moi aussi j'ai envie de guérir. Pour ça, je sais ce qu'il me reste à faire.

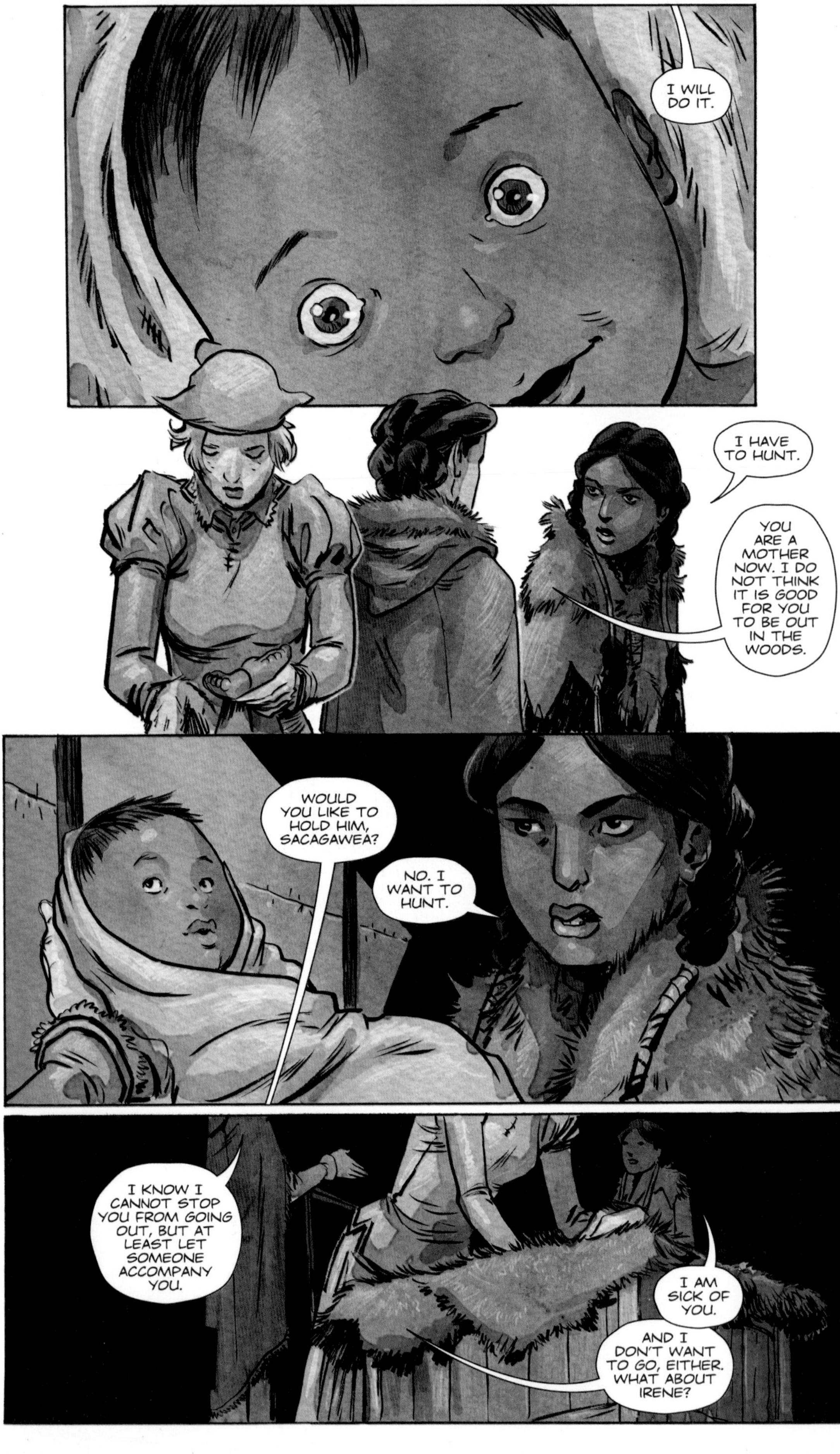
I WILL DO IT.
I HAVE TO HUNT.
YOU ARE A MOTHER NOW. I DO NOT THINK IT IS GOOD FOR YOU TO BE OUT IN THE WOODS.
WOULD YOU LIKE TO HOLD HIM, SACAGAWEA?
NO. I WANT TO HUNT.
I KNOW I CANNOT STOP YOU FROM GOING OUT, BUT AT LEAST LET SOMEONE ACCOMPANY YOU.
I AM SICK OF YOU.
AND I DON'T WANT TO GO, EITHER. WHAT ABOUT IRENE?

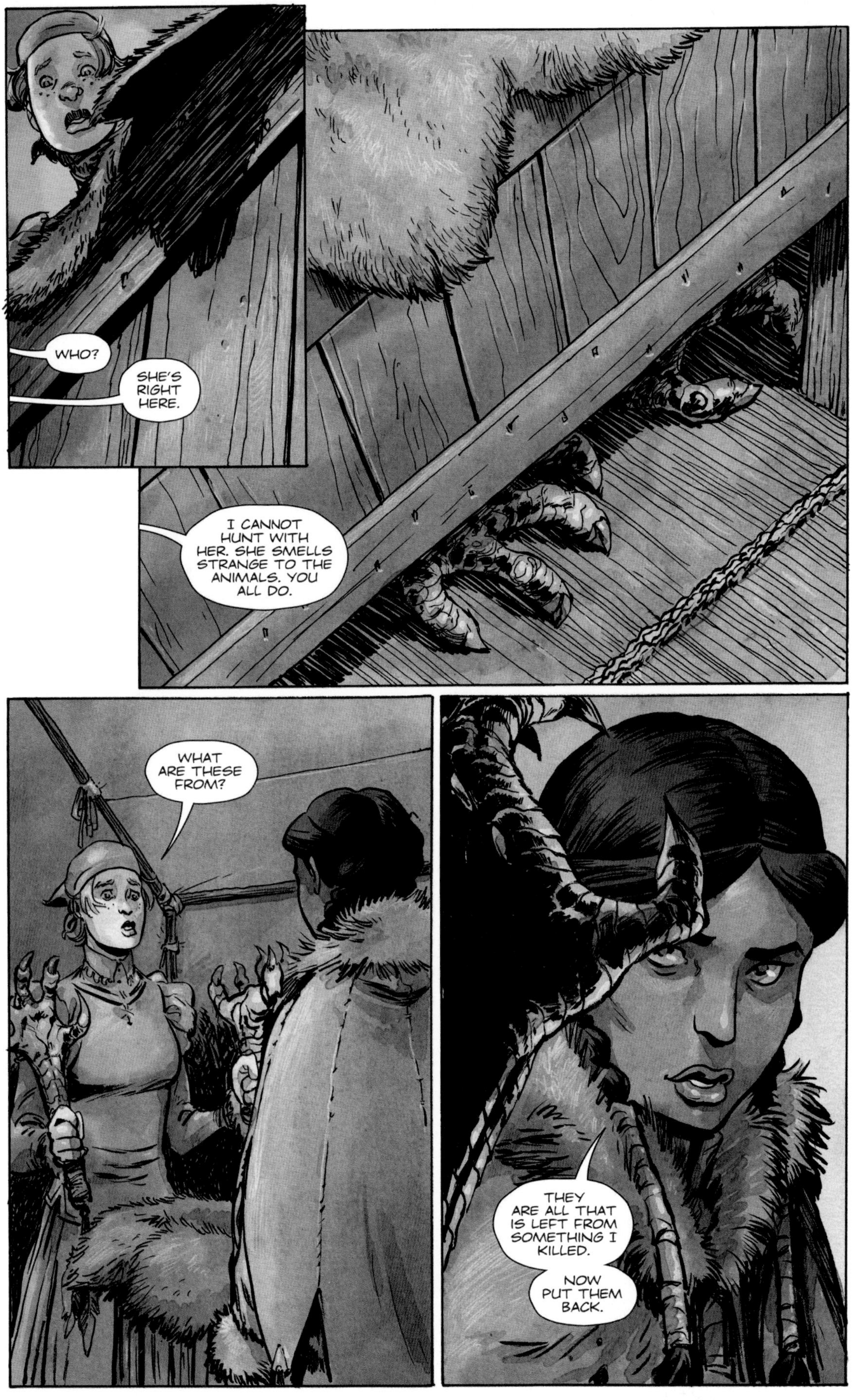
WHO?
SHE'S RIGHT HERE.
I CANNOT HUNT WITH HER. SHE SMELLS STRANGE TO THE ANIMALS. YOU ALL DO.
WHAT ARE THESE FROM?
THEY ARE ALL THAT IS LEFT FROM SOMETHING I KILLED.
NOW PUT THEM BACK.

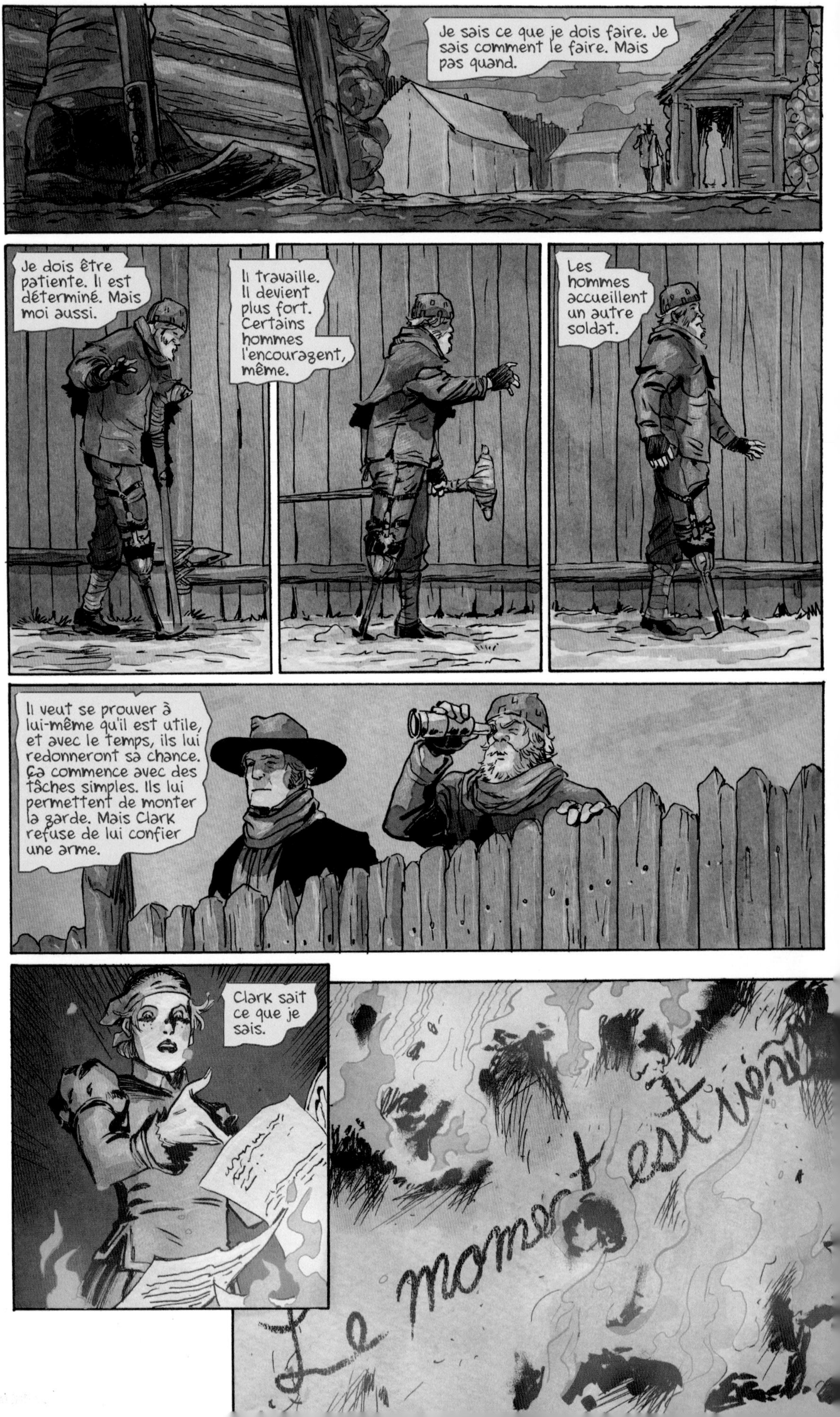
Je sais ce que je dois faire. Je sais comment le faire. Mais pas quand.
Je dois être patiente. Il est déterminé. Mais moi aussi.
Il travaille. Il devient plus fort. Certains hommes l'encouragent, même.
Les hommes accueillent un autre soldat.
Il veut se prouver à lui-même qu'il est utile, et avec le temps, ils lui redonneront sa chance. Ça commence avec des tâches simples. Ils lui permettent de monter la garde. Mais Clark refuse de lui confier une arme.
Clark sait ce que je sais.
Le moment est venu

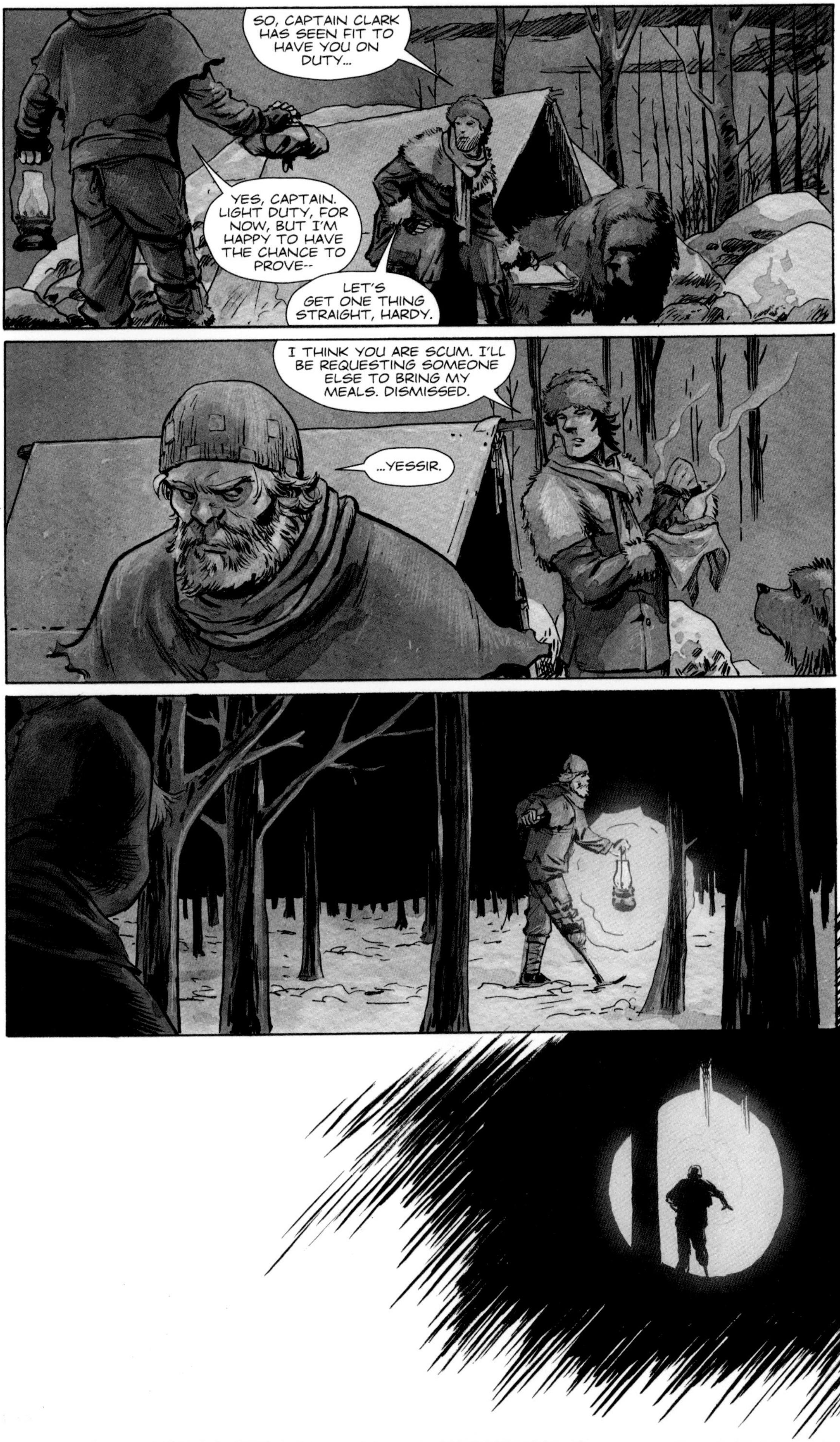
SO, CAPTAIN CLARK HAS SEEN FIT TO HAVE YOU ON DUTY...
YES, CAPTAIN. LIGHT DUTY, FOR NOW, BUT I'M HAPPY TO HAVE THE CHANCE TO PROVE--
LET'S GET ONE THING STRAIGHT, HARDY.
I THINK YOU ARE SCUM. I'LL BE REQUESTING SOMEONE ELSE TO BRING MY MEALS. DISMISSED.
...YESSIR.

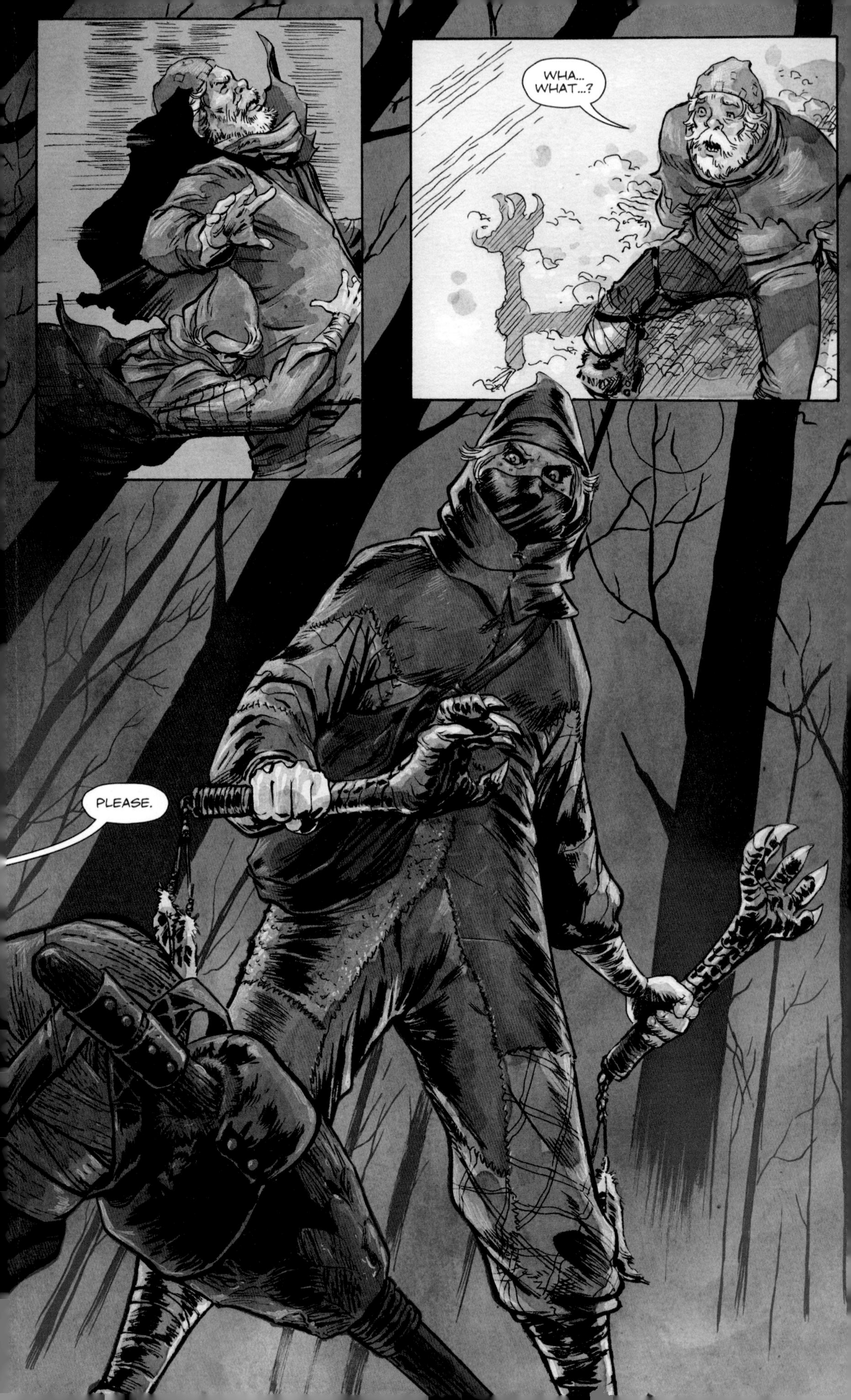
WHA... WHAT...?
PLEASE.

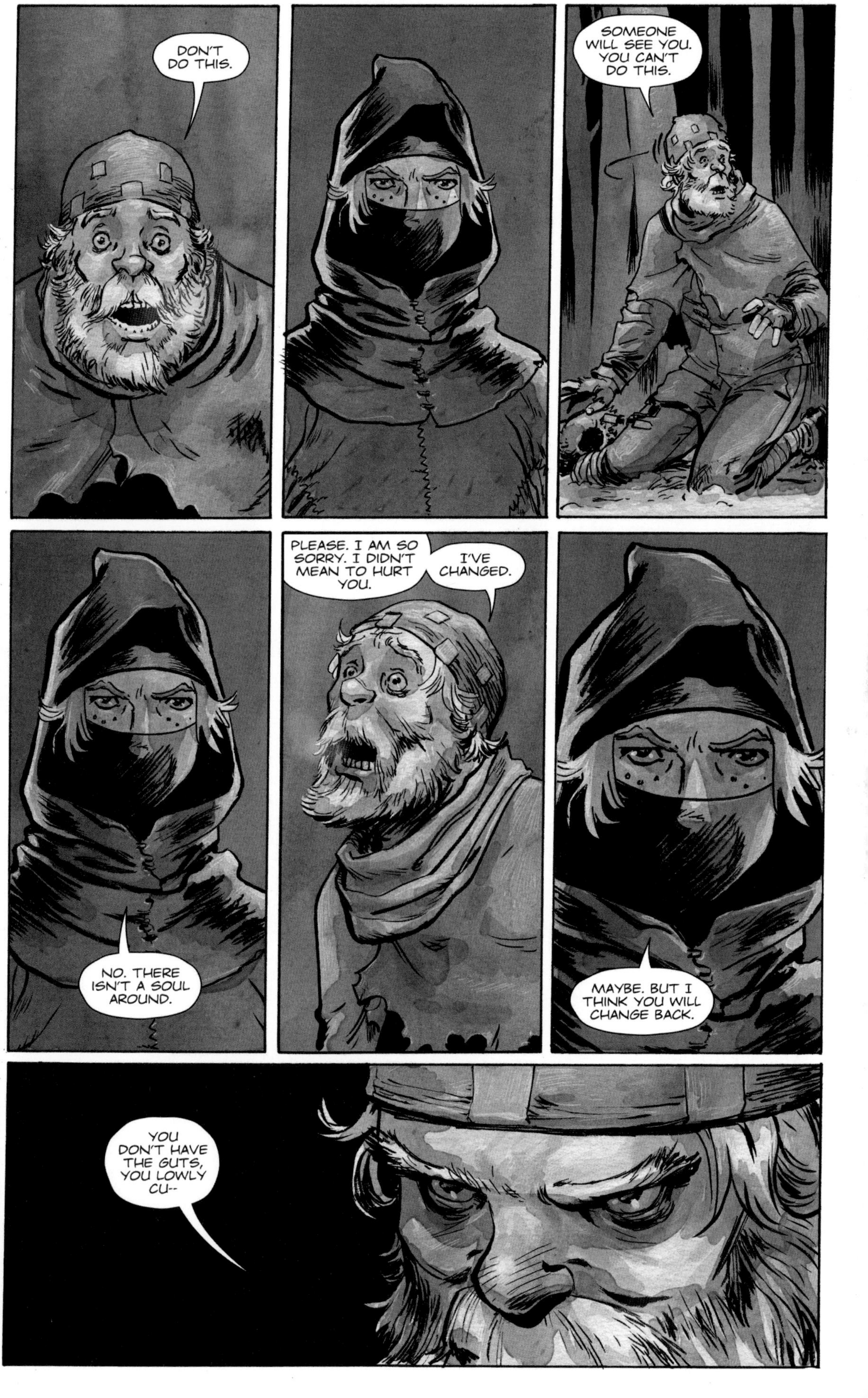
DON'T DO THIS.
SOMEONE WILL SEE YOU. YOU CAN'T DO THIS.
NO. THERE ISN'T A SOUL AROUND.
PLEASE. I AM SO SORRY. I DIDN'T MEAN TO HURT YOU.
I'VE CHANGED.
MAYBE. BUT I THINK YOU WILL CHANGE BACK.
YOU DON'T HAVE THE GUTS, YOU LOWLY CU--

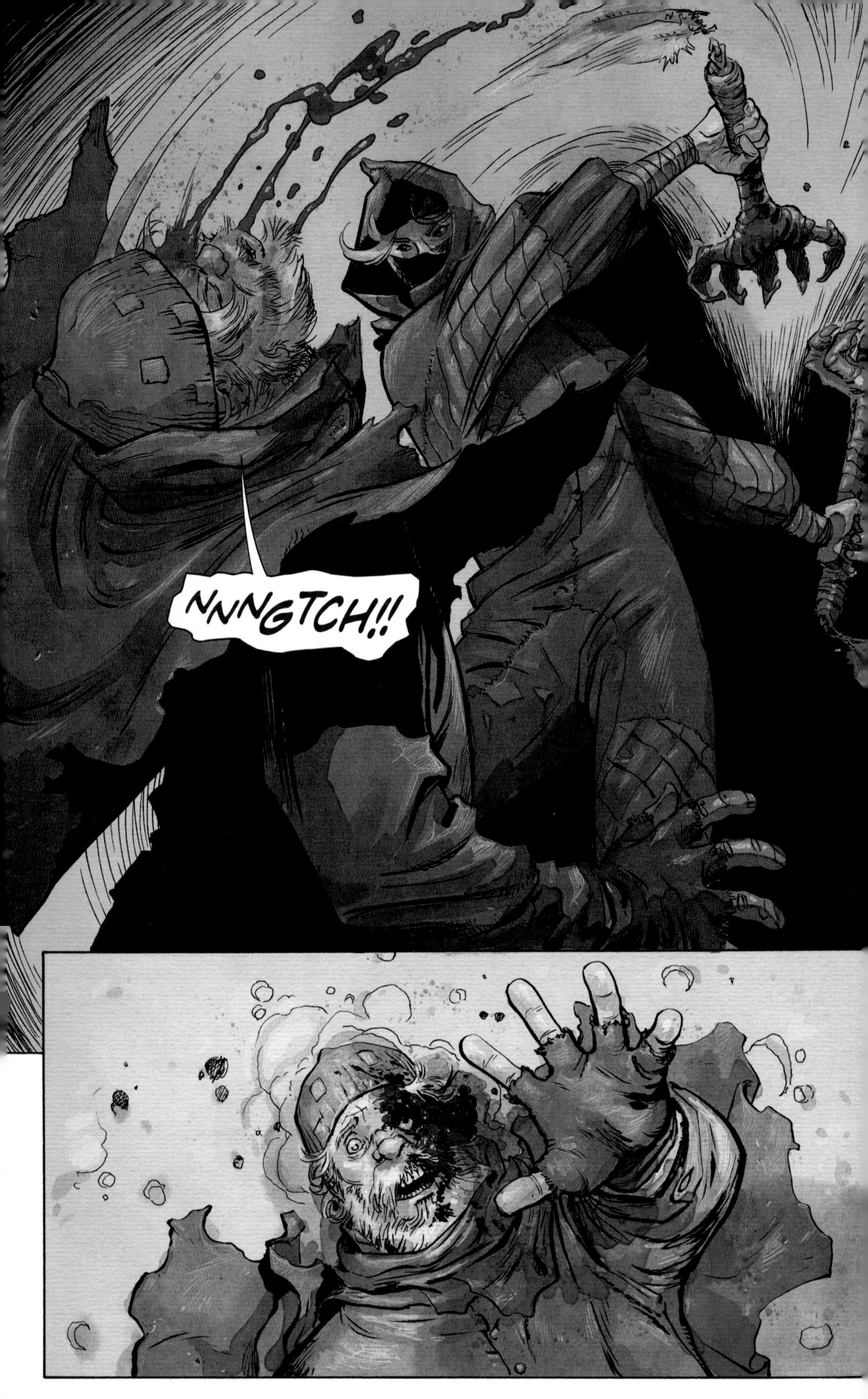
NNNGTCH!!

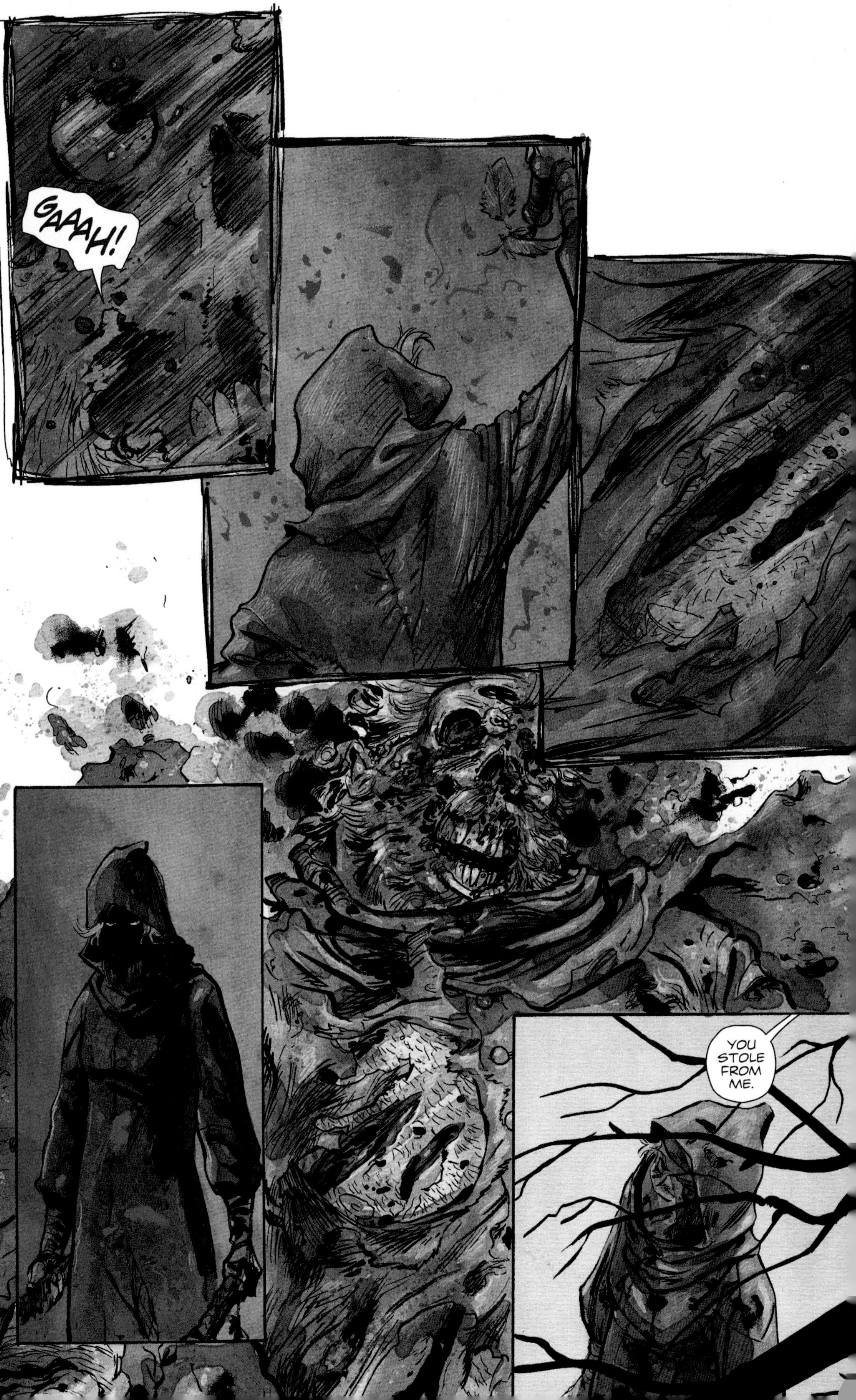
GAAAH!
YOU STOLE FROM ME.

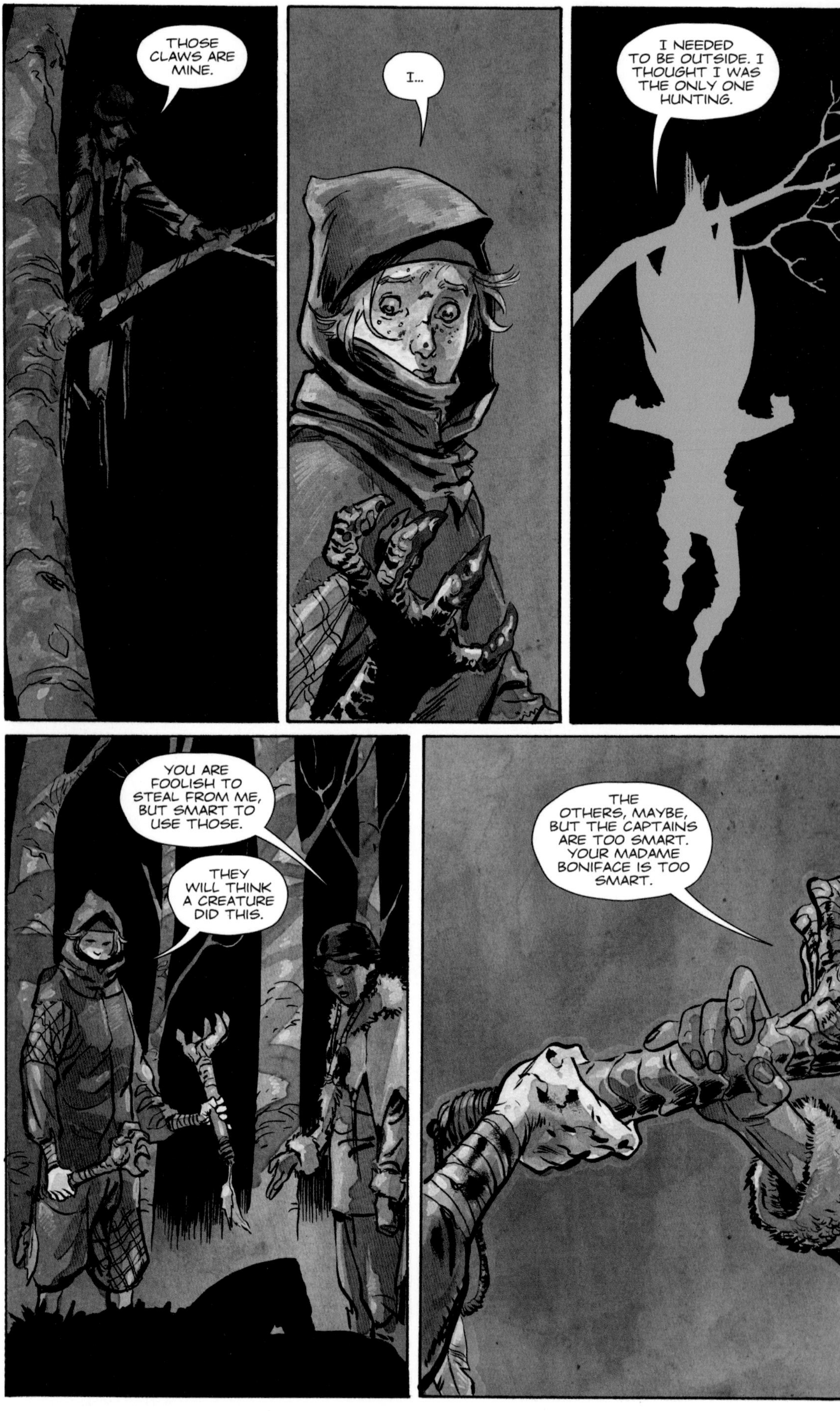
THOSE CLAWS ARE MINE.
I...
I NEEDED TO BE OUTSIDE. I THOUGHT I WAS THE ONLY ONE HUNTING.
YOU ARE FOOLISH TO STEAL FROM ME, BUT SMART TO USE THOSE.
THEY WILL THINK A CREATURE DID THIS.
THE OTHERS, MAYBE, BUT THE CAPTAINS ARE TOO SMART. YOUR MADAME BONIFACE IS TOO SMART.

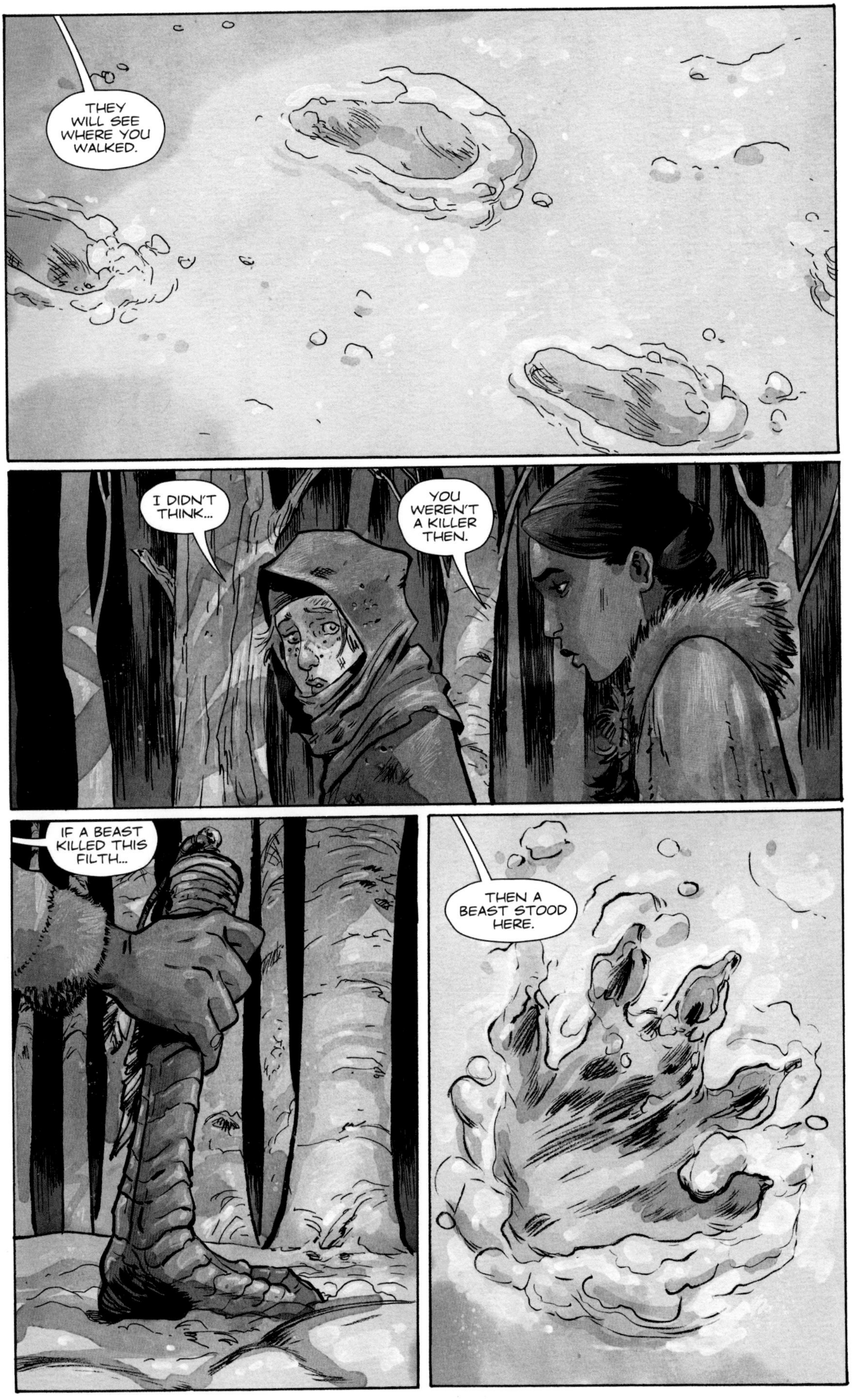
THEY WILL SEE WHERE YOU WALKED.
I DIDN'T THINK...
YOU WEREN'T A KILLER THEN.
IF A BEAST KILLED THIS FILTH...
THEN A BEAST STOOD HERE.

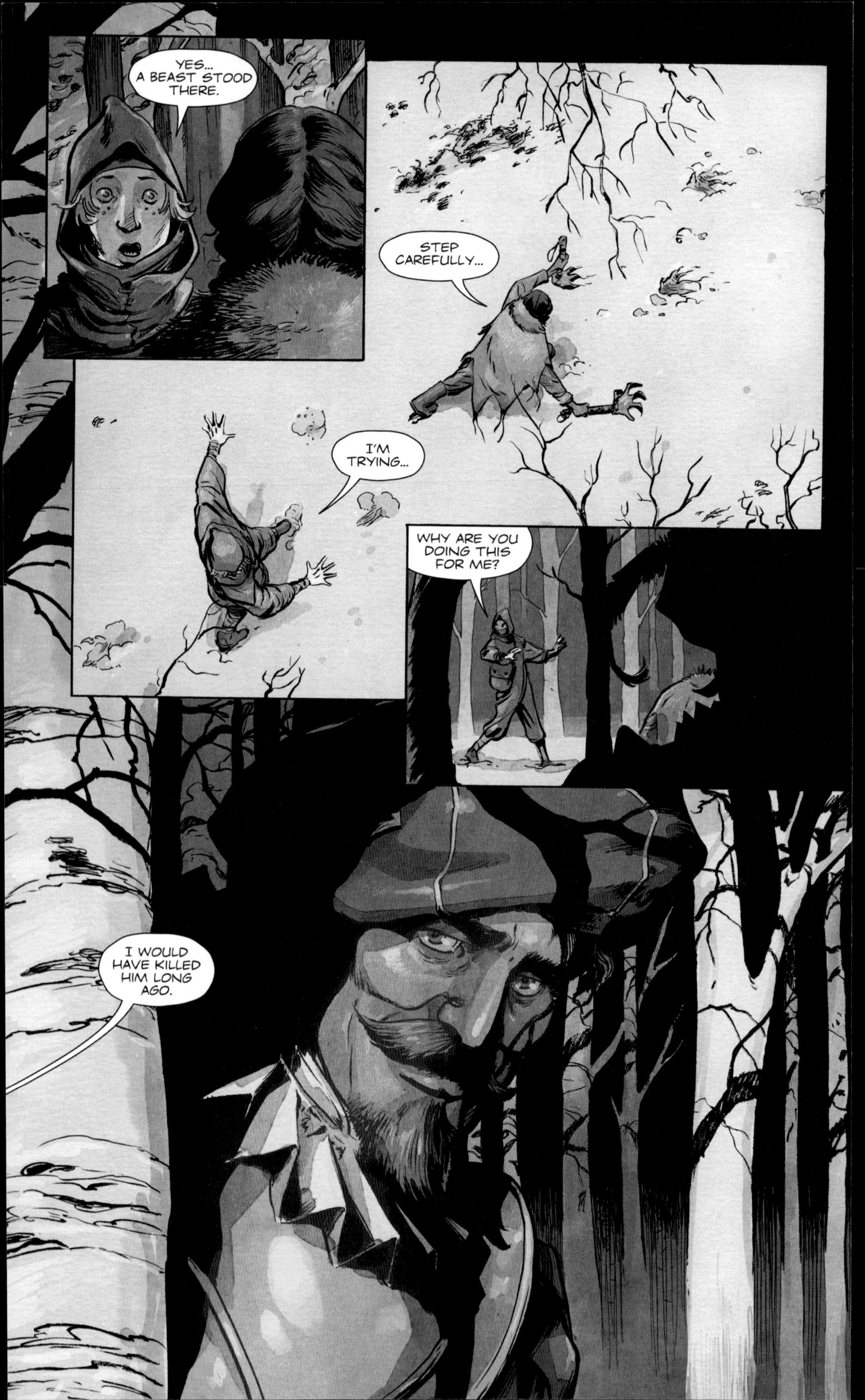
YES... A BEAST STOOD THERE.
STEP CAREFULLY...
I'M TRYING...
WHY ARE YOU DOING THIS FOR ME?
I WOULD HAVE KILLED HIM LONG AGO.

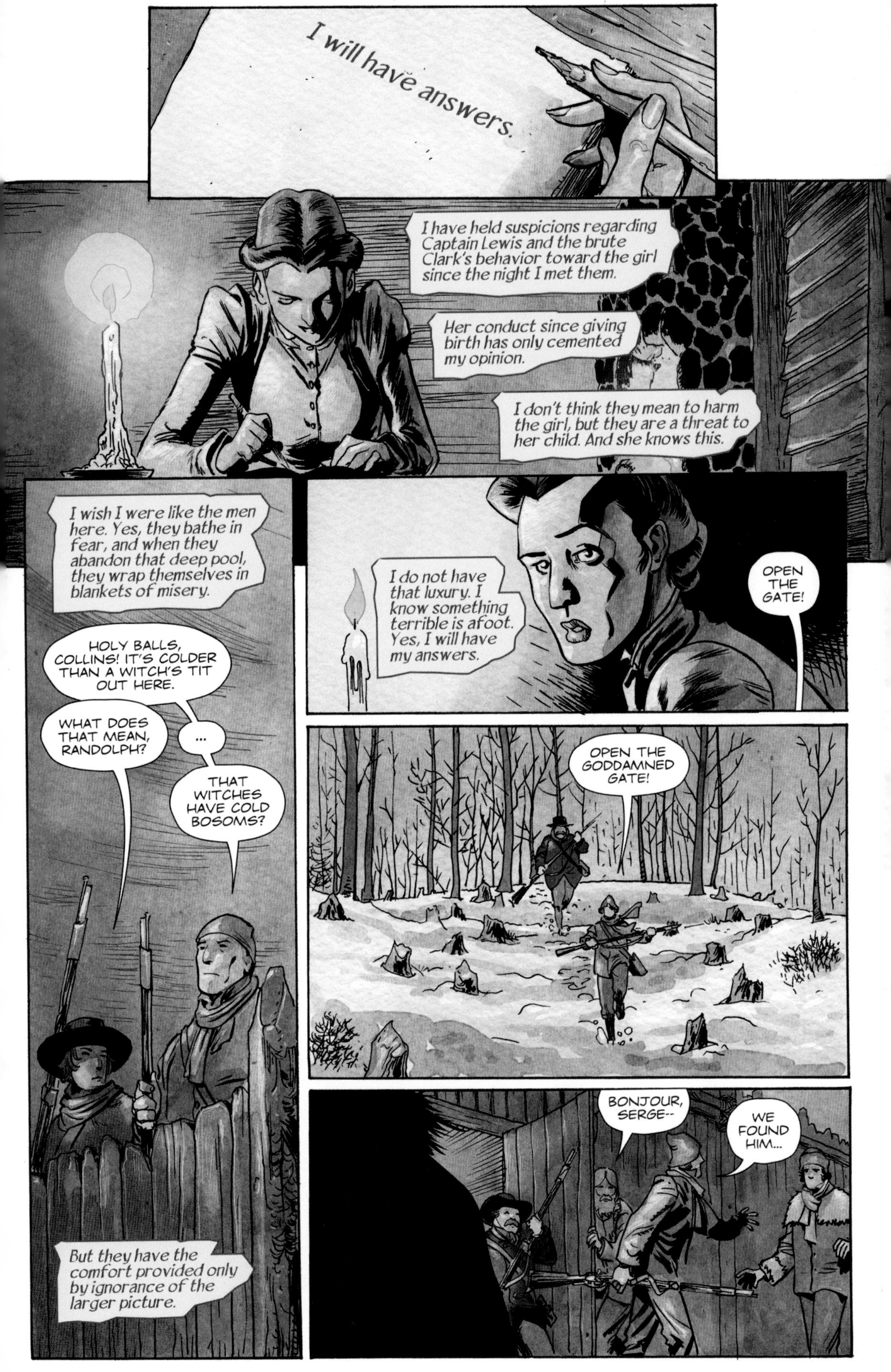

I will have answers.
I have held suspicions regarding Captain Lewis and the brute Clark's behavior toward the girl since the night I met them.
Her conduct since giving birth has only cemented my opinion.
I don't think they mean to harm the girl, but they are a threat to her child. And she knows this.
I wish I were like the men here. Yes, they bathe in fear, and when they abandon that deep pool, they wrap themselves in blankets of misery.
I do not have that luxury. I know something terrible is afoot. Yes, I will have my answers.
OPEN THE GATE!
HOLY BALLS, COLLINS! IT'S COLDER THAN A WITCH'S TIT OUT HERE.
...
WHAT DOES THAT MEAN, RANDOLPH?
THAT WITCHES HAVE COLD BOSOMS?
OPEN THE GODDAMNED GATE!
But they have the comfort provided only by ignorance of the larger picture.
BONJOUR, SERGE--
WE FOUND HIM...

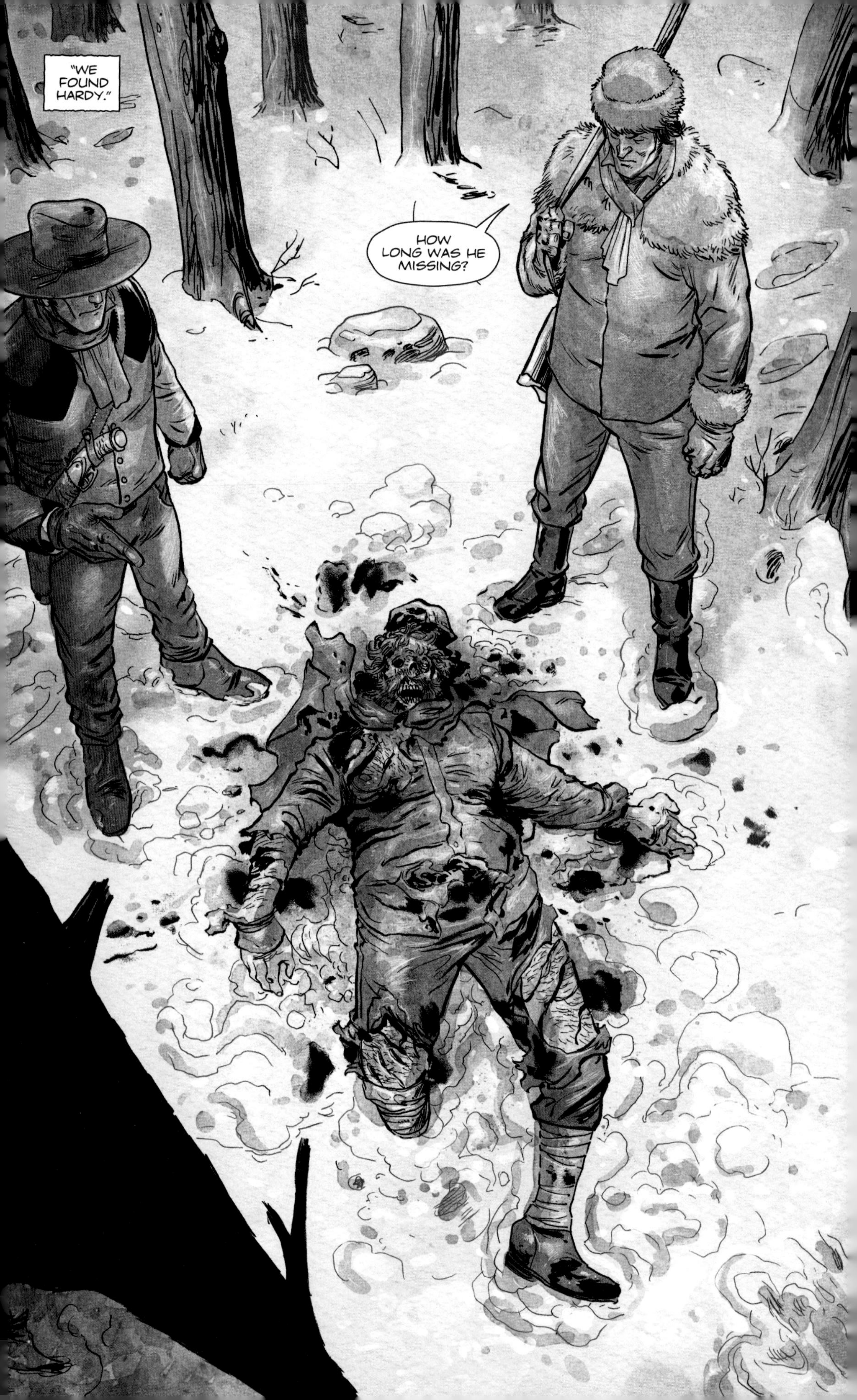
"WE FOUND HARDY."
HOW LONG WAS HE MISSING?

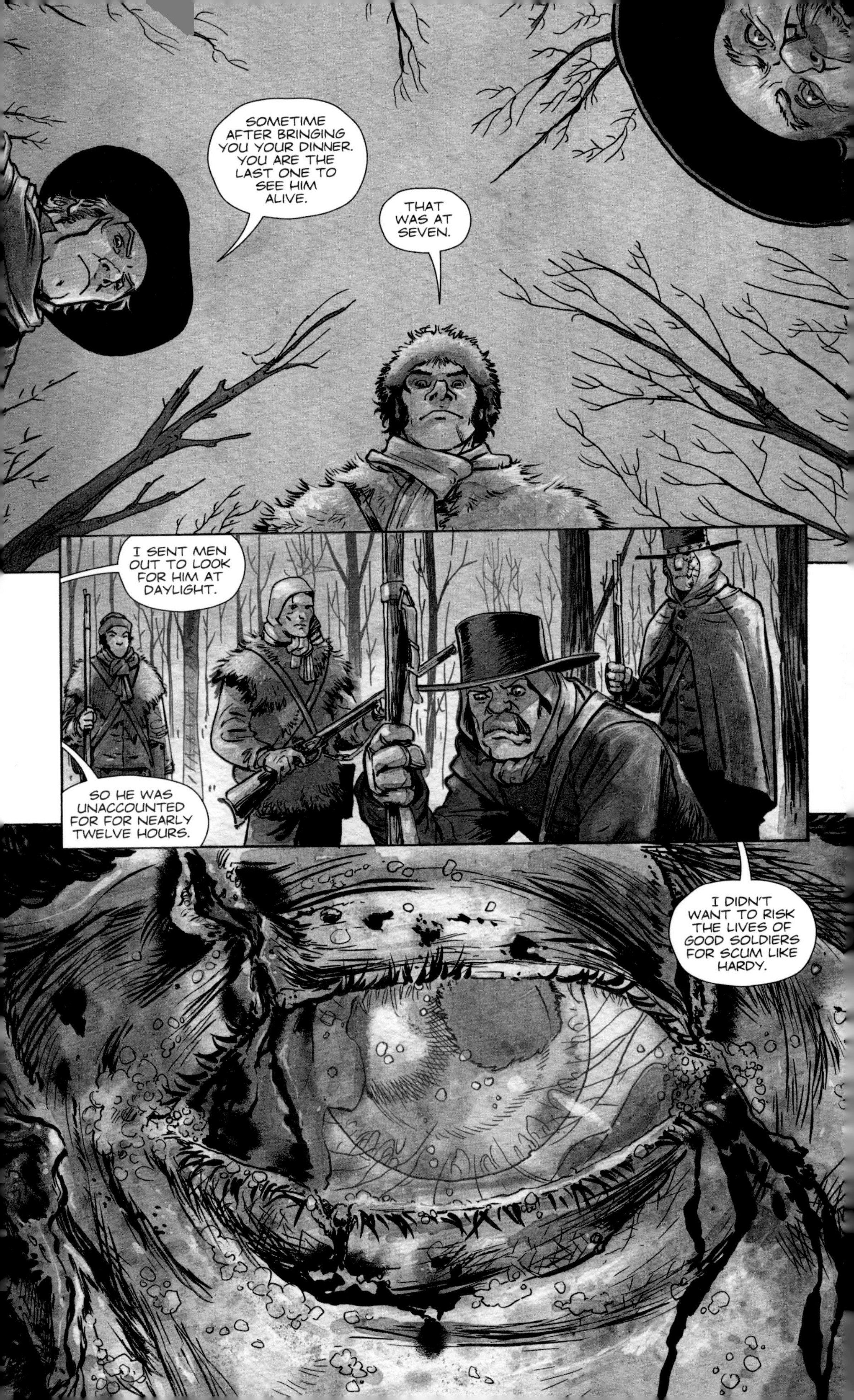
SOMETIME AFTER BRINGING YOU YOUR DINNER. YOU ARE THE LAST ONE TO SEE HIM ALIVE.
THAT WAS AT SEVEN.
I SENT MEN OUT TO LOOK FOR HIM AT DAYLIGHT.
SO HE WAS UNACCOUNTED FOR FOR NEARLY TWELVE HOURS.
I DIDN'T WANT TO RISK THE LIVES OF GOOD SOLDIERS FOR SCUM LIKE HARDY.

TURNS OUT I WAS RIGHT. WHATEVER RIPPED HIM APART COULD HAVE DONE THE SAME TO ANYONE ELSE.

THAT INCLUDES YOU. IN YOUR TENT. WATCHING YOUR ARCH.

WHAT IS THAT SUPPOSED TO MEAN?

WE CAN DISCUSS THIS LATER.

BRING HIM BACK TO THE FORT, GENTLEMEN. I'M SURE CAPTAIN LEWIS WANTS TO GET A GOOD LOOK AT HIM.

AND BE CAREFUL WHERE YOU STEP...

THERE'S TRACKS WE NEED TO EXAMINE AS WELL.

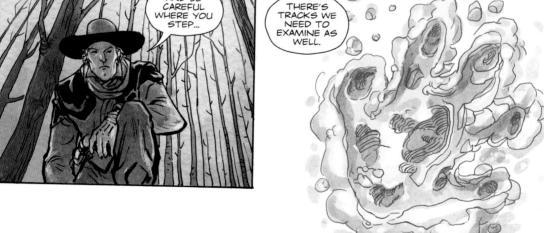

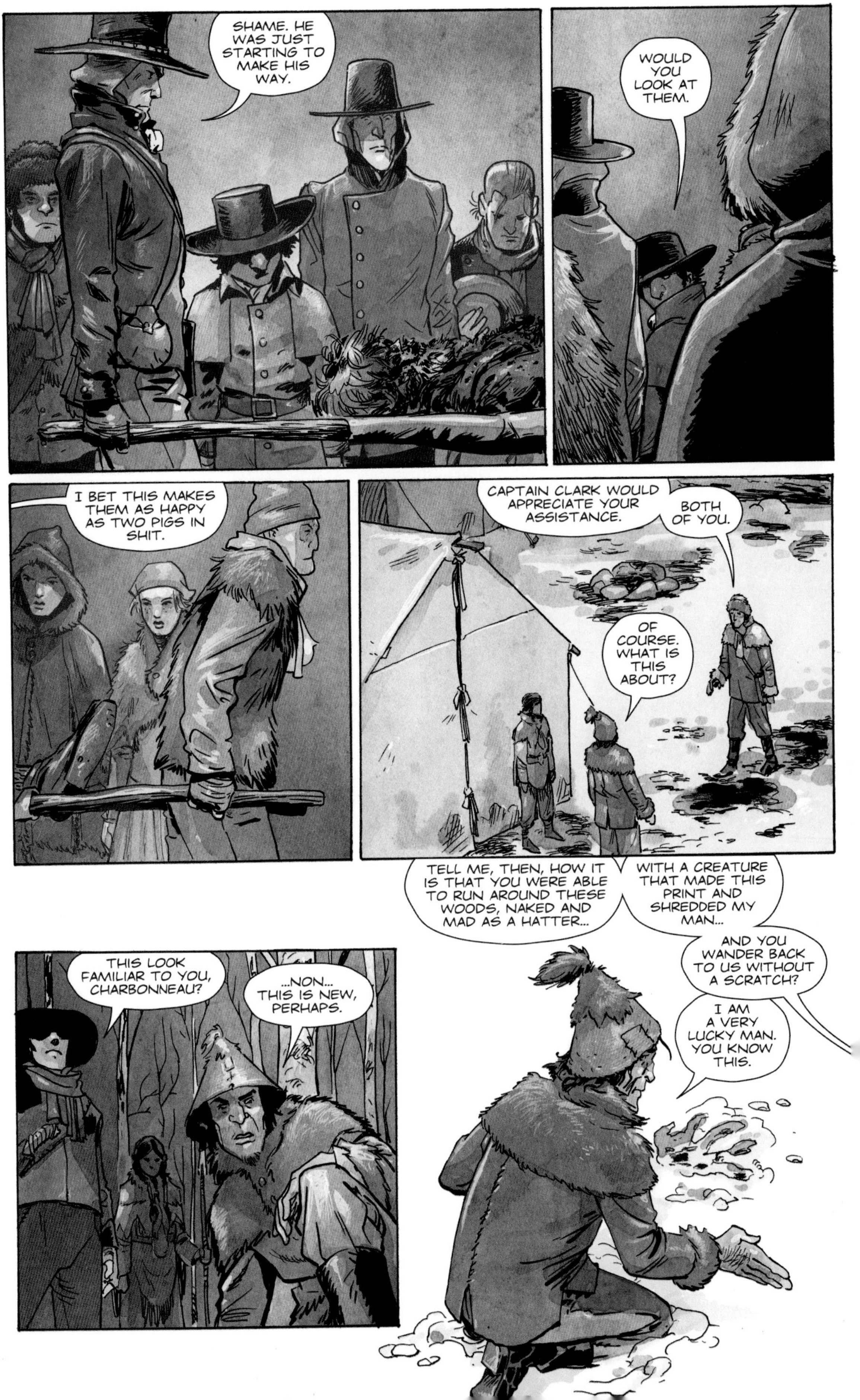
SHAME. HE WAS JUST STARTING TO MAKE HIS WAY.
WOULD YOU LOOK AT THEM.
I BET THIS MAKES THEM AS HAPPY AS TWO PIGS IN SHIT.
CAPTAIN CLARK WOULD APPRECIATE YOUR ASSISTANCE.
BOTH OF YOU.
OF COURSE. WHAT IS THIS ABOUT?
THIS LOOK FAMILIAR TO YOU, CHARBONNEAU?
...NON... THIS IS NEW, PERHAPS.
TELL ME, THEN, HOW IT IS THAT YOU WERE ABLE TO RUN AROUND THESE WOODS, NAKED AND MAD AS A HATTER...
WITH A CREATURE THAT MADE THIS PRINT AND SHREDDED MY MAN...
AND YOU WANDER BACK TO US WITHOUT A SCRATCH?
I AM A VERY LUCKY MAN. YOU KNOW THIS.

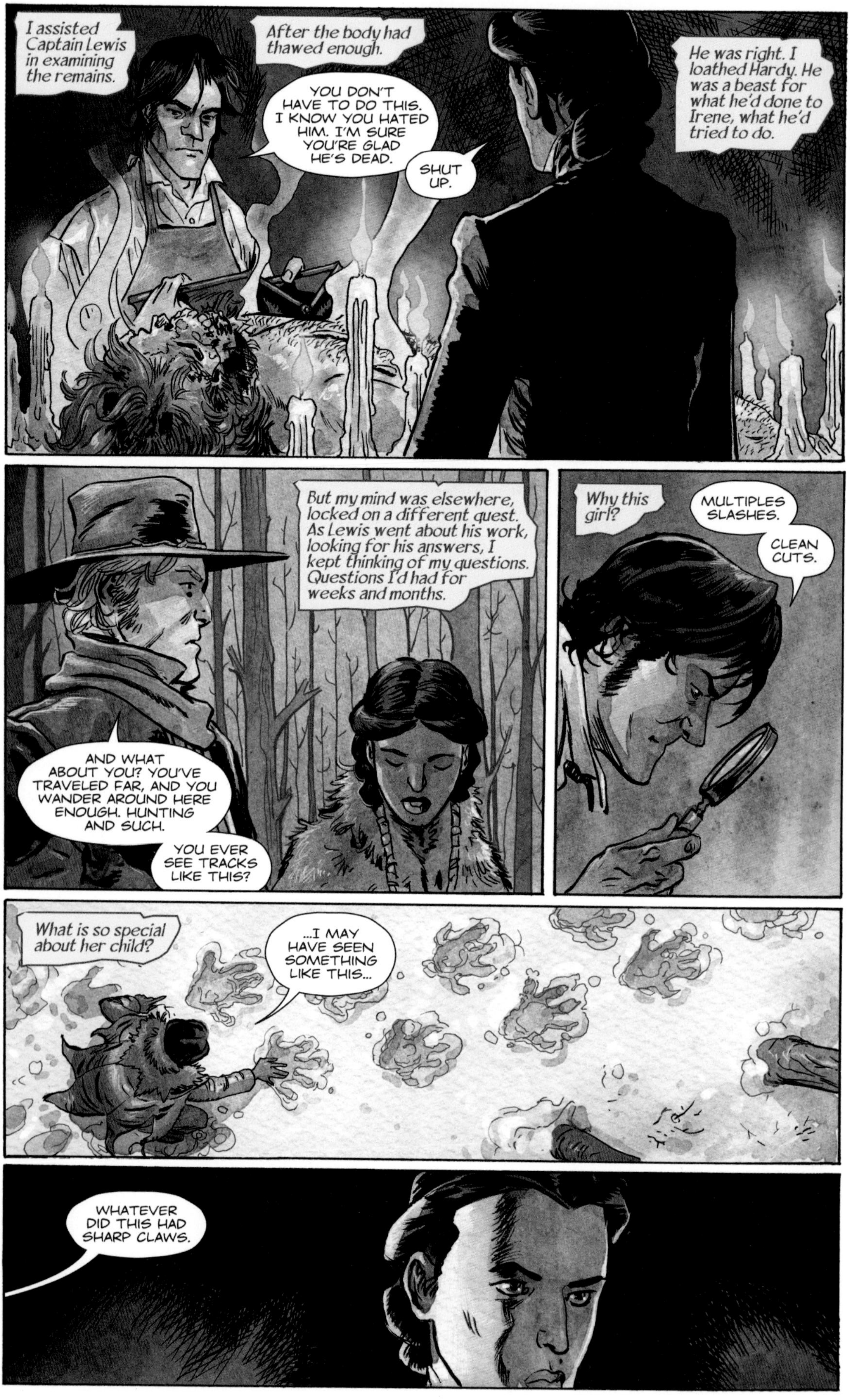
I assisted Captain Lewis in examining the remains.
After the body had thawed enough.
YOU DON'T HAVE TO DO THIS. I KNOW YOU HATED HIM. I'M SURE YOU'RE GLAD HE'S DEAD.
SHUT UP.
He was right. I loathed Hardy. He was a beast for what he'd done to Irene, what he'd tried to do.
But my mind was elsewhere, locked on a different quest. As Lewis went about his work, looking for his answers, I kept thinking of my questions. Questions I'd had for weeks and months.
AND WHAT ABOUT YOU? YOU'VE TRAVELED FAR, AND YOU WANDER AROUND HERE ENOUGH. HUNTING AND SUCH.
YOU EVER SEE TRACKS LIKE THIS?
Why this girl?
MULTIPLES SLASHES.
CLEAN CUTS.
What is so special about her child?
...I MAY HAVE SEEN SOMETHING LIKE THIS...
WHATEVER DID THIS HAD SHARP CLAWS.

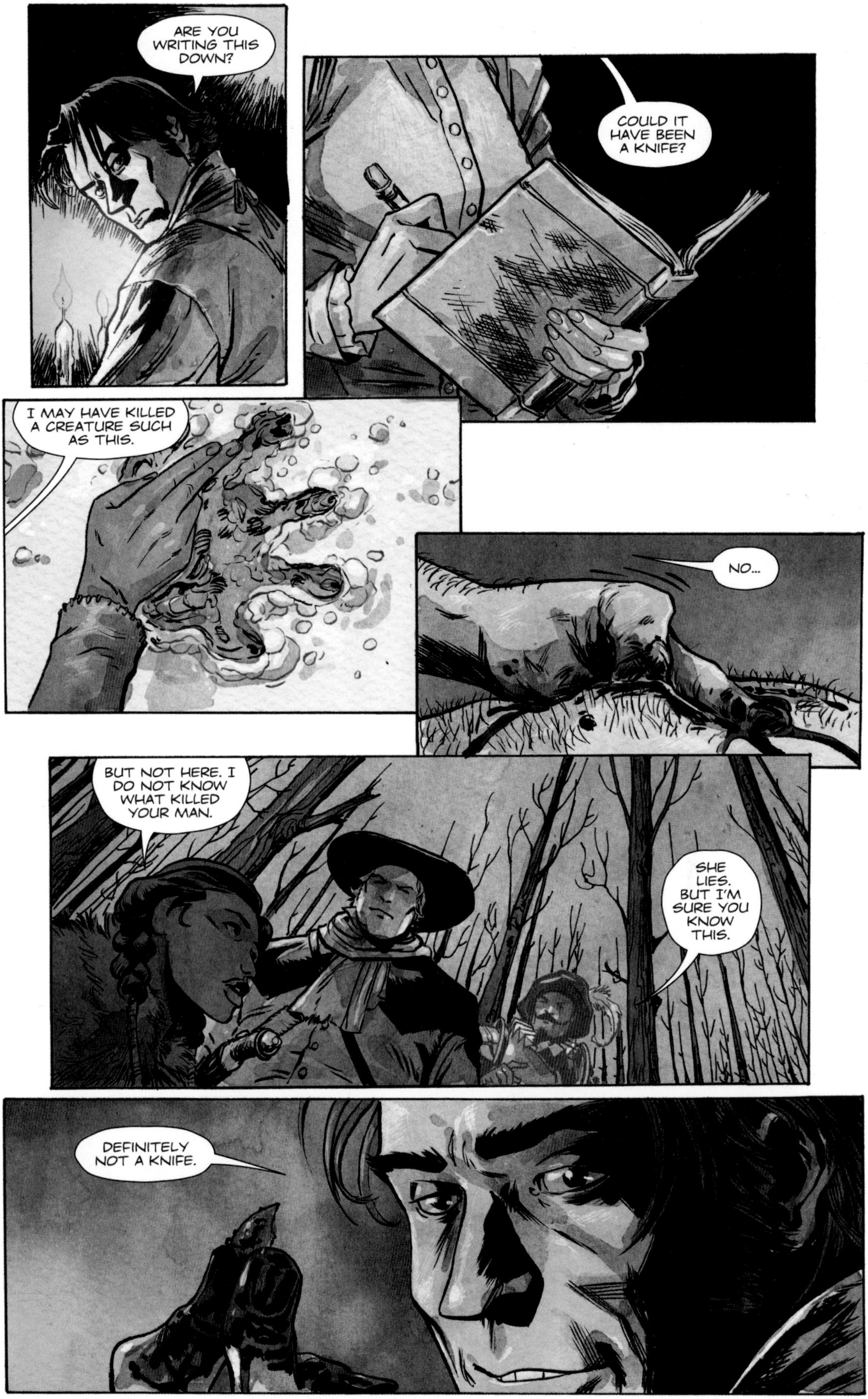
ARE YOU WRITING THIS DOWN?
COULD IT HAVE BEEN A KNIFE?
I MAY HAVE KILLED A CREATURE SUCH AS THIS.
NO...
BUT NOT HERE. I DO NOT KNOW WHAT KILLED YOUR MAN.
SHE LIES. BUT I'M SURE YOU KNOW THIS.
DEFINITELY NOT A KNIFE.

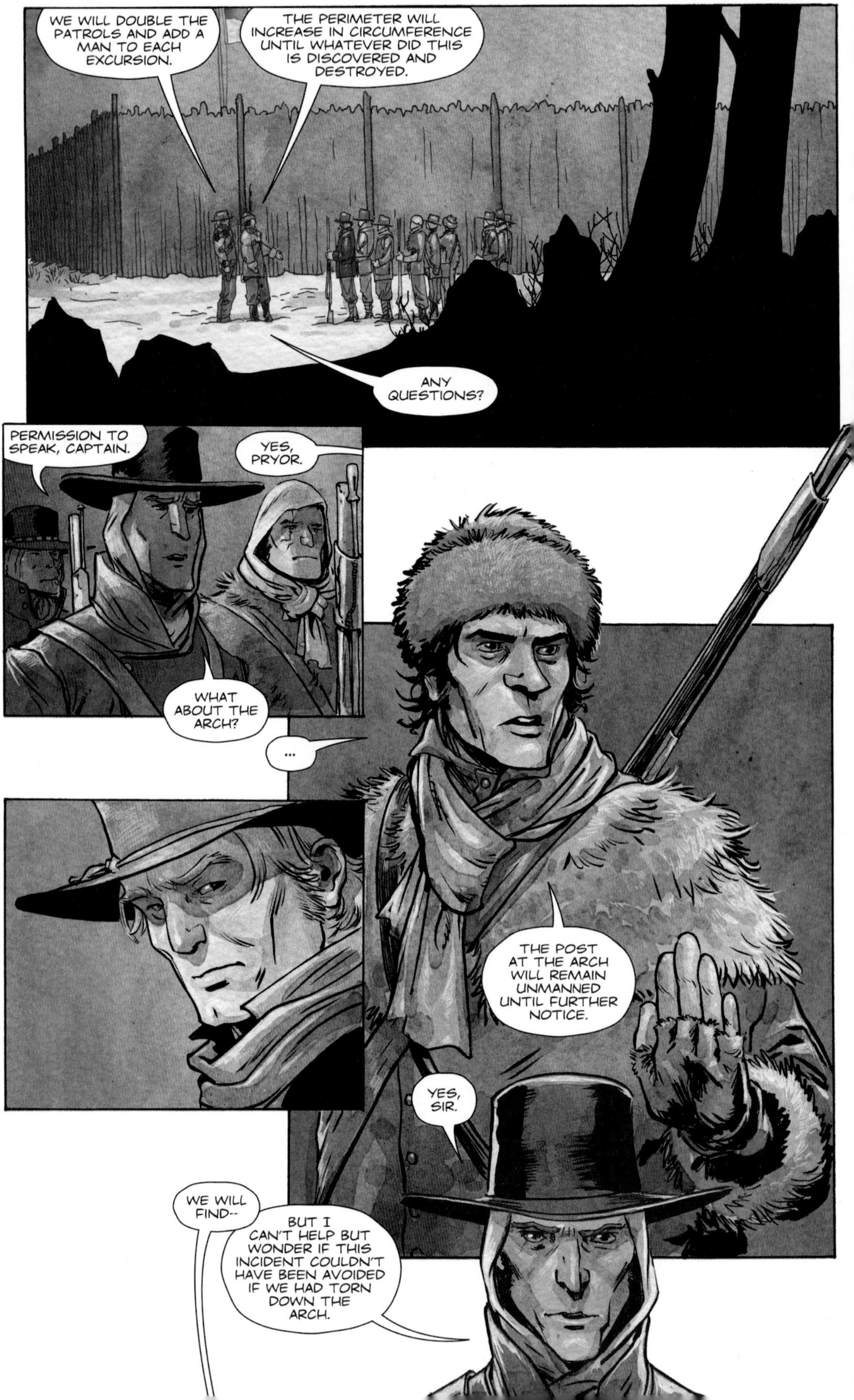
WE WILL DOUBLE THE PATROLS AND ADD A MAN TO EACH EXCURSION.
THE PERIMETER WILL INCREASE IN CIRCUMFERENCE UNTIL WHATEVER DID THIS IS DISCOVERED AND DESTROYED.
ANY QUESTIONS?
PERMISSION TO SPEAK, CAPTAIN.
YES, PRYOR.
WHAT ABOUT THE ARCH?
...
THE POST AT THE ARCH WILL REMAIN UNMANNED UNTIL FURTHER NOTICE.
YES, SIR.
WE WILL FIND--
BUT I CAN'T HELP BUT WONDER IF THIS INCIDENT COULDN'T HAVE BEEN AVOIDED IF WE HAD TORN DOWN THE ARCH.

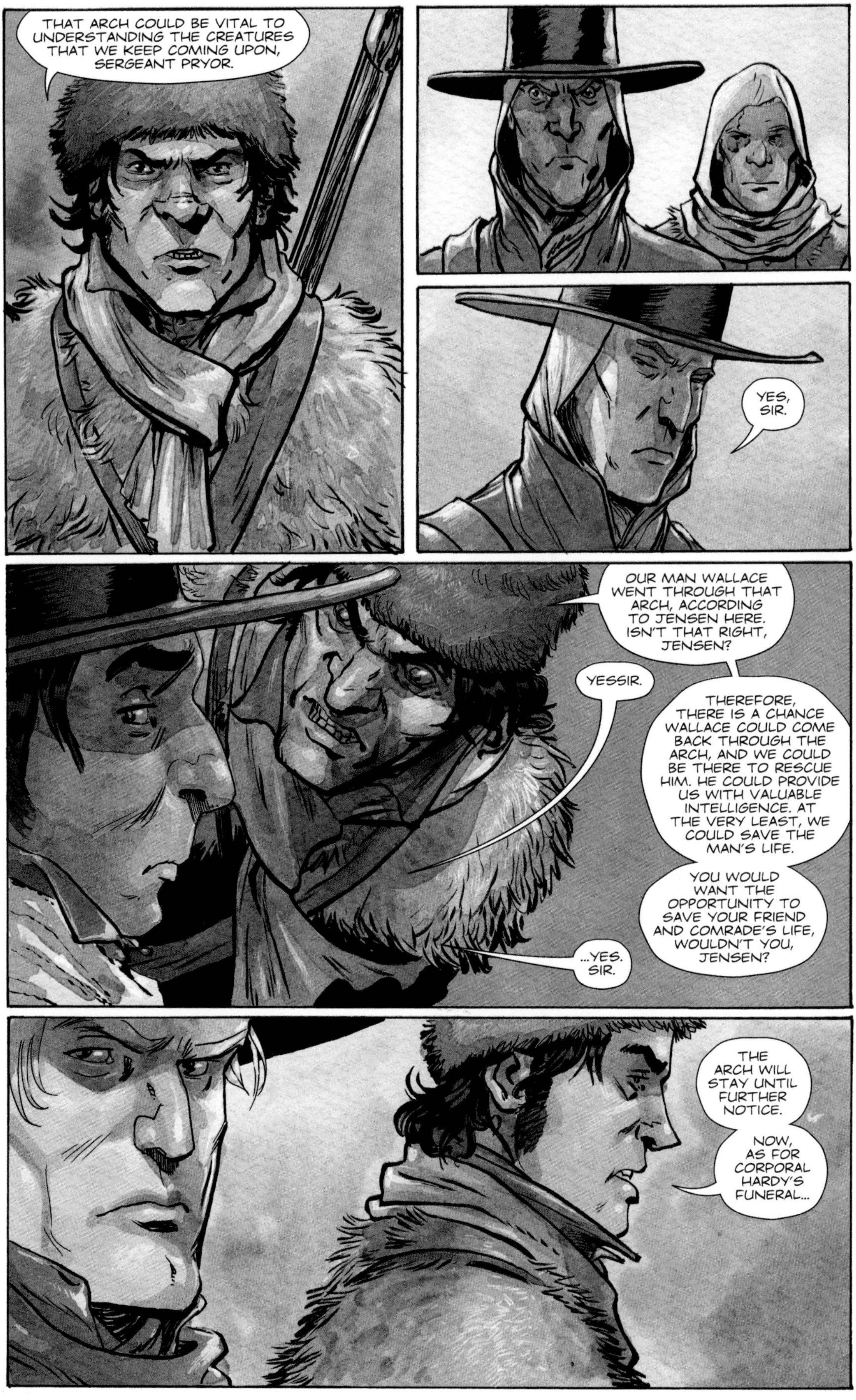
THAT ARCH COULD BE VITAL TO UNDERSTANDING THE CREATURES THAT WE KEEP COMING UPON, SERGEANT PRYOR.
YES, SIR.
OUR MAN WALLACE WENT THROUGH THAT ARCH, ACCORDING TO JENSEN HERE. ISN'T THAT RIGHT, JENSEN?
YESSIR.
THEREFORE, THERE IS A CHANCE WALLACE COULD COME BACK THROUGH THE ARCH, AND WE COULD BE THERE TO RESCUE HIM. HE COULD PROVIDE US WITH VALUABLE INTELLIGENCE. AT THE VERY LEAST, WE COULD SAVE THE MAN'S LIFE.
YOU WOULD WANT THE OPPORTUNITY TO SAVE YOUR FRIEND AND COMRADE'S LIFE, WOULDN'T YOU, JENSEN?
...YES. SIR.
THE ARCH WILL STAY UNTIL FURTHER NOTICE.
NOW, AS FOR CORPORAL HARDY'S FUNERAL...

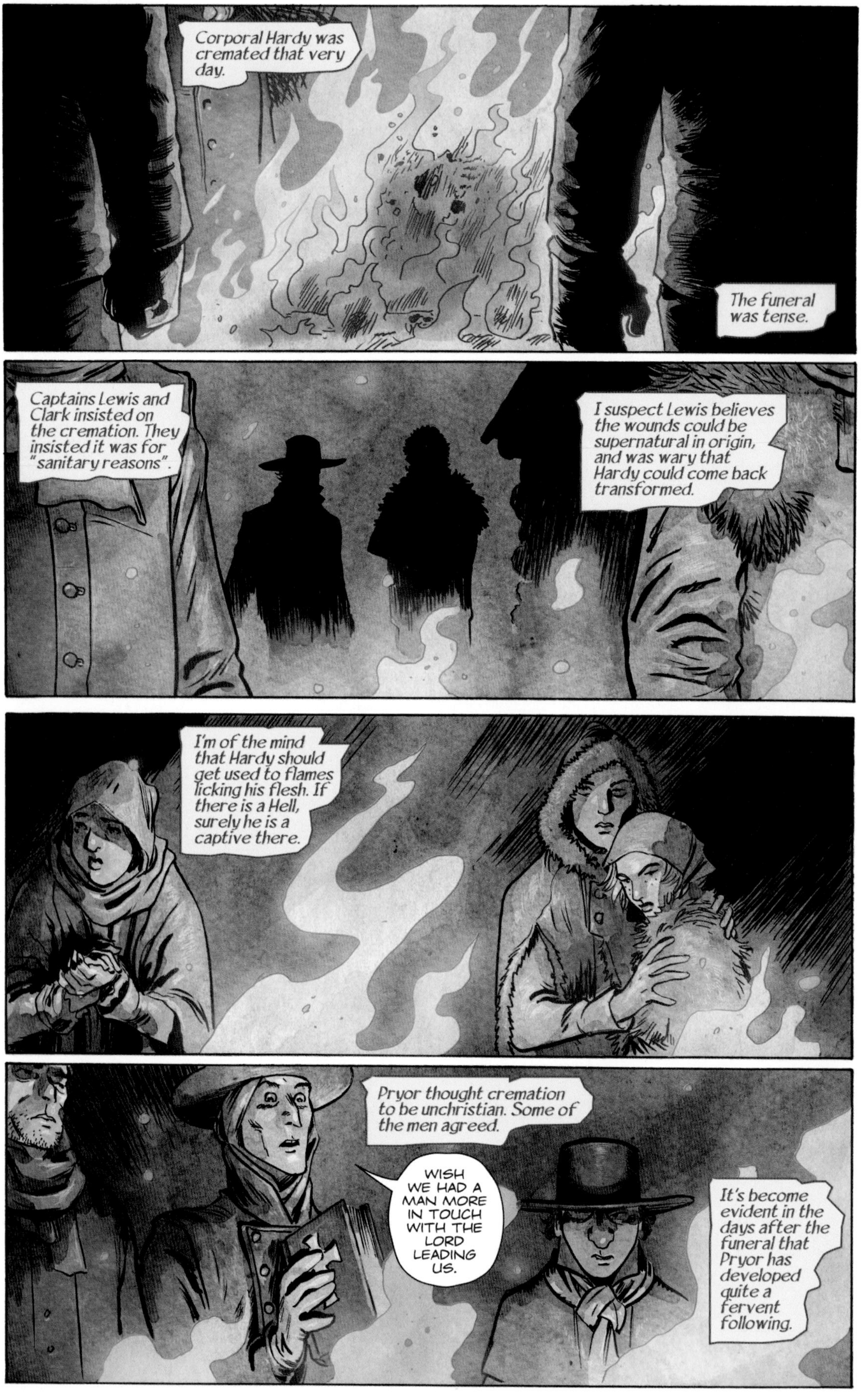
Corporal Hardy was cremated that very day.
The funeral was tense.
Captains Lewis and Clark insisted on the cremation. They insisted it was for "sanitary reasons".
I suspect Lewis believes the wounds could be supernatural in origin, and was wary that Hardy could come back transformed.
I'm of the mind that Hardy should get used to flames licking his flesh. If there is a Hell, surely he is a captive there.
Pryor thought cremation to be unchristian. Some of the men agreed.
WISH WE HAD A MAN MORE IN TOUCH WITH THE LORD LEADING US.
It's become evident in the days after the funeral that Pryor has developed quite a fervent following.

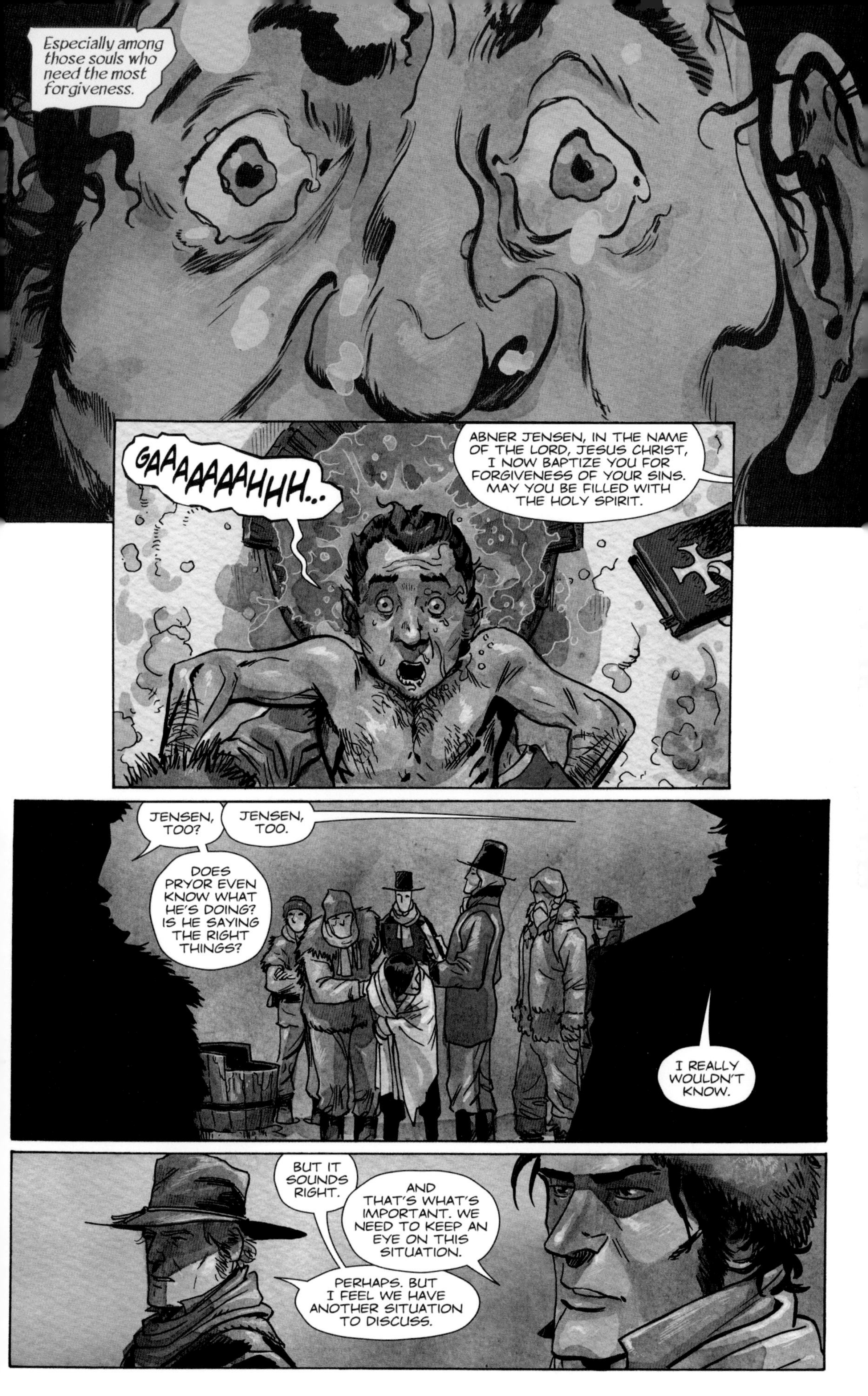
Especially among those souls who need the most forgiveness.
GAAAAAAHHH...
ABNER JENSEN, IN THE NAME OF THE LORD, JESUS CHRIST, I NOW BAPTIZE YOU FOR FORGIVENESS OF YOUR SINS. MAY YOU BE FILLED WITH THE HOLY SPIRIT.
JENSEN, TOO?
JENSEN, TOO.
DOES PRYOR EVEN KNOW WHAT HE'S DOING? IS HE SAYING THE RIGHT THINGS?
I REALLY WOULDN'T KNOW.
BUT IT SOUNDS RIGHT.
AND THAT'S WHAT'S IMPORTANT. WE NEED TO KEEP AN EYE ON THIS SITUATION.
PERHAPS. BUT I FEEL WE HAVE ANOTHER SITUATION TO DISCUSS.

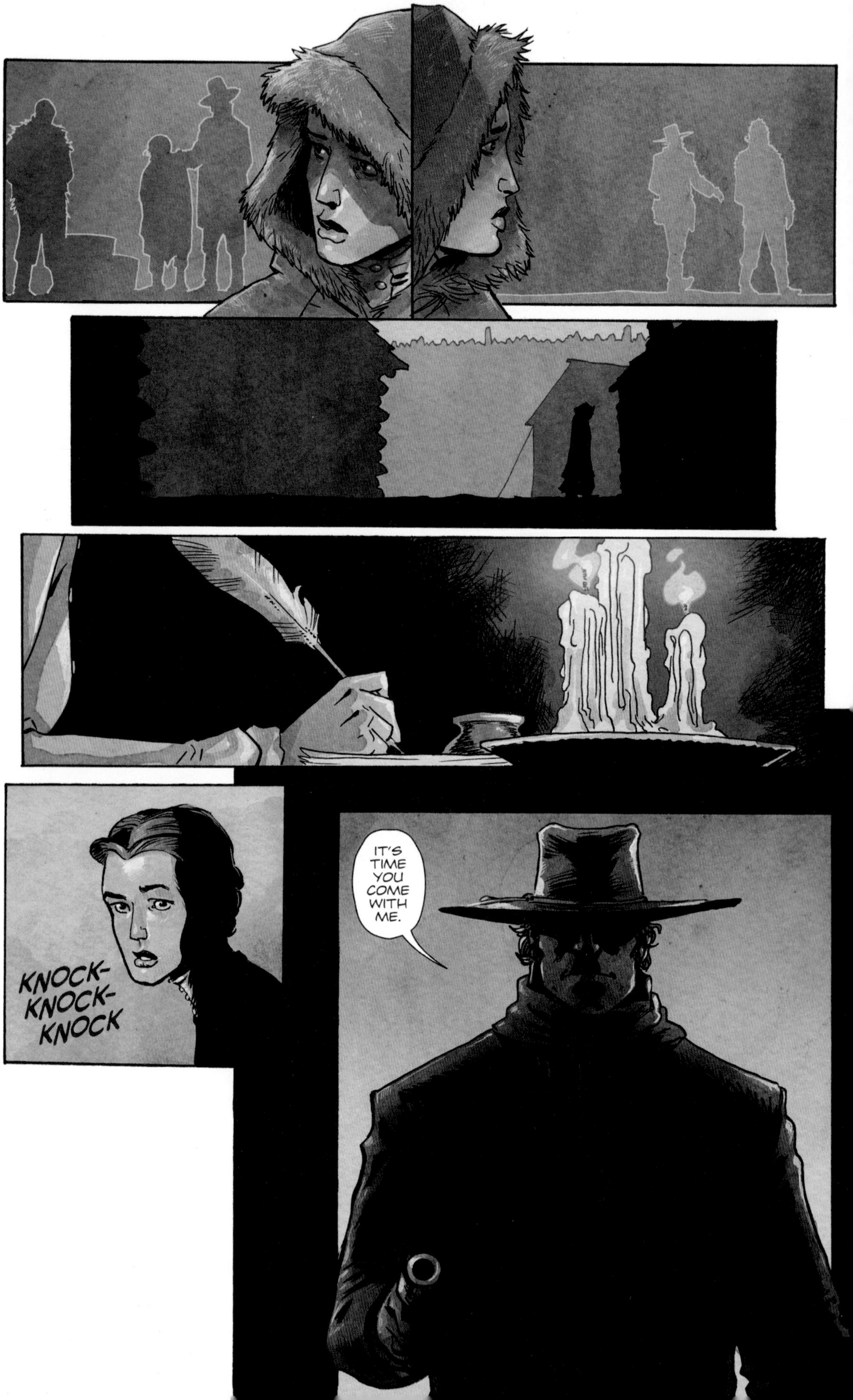
KNOCK-
KNOCK-
KNOCK
IT'S TIME YOU COME WITH ME.

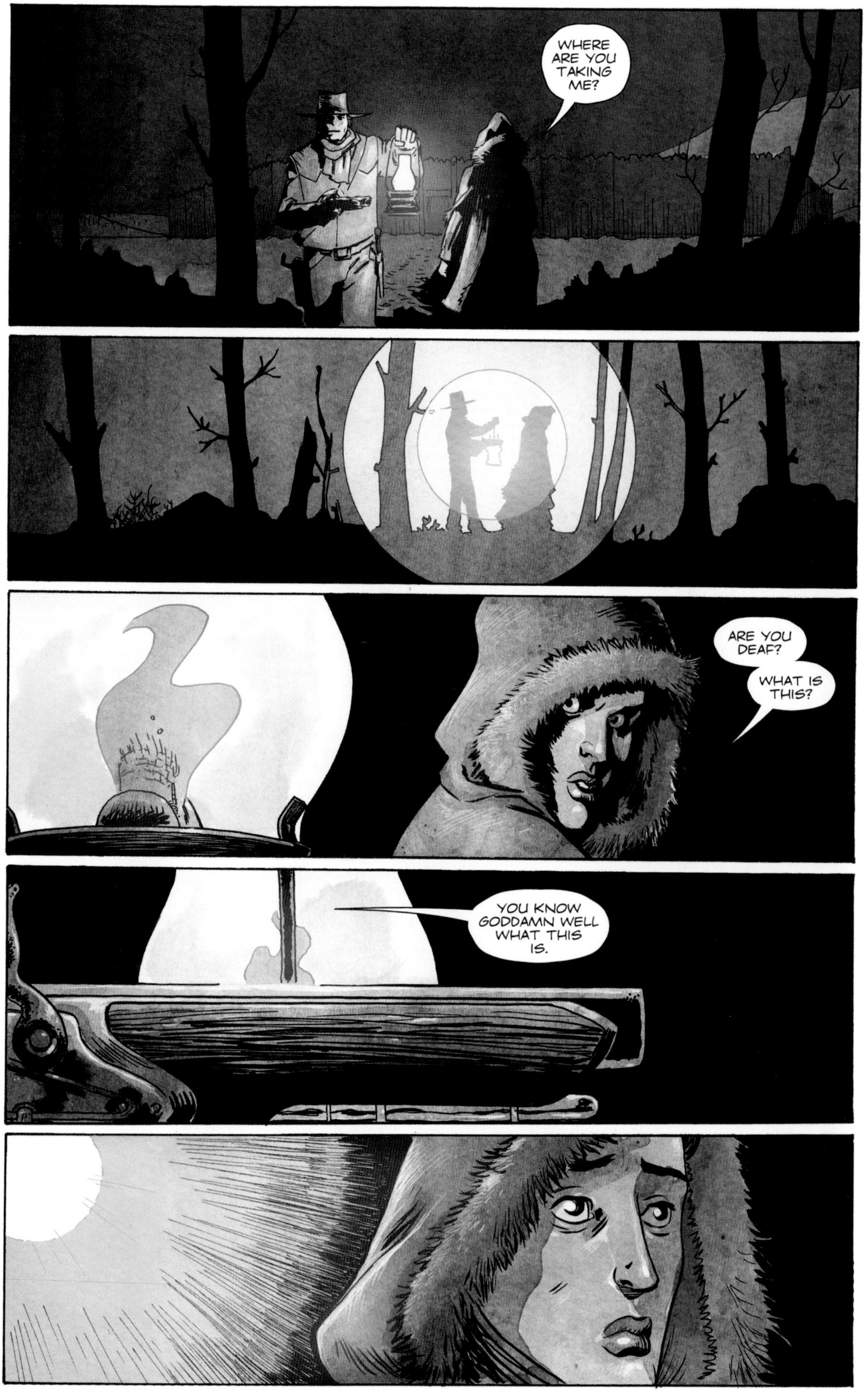
WHERE ARE YOU TAKING ME?
ARE YOU DEAF?
WHAT IS THIS?
YOU KNOW GODDAMN WELL WHAT THIS IS.

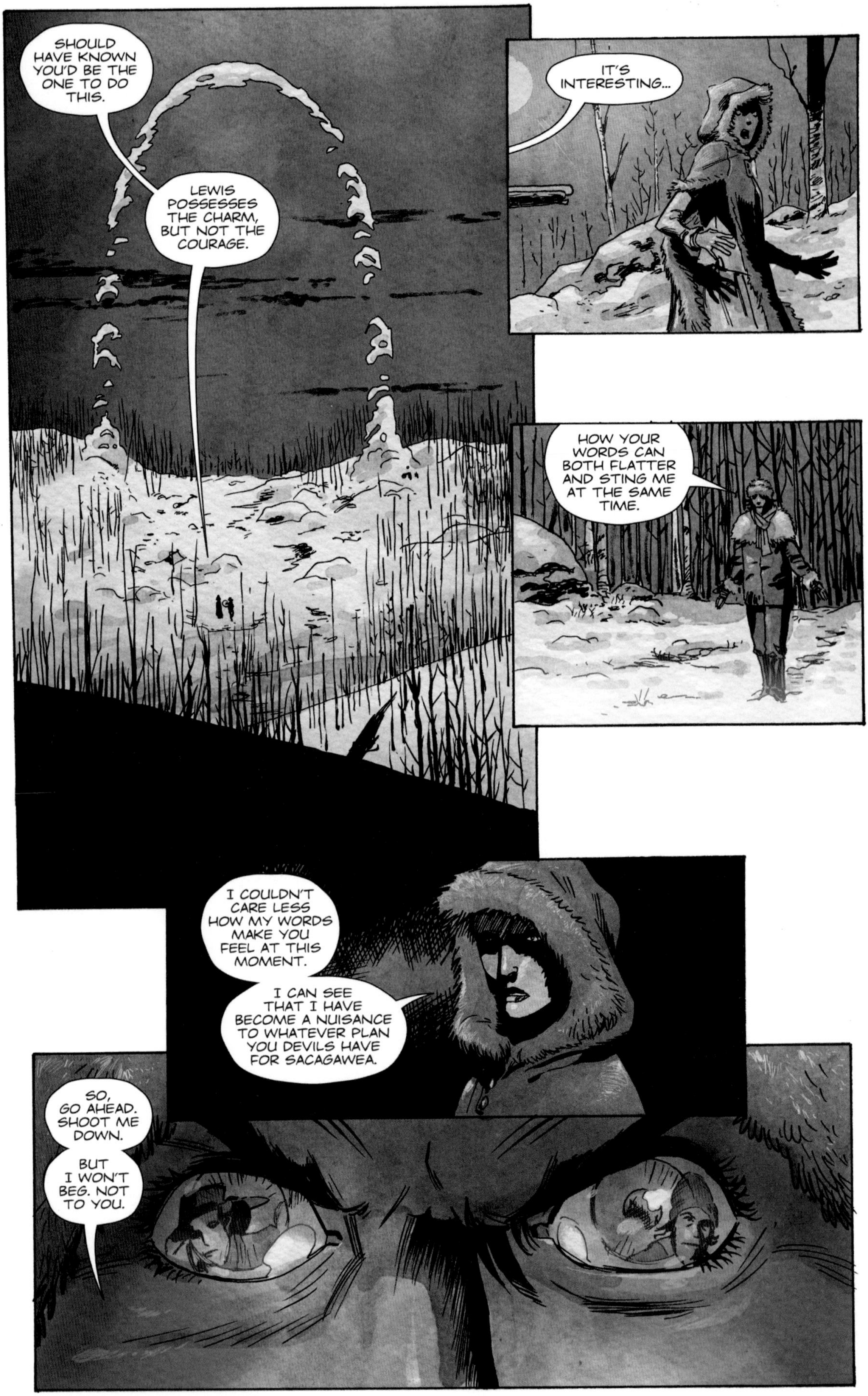
SHOULD HAVE KNOWN YOU'D BE THE ONE TO DO THIS.
LEWIS POSSESSES THE CHARM, BUT NOT THE COURAGE.
IT'S INTERESTING...
HOW YOUR WORDS CAN BOTH FLATTER AND STING ME AT THE SAME TIME.
I COULDN'T CARE LESS HOW MY WORDS MAKE YOU FEEL AT THIS MOMENT.
I CAN SEE THAT I HAVE BECOME A NUISANCE TO WHATEVER PLAN YOU DEVILS HAVE FOR SACAGAWEA.
SO, GO AHEAD. SHOOT ME DOWN.
BUT I WON'T BEG. NOT TO YOU.

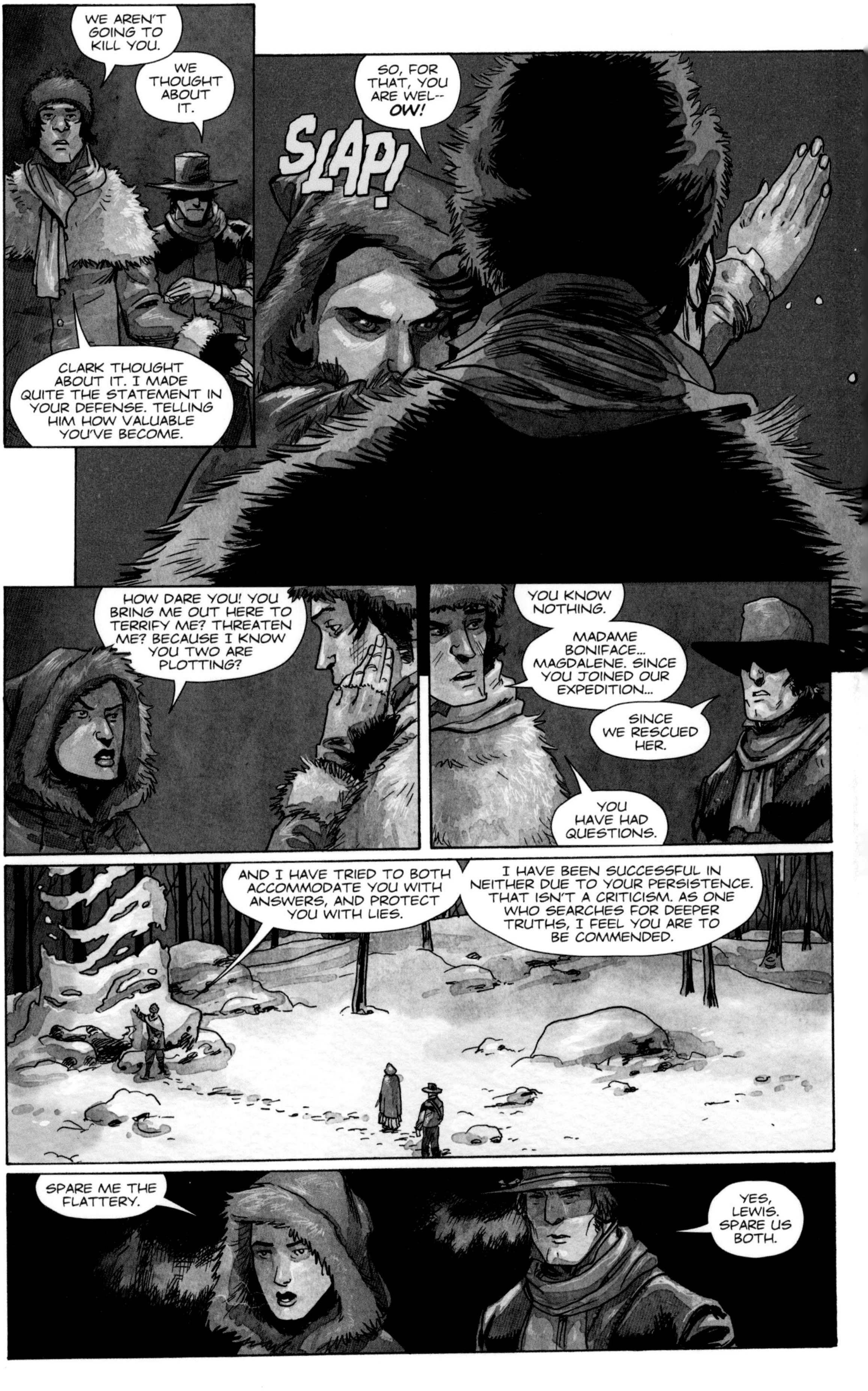

WE AREN'T GOING TO KILL YOU.
WE THOUGHT ABOUT IT.
CLARK THOUGHT ABOUT IT. I MADE QUITE THE STATEMENT IN YOUR DEFENSE. TELLING HIM HOW VALUABLE YOU'VE BECOME.
SO, FOR THAT, YOU ARE WEL-- OW!
SLAP!
HOW DARE YOU! YOU BRING ME OUT HERE TO TERRIFY ME? THREATEN ME? BECAUSE I KNOW YOU TWO ARE PLOTTING?
YOU KNOW NOTHING.
MADAME BONIFACE... MAGDALENE. SINCE YOU JOINED OUR EXPEDITION...
SINCE WE RESCUED HER.
YOU HAVE HAD QUESTIONS.
AND I HAVE TRIED TO BOTH ACCOMMODATE YOU WITH ANSWERS, AND PROTECT YOU WITH LIES.
I HAVE BEEN SUCCESSFUL IN NEITHER DUE TO YOUR PERSISTENCE. THAT ISN'T A CRITICISM. AS ONE WHO SEARCHES FOR DEEPER TRUTHS, I FEEL YOU ARE TO BE COMMENDED.
SPARE ME THE FLATTERY.
YES, LEWIS. SPARE US BOTH.

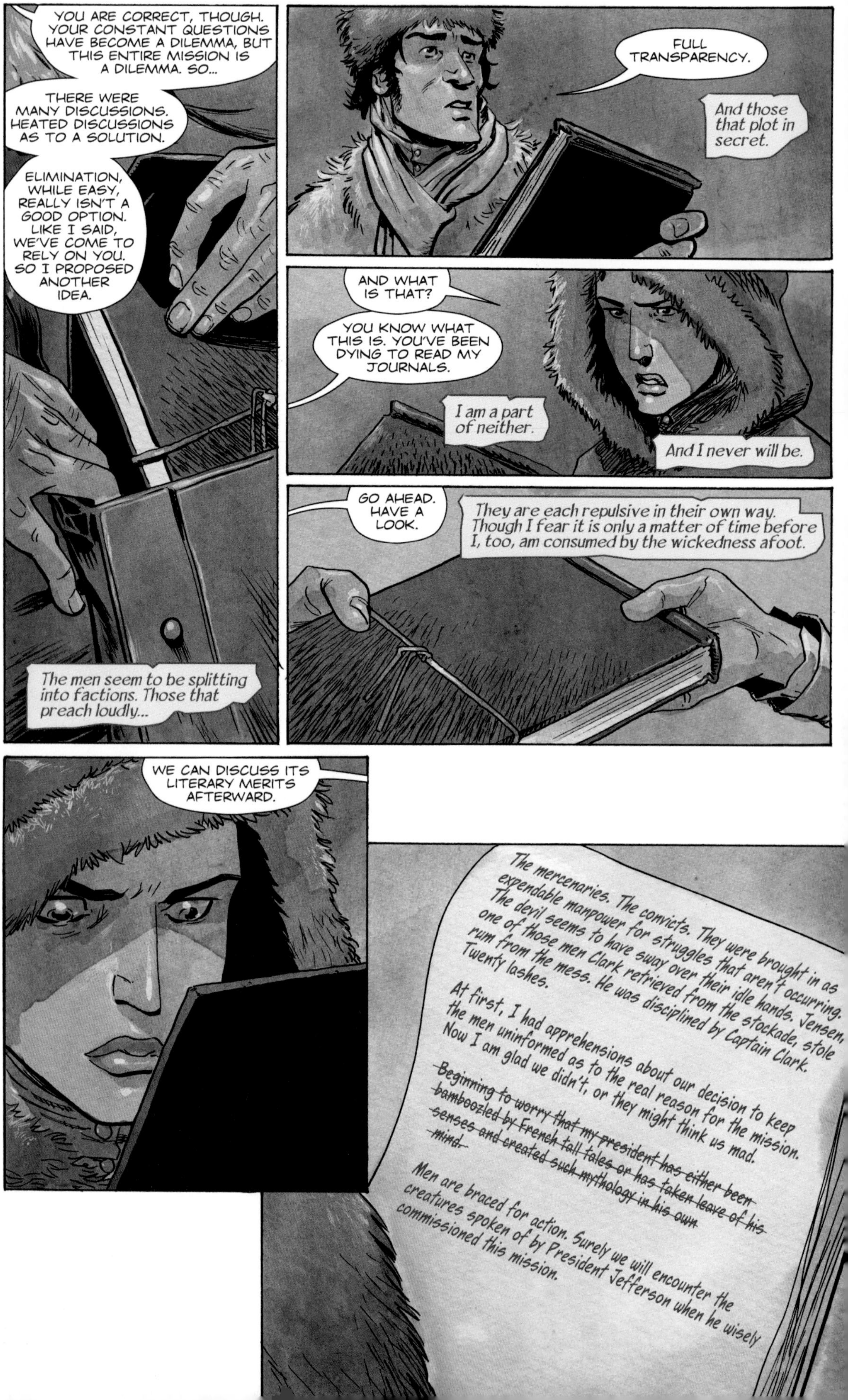
YOU ARE CORRECT, THOUGH. YOUR CONSTANT QUESTIONS HAVE BECOME A DILEMMA, BUT THIS ENTIRE MISSION IS A DILEMMA. SO...
THERE WERE MANY DISCUSSIONS. HEATED DISCUSSIONS AS TO A SOLUTION.
ELIMINATION, WHILE EASY, REALLY ISN'T A GOOD OPTION. LIKE I SAID, WE'VE COME TO RELY ON YOU. SO I PROPOSED ANOTHER IDEA.
The men seem to be splitting into factions. Those that preach loudly...
FULL TRANSPARENCY.
And those that plot in secret.
AND WHAT IS THAT?
YOU KNOW WHAT THIS IS. YOU'VE BEEN DYING TO READ MY JOURNALS.
I am a part of neither.
And I never will be.
GO AHEAD. HAVE A LOOK.
They are each repulsive in their own way. Though I fear it is only a matter of time before I, too, am consumed by the wickedness afoot.
WE CAN DISCUSS ITS LITERARY MERITS AFTERWARD.
The mercenaries. The convicts. They were brought in as expendable manpower for struggles that aren't occurring. The devil seems to have sway over their idle hands. Jensen, one of those men Clark retrieved from the stockade, stole rum from the mess. He was disciplined by Captain Clark. Twenty lashes.
At first, I had apprehensions about our decision to keep the men uninformed as to the real reason for the mission. Now I am glad we didn't, or they might think us mad.
~~Beginning to worry that my president has either been bamboozled by French tall tales or has taken leave of his senses and created such mythology in his own mind.~~
Men are braced for action. Surely we will encounter the creatures spoken of by President Jefferson when he wisely commissioned this mission.

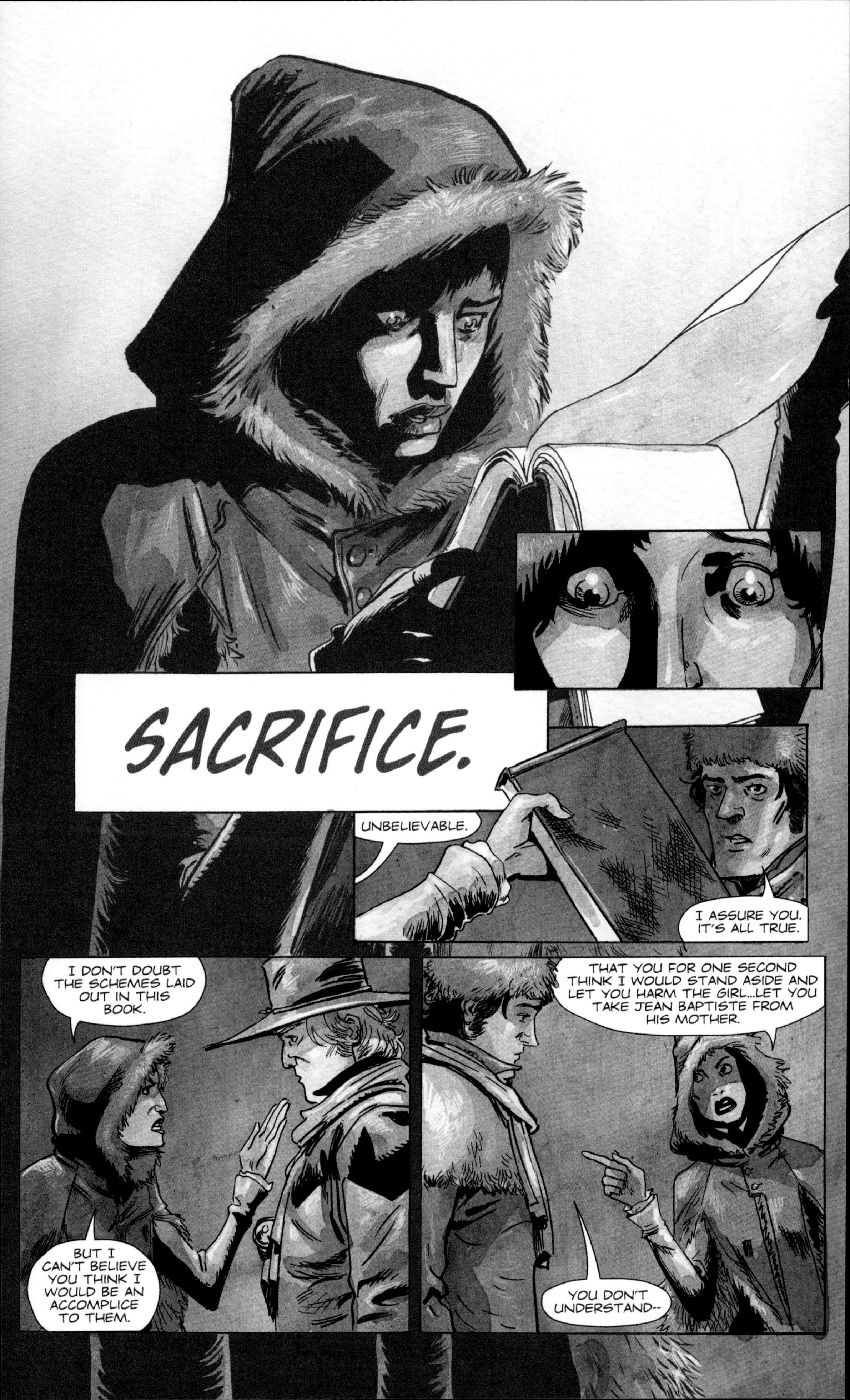
SACRIFICE.
UNBELIEVABLE.
I ASSURE YOU. IT'S ALL TRUE.
I DON'T DOUBT THE SCHEMES LAID OUT IN THIS BOOK.
BUT I CAN'T BELIEVE YOU THINK I WOULD BE AN ACCOMPLICE TO THEM.
THAT YOU FOR ONE SECOND THINK I WOULD STAND ASIDE AND LET YOU HARM THE GIRL...LET YOU TAKE JEAN BAPTISTE FROM HIS MOTHER.
YOU DON'T UNDERSTAND--

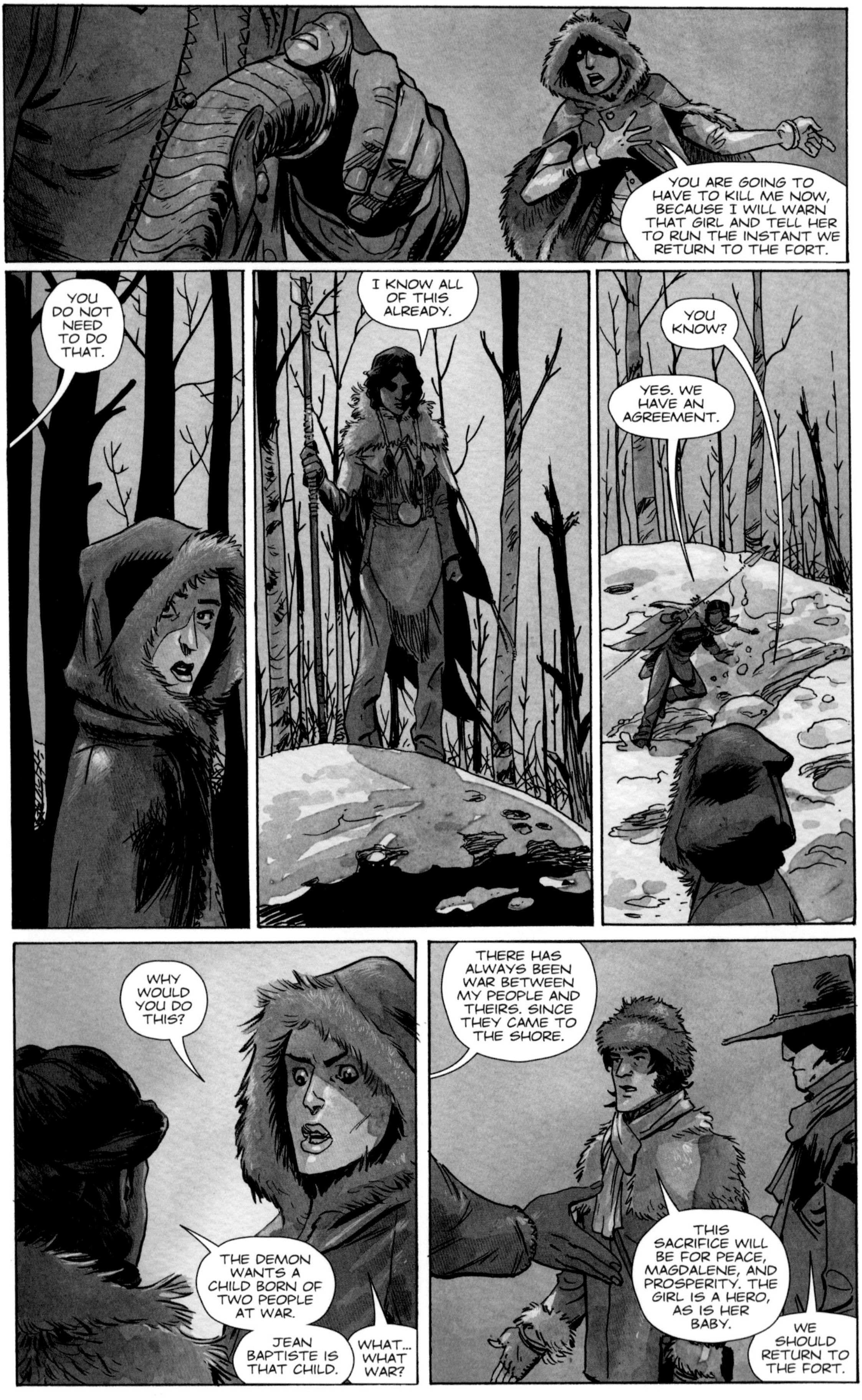

YOU ARE GOING TO HAVE TO KILL ME NOW, BECAUSE I WILL WARN THAT GIRL AND TELL HER TO RUN THE INSTANT WE RETURN TO THE FORT.
YOU DO NOT NEED TO DO THAT.
I KNOW ALL OF THIS ALREADY.
YOU KNOW?
YES. WE HAVE AN AGREEMENT.
WHY WOULD YOU DO THIS?
THE DEMON WANTS A CHILD BORN OF TWO PEOPLE AT WAR.
JEAN BAPTISTE IS THAT CHILD.
WHAT... WHAT WAR?
THERE HAS ALWAYS BEEN WAR BETWEEN MY PEOPLE AND THEIRS. SINCE THEY CAME TO THE SHORE.
THIS SACRIFICE WILL BE FOR PEACE, MAGDALENE, AND PROSPERITY. THE GIRL IS A HERO, AS IS HER BABY.
WE SHOULD RETURN TO THE FORT.

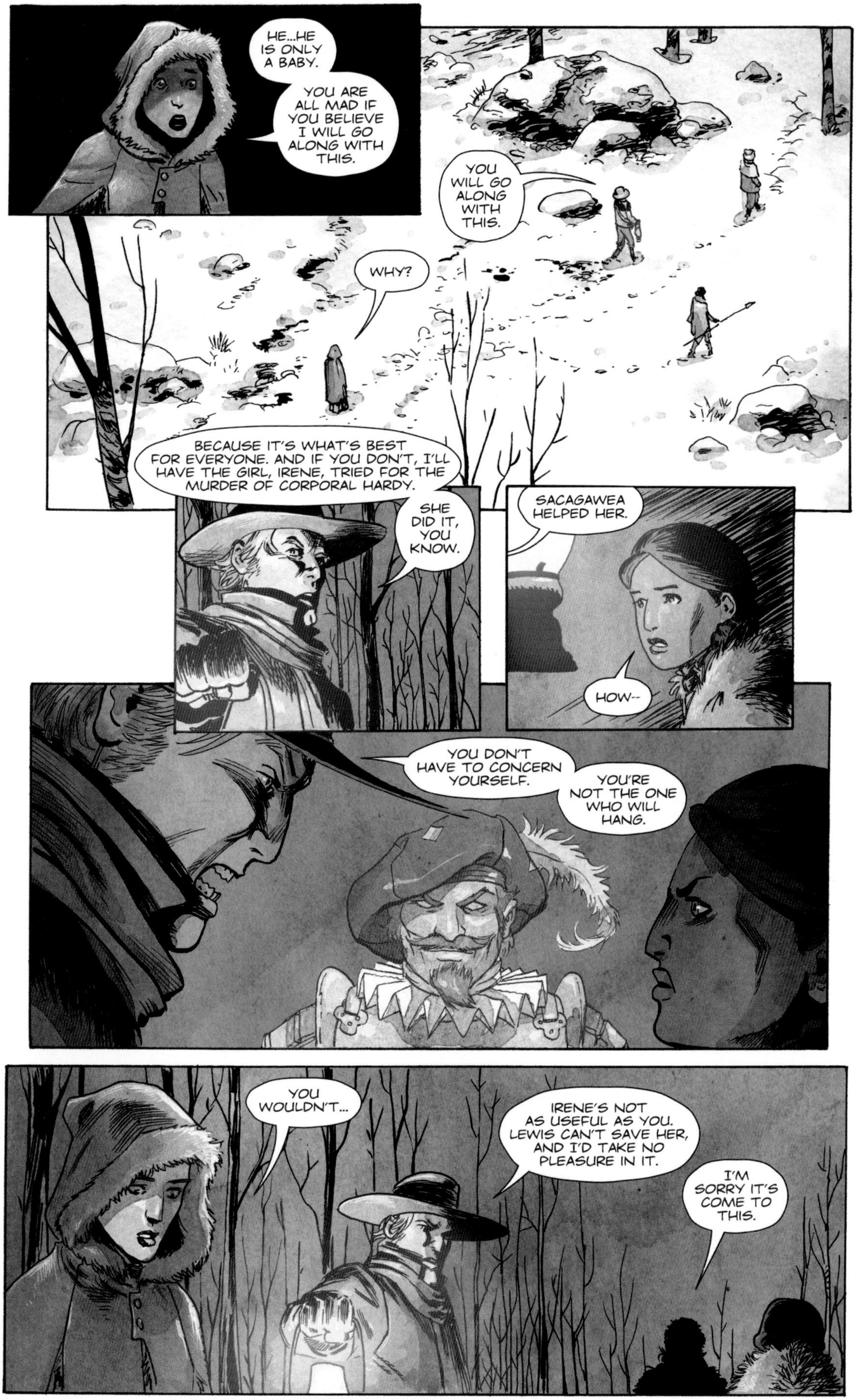
HE...HE IS ONLY A BABY.
YOU ARE ALL MAD IF YOU BELIEVE I WILL GO ALONG WITH THIS.
YOU WILL GO ALONG WITH THIS.
WHY?
BECAUSE IT'S WHAT'S BEST FOR EVERYONE. AND IF YOU DON'T, I'LL HAVE THE GIRL, IRENE, TRIED FOR THE MURDER OF CORPORAL HARDY.
SHE DID IT, YOU KNOW.
SACAGAWEA HELPED HER.
HOW--
YOU DON'T HAVE TO CONCERN YOURSELF.
YOU'RE NOT THE ONE WHO WILL HANG.
YOU WOULDN'T...
IRENE'S NOT AS USEFUL AS YOU. LEWIS CAN'T SAVE HER, AND I'D TAKE NO PLEASURE IN IT.
I'M SORRY IT'S COME TO THIS.

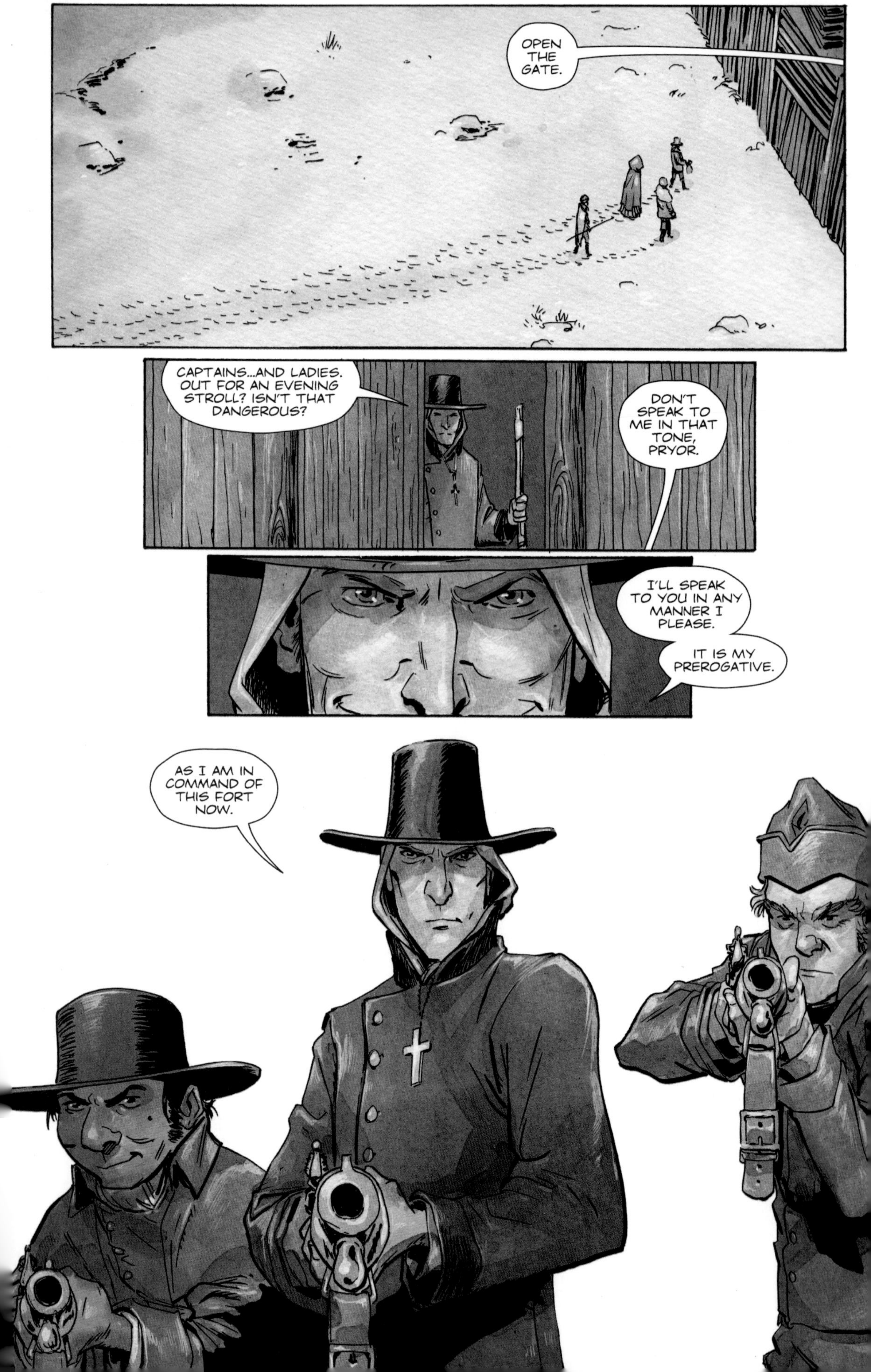
OPEN THE GATE.
CAPTAINS...AND LADIES. OUT FOR AN EVENING STROLL? ISN'T THAT DANGEROUS?
DON'T SPEAK TO ME IN THAT TONE, PRYOR.
I'LL SPEAK TO YOU IN ANY MANNER I PLEASE.
IT IS MY PREROGATIVE.
AS I AM IN COMMAND OF THIS FORT NOW.

PRYOR. YOU HAVE LOST YOUR MIND.

NO, CAPTAIN. I AM BRINGING SANITY BACK TO THIS CORP.

WE'VE FOLLOWED YOU ON THE DEVIL'S PATH FOR TOO LONG. WE HAVE TURNED BACK TOWARD THE LIGHT.

I'D PREFER THIS TO BE A PEACEFUL, CHRISTIAN CHANGE OF POWER.

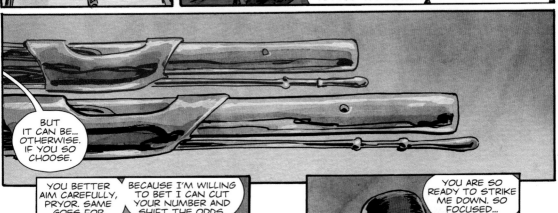

BUT IT CAN BE... OTHERWISE. IF YOU SO CHOOSE.

YOU BETTER AIM CAREFULLY, PRYOR. SAME GOES FOR YOU TWO.

BECAUSE I'M WILLING TO BET I CAN CUT YOUR NUMBER AND SHIFT THE ODDS.

AT THE VERY LEAST, I CAN KILL YOU.

YOU ARE SO READY TO STRIKE ME DOWN. SO FOCUSED...

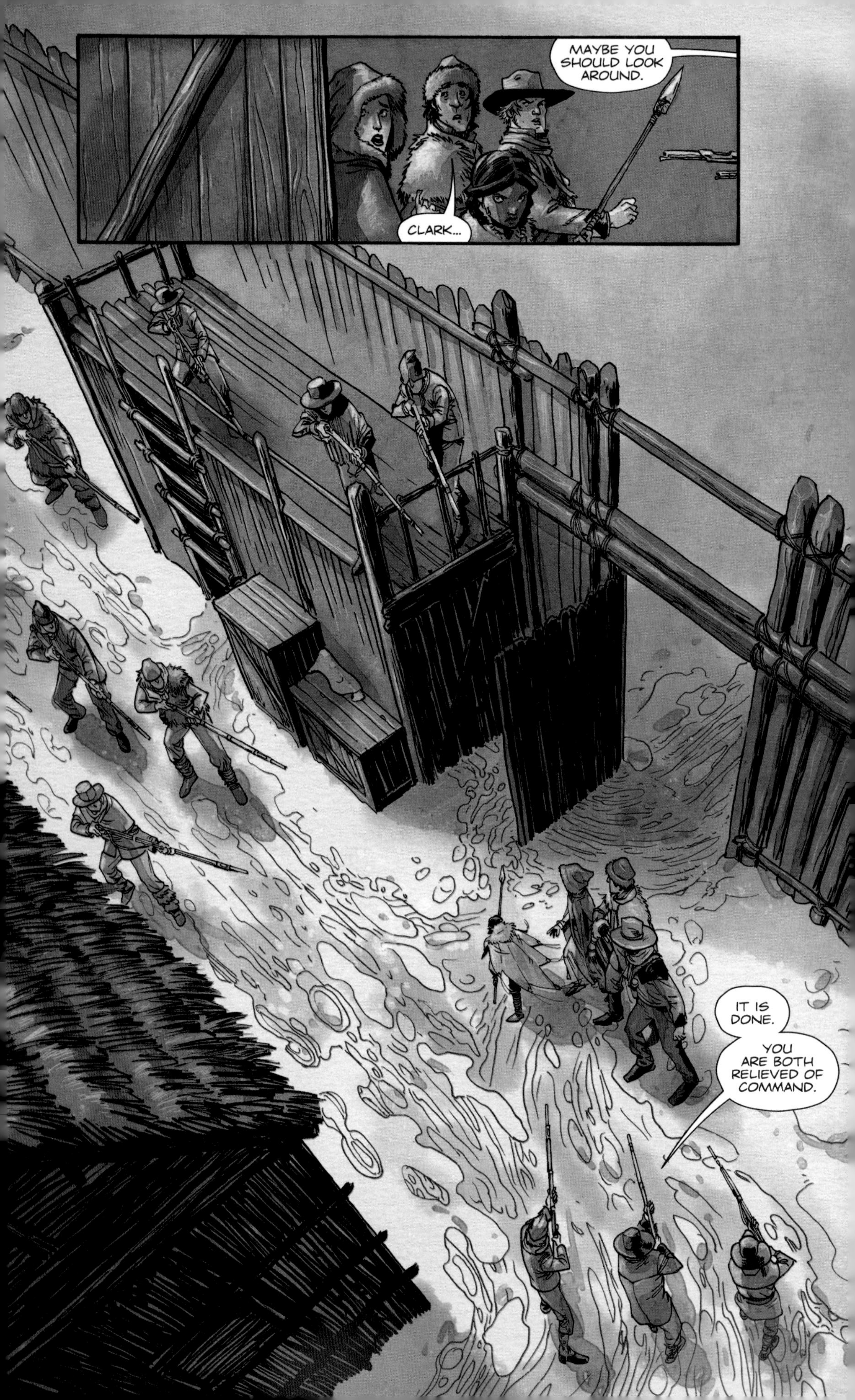
MAYBE YOU SHOULD LOOK AROUND.
CLARK...
IT IS DONE.
YOU ARE BOTH RELIEVED OF COMMAND.

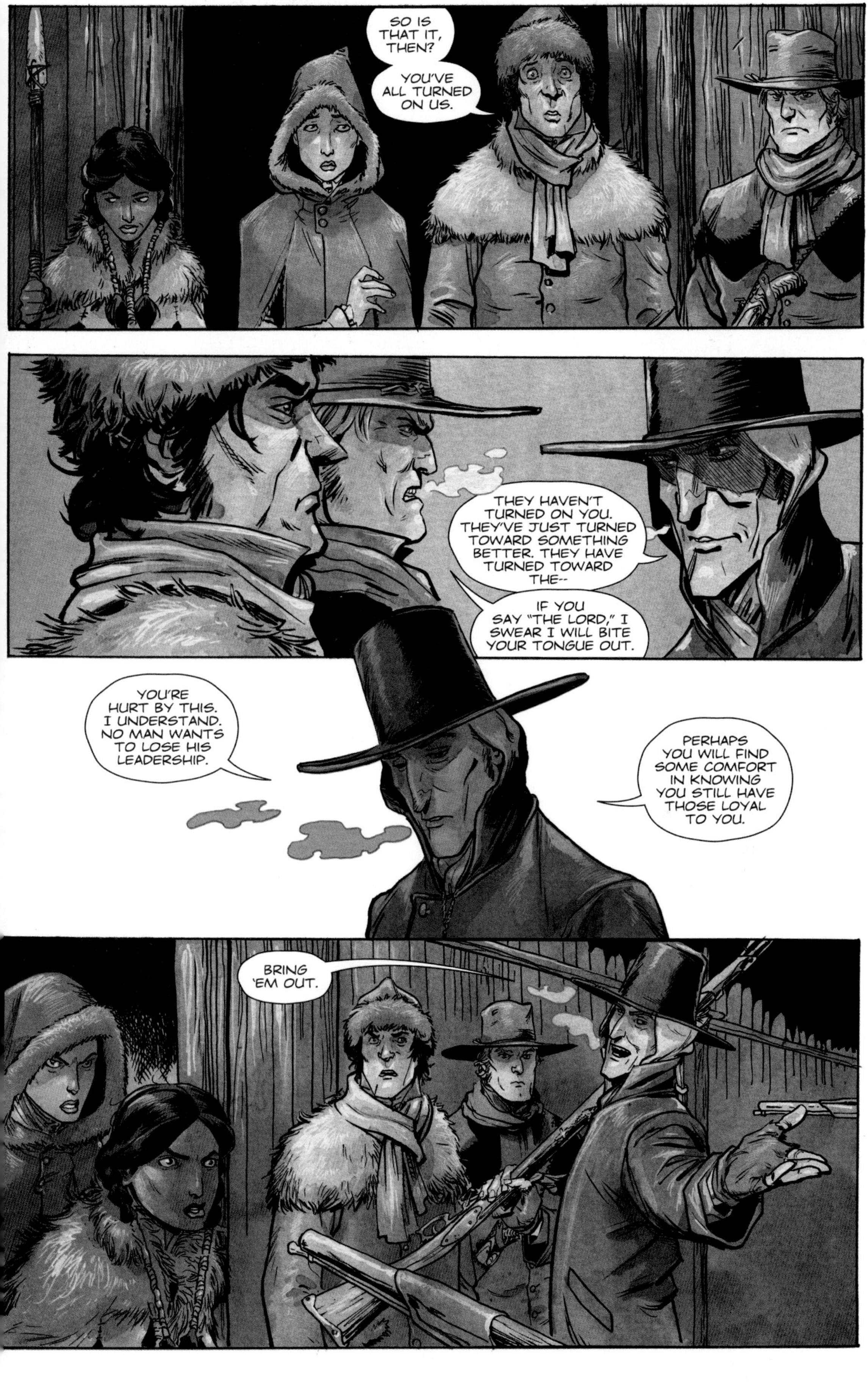
SO IS THAT IT, THEN?
YOU'VE ALL TURNED ON US.
THEY HAVEN'T TURNED ON YOU. THEY'VE JUST TURNED TOWARD SOMETHING BETTER. THEY HAVE TURNED TOWARD THE--
IF YOU SAY "THE LORD," I SWEAR I WILL BITE YOUR TONGUE OUT.
YOU'RE HURT BY THIS. I UNDERSTAND. NO MAN WANTS TO LOSE HIS LEADERSHIP.
PERHAPS YOU WILL FIND SOME COMFORT IN KNOWING YOU STILL HAVE THOSE LOYAL TO YOU.
BRING 'EM OUT.

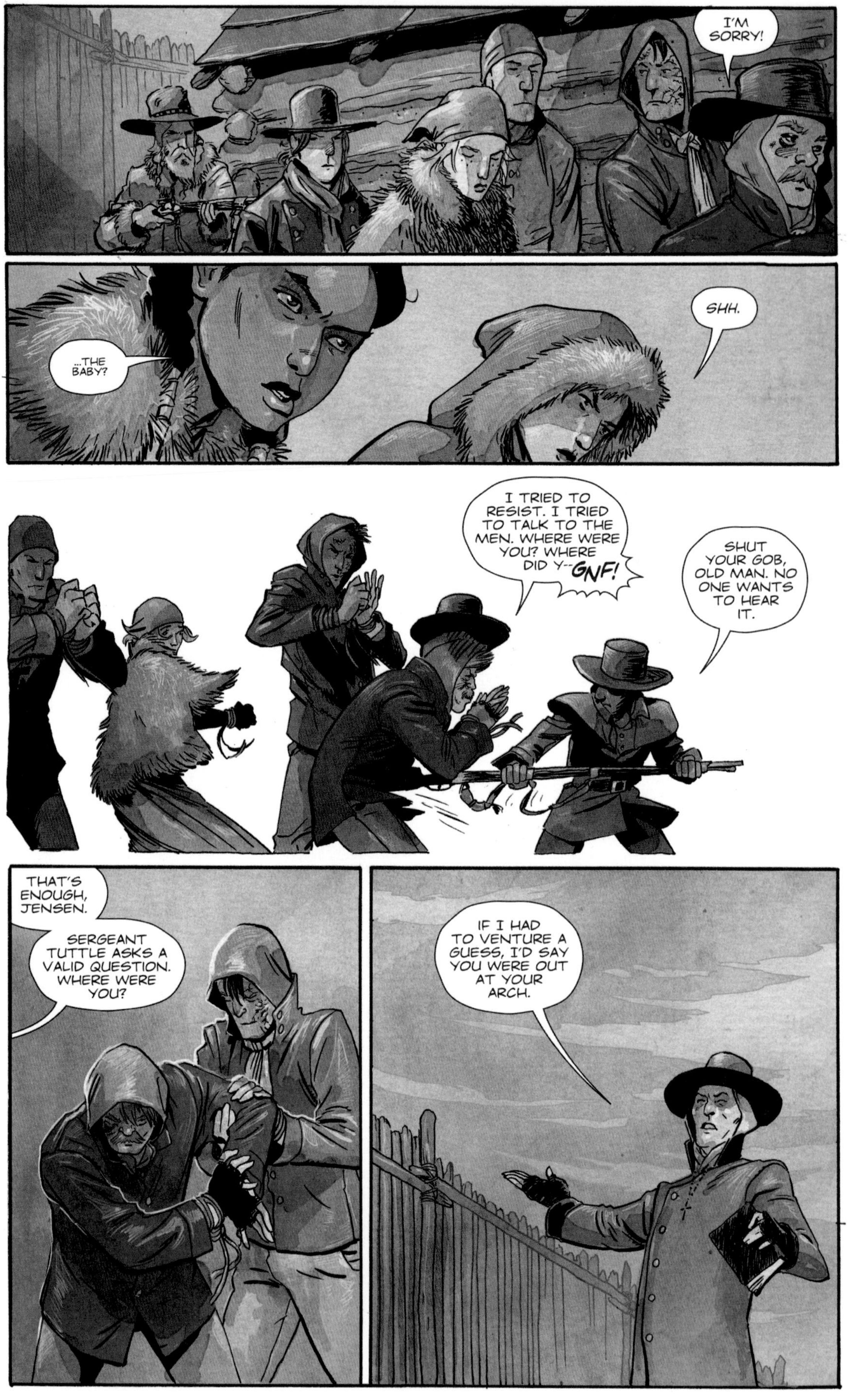

I'M SORRY!
...THE BABY?
SHH.
I TRIED TO RESIST. I TRIED TO TALK TO THE MEN. WHERE WERE YOU? WHERE DID Y--GNF!
SHUT YOUR GOB, OLD MAN. NO ONE WANTS TO HEAR IT.
THAT'S ENOUGH, JENSEN.
SERGEANT TUTTLE ASKS A VALID QUESTION. WHERE WERE YOU?
IF I HAD TO VENTURE A GUESS, I'D SAY YOU WERE OUT AT YOUR ARCH.

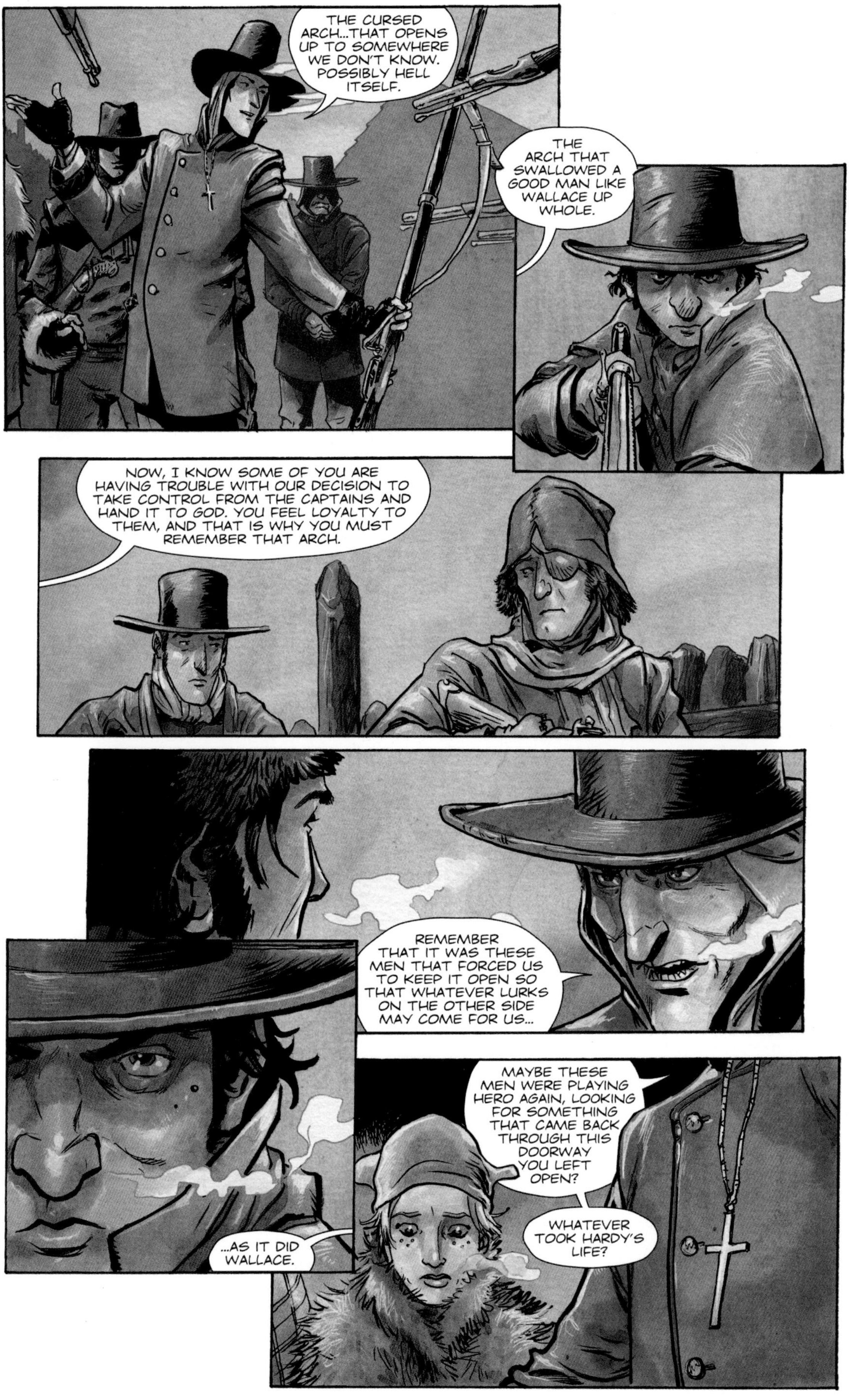
THE CURSED ARCH...THAT OPENS UP TO SOMEWHERE WE DON'T KNOW. POSSIBLY HELL ITSELF.
THE ARCH THAT SWALLOWED A GOOD MAN LIKE WALLACE UP WHOLE.
NOW, I KNOW SOME OF YOU ARE HAVING TROUBLE WITH OUR DECISION TO TAKE CONTROL FROM THE CAPTAINS AND HAND IT TO GOD. YOU FEEL LOYALTY TO THEM, AND THAT IS WHY YOU MUST REMEMBER THAT ARCH.
REMEMBER THAT IT WAS THESE MEN THAT FORCED US TO KEEP IT OPEN SO THAT WHATEVER LURKS ON THE OTHER SIDE MAY COME FOR US...
...AS IT DID WALLACE.
MAYBE THESE MEN WERE PLAYING HERO AGAIN, LOOKING FOR SOMETHING THAT CAME BACK THROUGH THIS DOORWAY YOU LEFT OPEN?
WHATEVER TOOK HARDY'S LIFE?

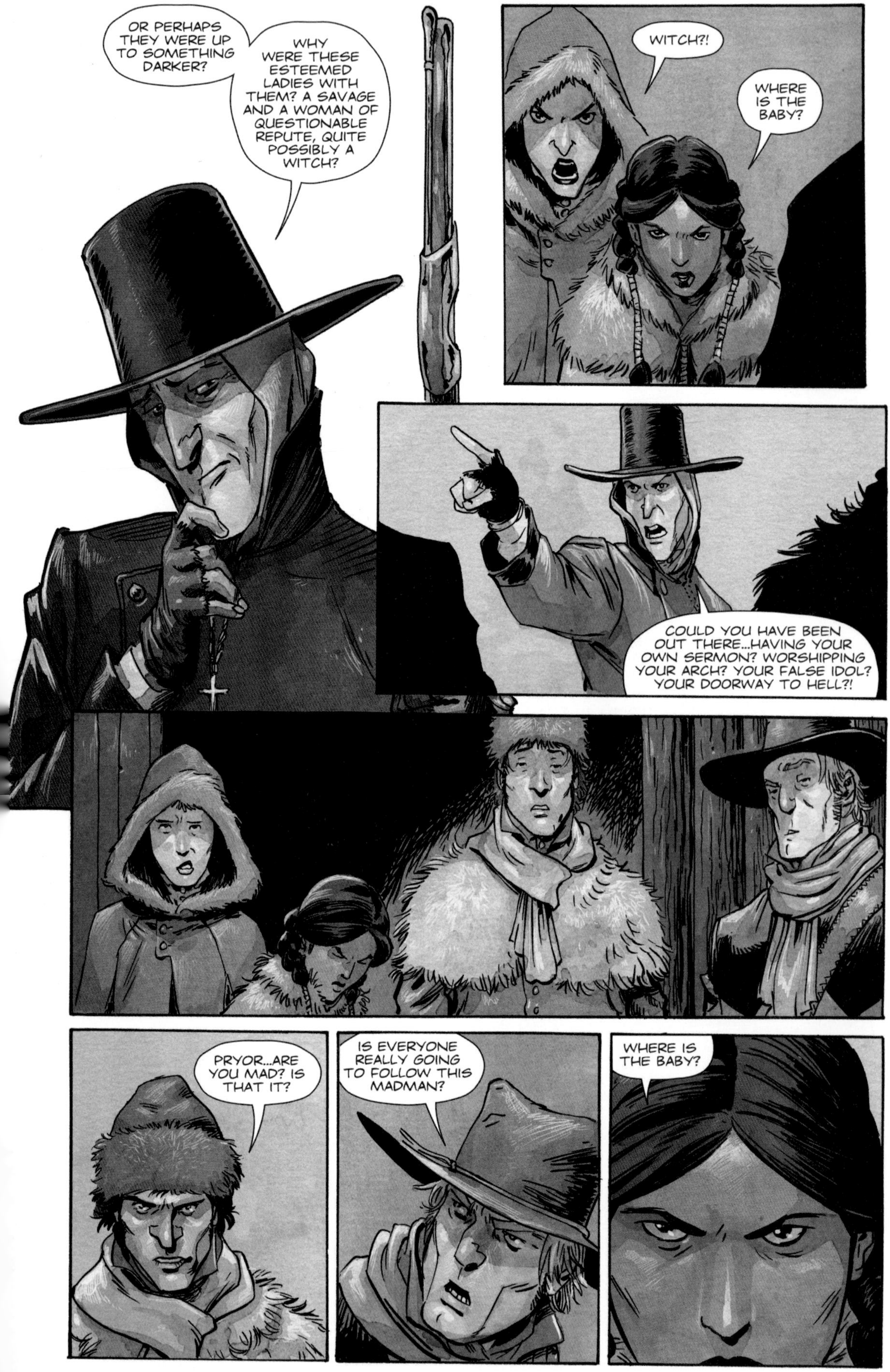
OR PERHAPS THEY WERE UP TO SOMETHING DARKER?
WHY WERE THESE ESTEEMED LADIES WITH THEM? A SAVAGE AND A WOMAN OF QUESTIONABLE REPUTE, QUITE POSSIBLY A WITCH?
WITCH?!
WHERE IS THE BABY?
COULD YOU HAVE BEEN OUT THERE...HAVING YOUR OWN SERMON? WORSHIPPING YOUR ARCH? YOUR FALSE IDOL? YOUR DOORWAY TO HELL?!
PRYOR...ARE YOU MAD? IS THAT IT?
IS EVERYONE REALLY GOING TO FOLLOW THIS MADMAN?
WHERE IS THE BABY?

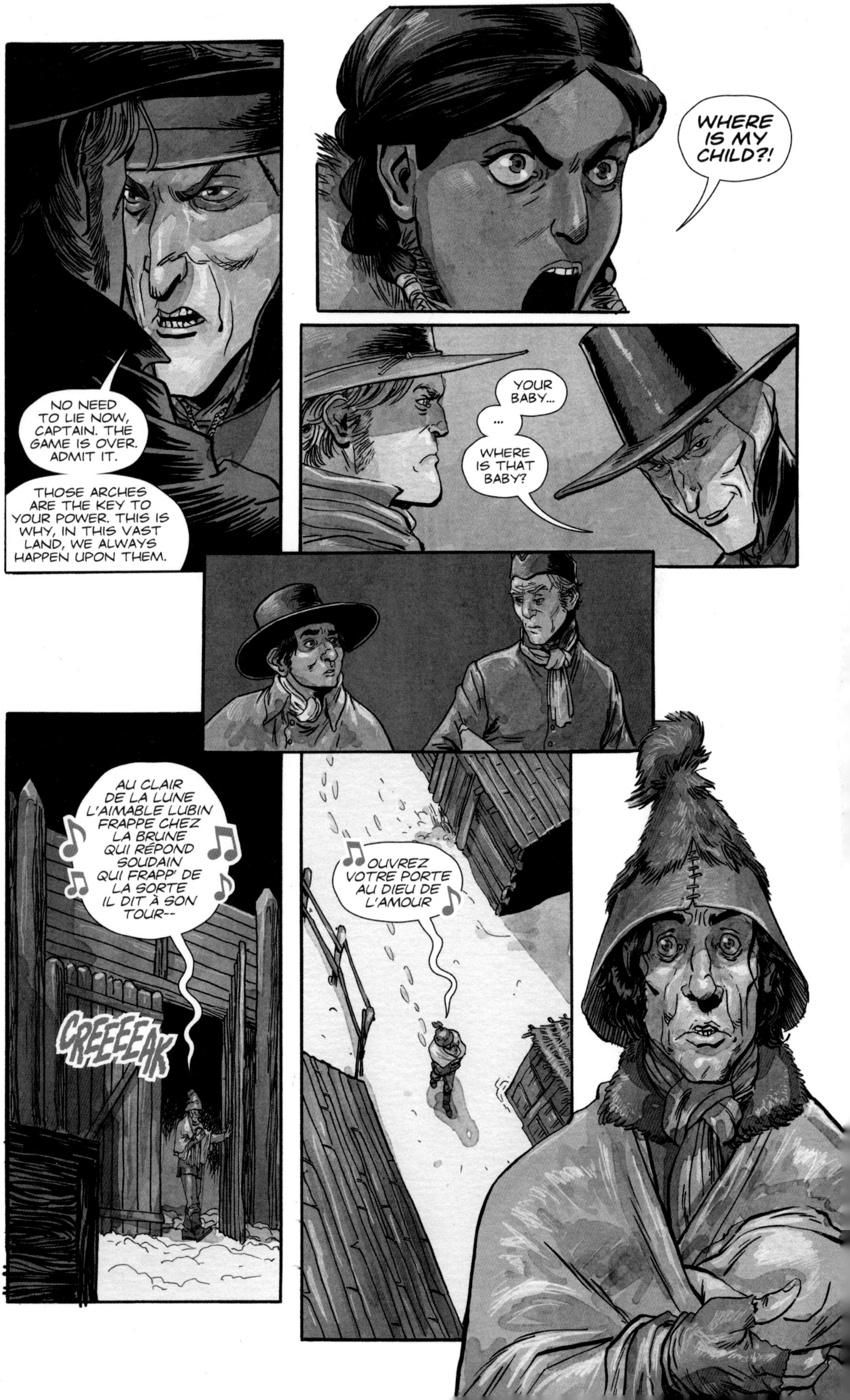
NO NEED TO LIE NOW, CAPTAIN. THE GAME IS OVER. ADMIT IT.
THOSE ARCHES ARE THE KEY TO YOUR POWER. THIS IS WHY, IN THIS VAST LAND, WE ALWAYS HAPPEN UPON THEM.
WHERE IS MY CHILD?!
YOUR BABY...
...
WHERE IS THAT BABY?
AU CLAIR DE LA LUNE L'AIMABLE LUBIN FRAPPE CHEZ LA BRUNE QUI RÉPOND SOUDAIN QUI FRAPP' DE LA SORTE IL DIT À SON TOUR--
CREEEEAK
OUVREZ VOTRE PORTE AU DIEU DE L'AMOUR

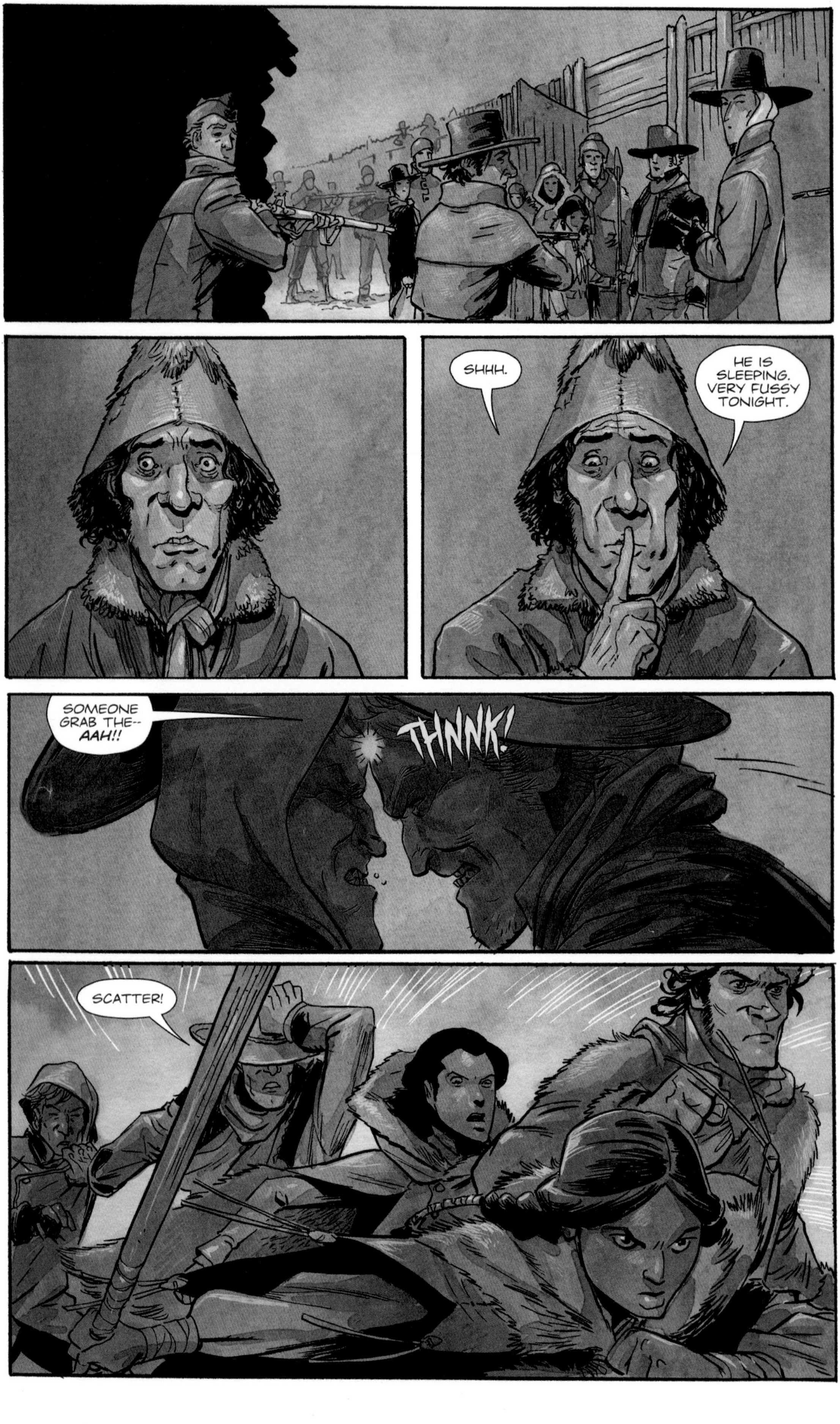
SHHH.
HE IS SLEEPING. VERY FUSSY TONIGHT.
SOMEONE GRAB THE-- AAH!!
THNK!
SCATTER!

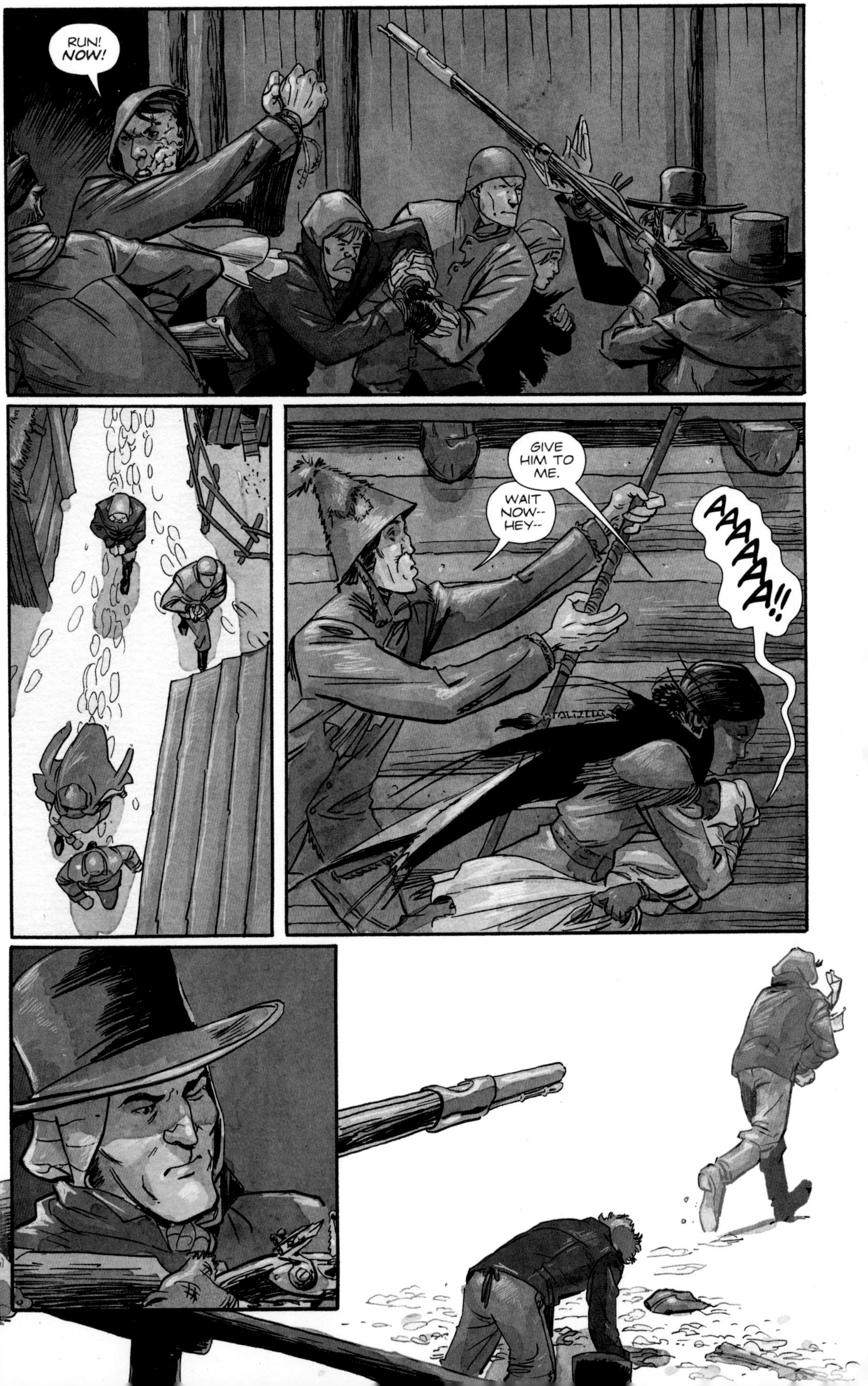
RUN! NOW!
GIVE HIM TO ME.
WAIT NOW-- HEY--
AAAAAA!!

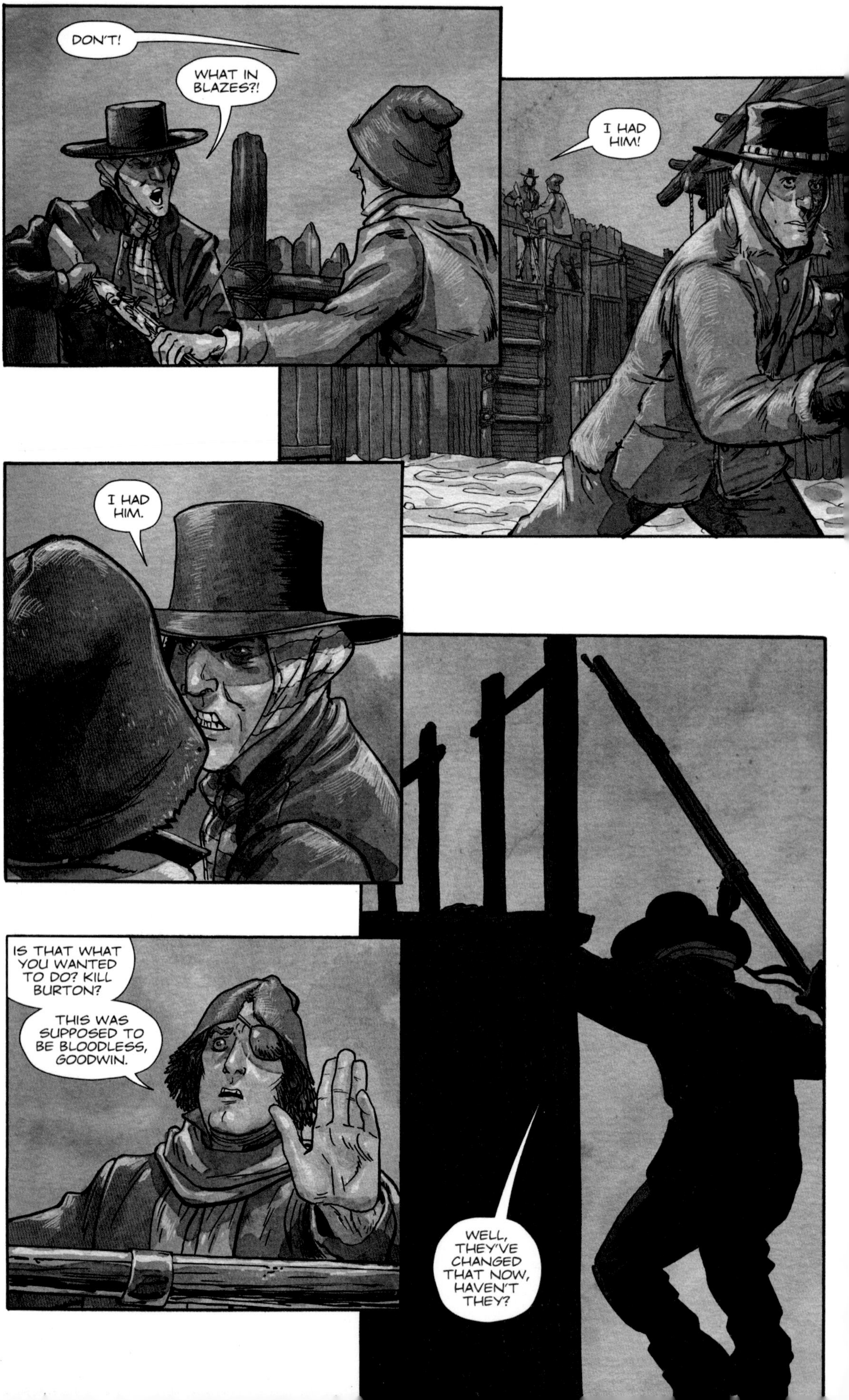
DON'T!
WHAT IN BLAZES?!
I HAD HIM!
I HAD HIM.
IS THAT WHAT YOU WANTED TO DO? KILL BURTON?
THIS WAS SUPPOSED TO BE BLOODLESS, GOODWIN.
WELL, THEY'VE CHANGED THAT NOW, HAVEN'T THEY?

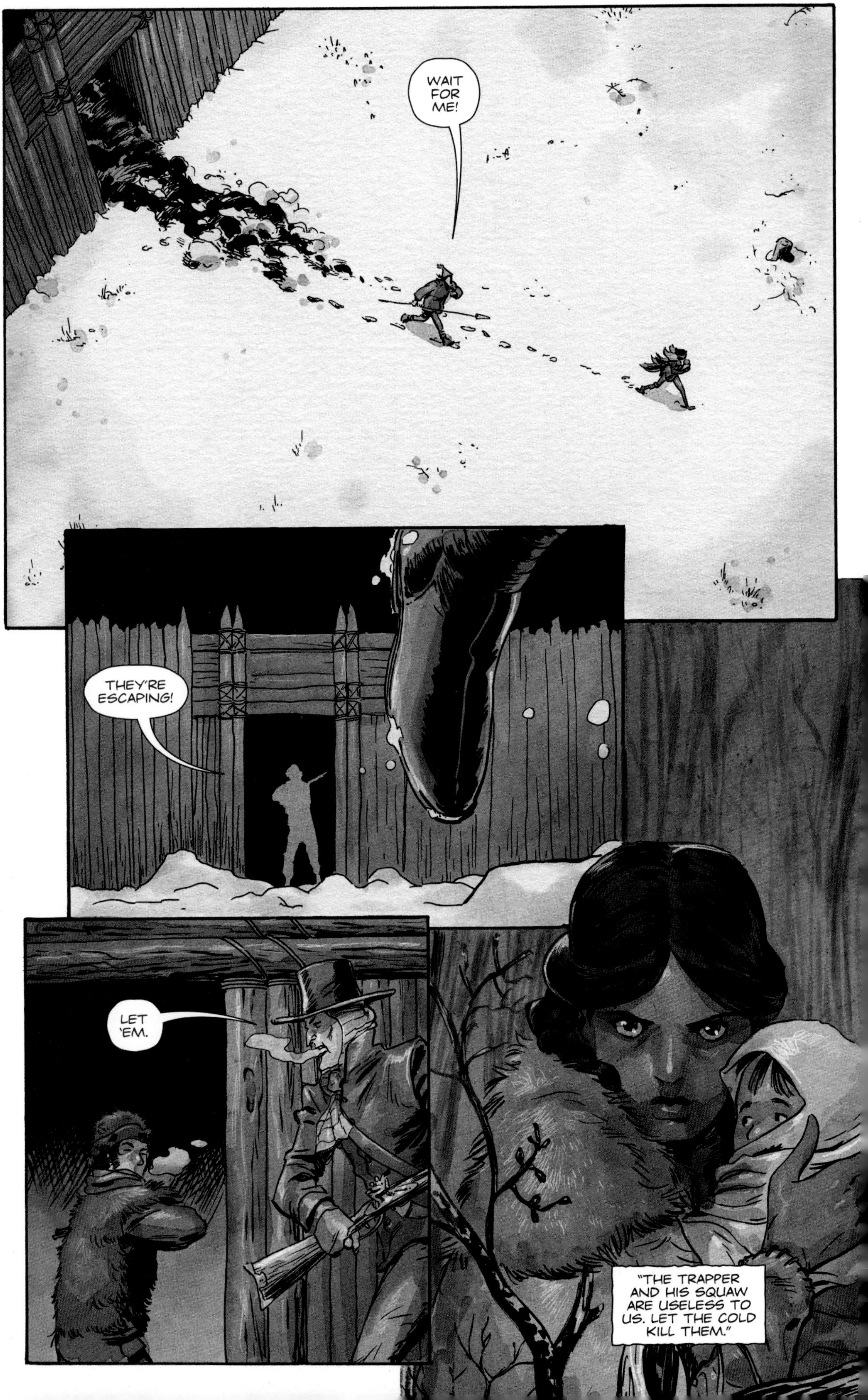
WAIT FOR ME!
THEY'RE ESCAPING!
LET 'EM.
"THE TRAPPER AND HIS SQUAW ARE USELESS TO US. LET THE COLD KILL THEM."

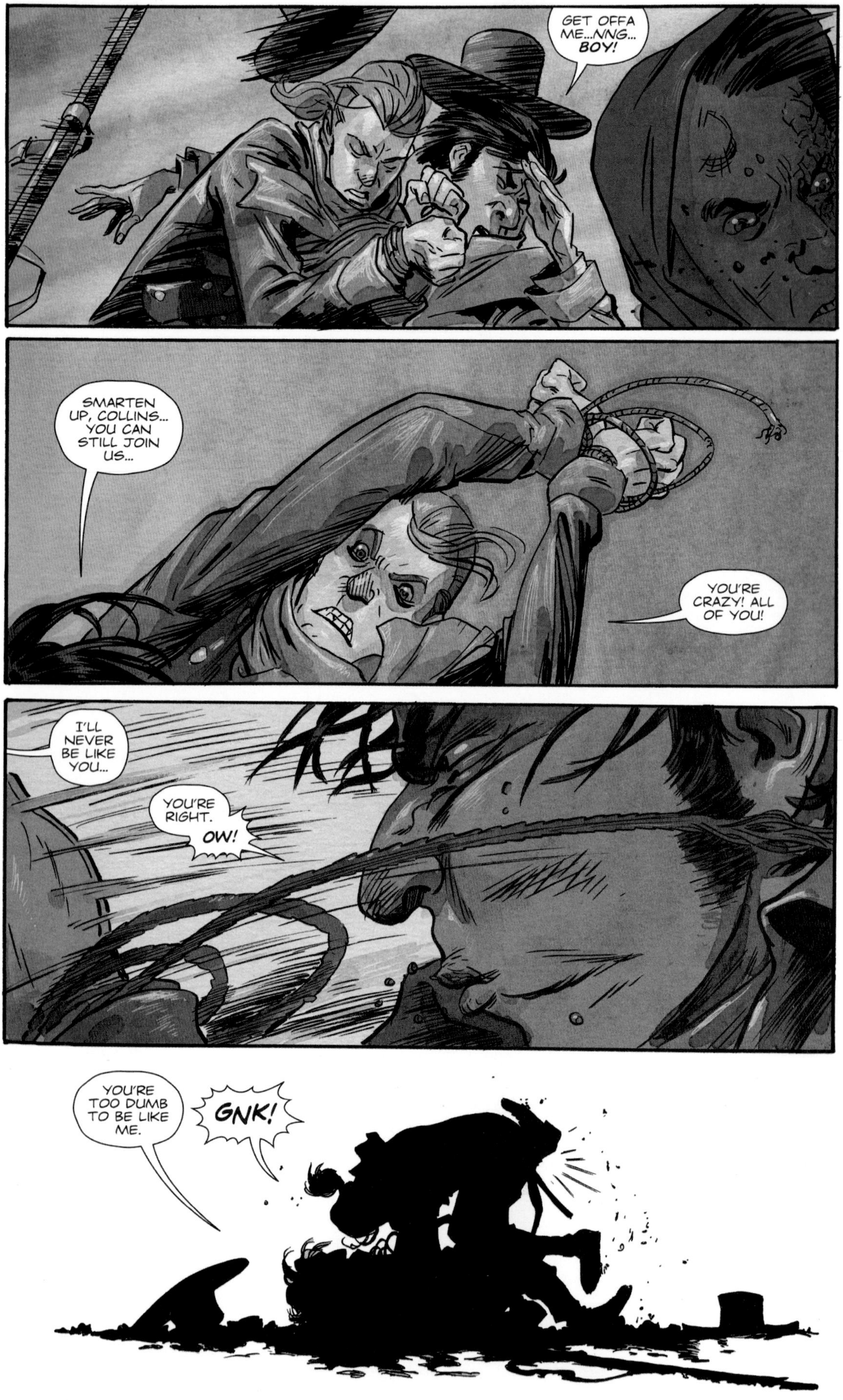

GET OFFA ME...NNG... BOY!
SMARTEN UP, COLLINS... YOU CAN STILL JOIN US...
YOU'RE CRAZY! ALL OF YOU!
I'LL NEVER BE LIKE YOU...
YOU'RE RIGHT.
OW!
YOU'RE TOO DUMB TO BE LIKE ME.
GNK!

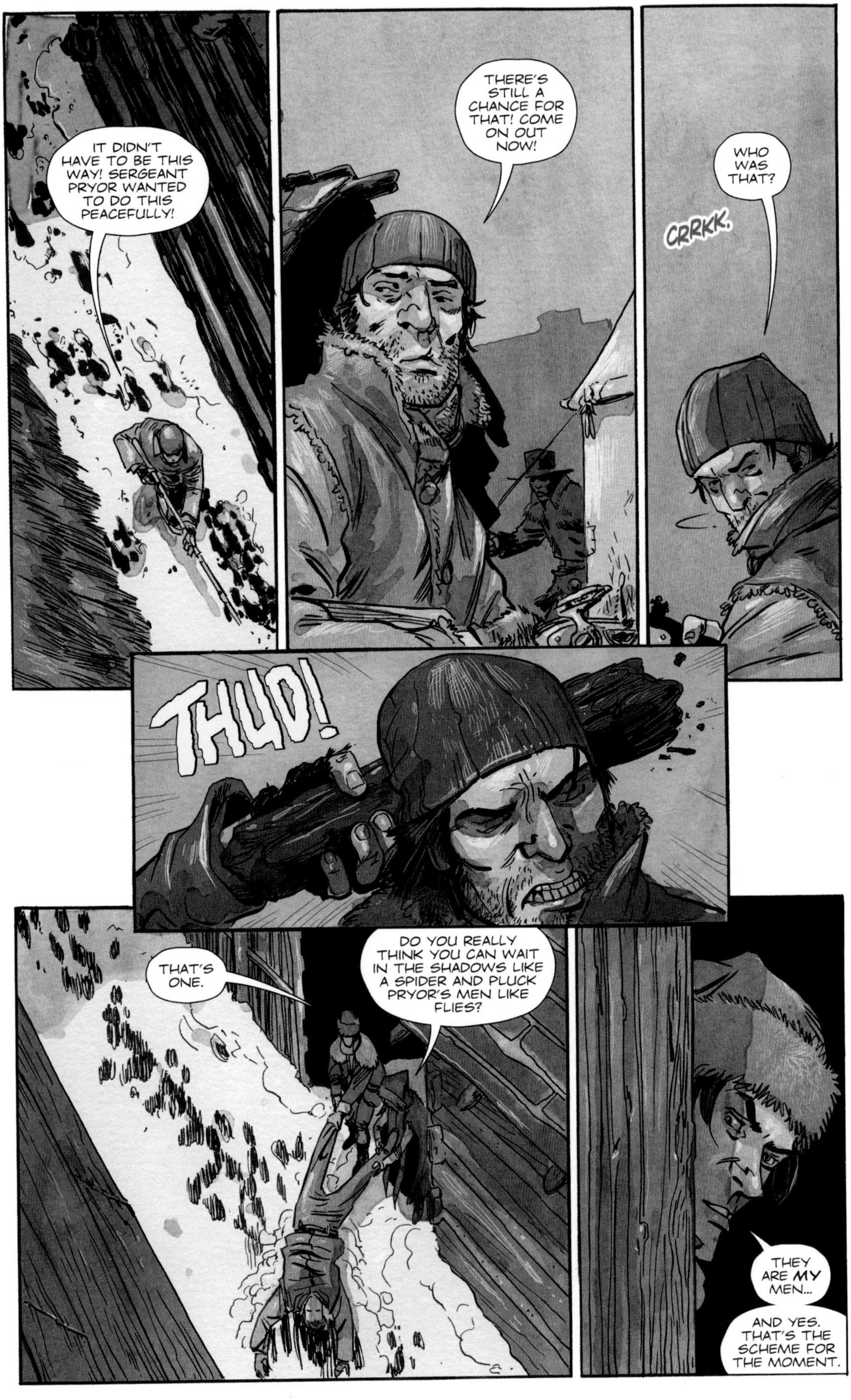
IT DIDN'T HAVE TO BE THIS WAY! SERGEANT PRYOR WANTED TO DO THIS PEACEFULLY!
THERE'S STILL A CHANCE FOR THAT! COME ON OUT NOW!
CRRKK.
WHO WAS THAT?
THUD!
THAT'S ONE.
DO YOU REALLY THINK YOU CAN WAIT IN THE SHADOWS LIKE A SPIDER AND PLUCK PRYOR'S MEN LIKE FLIES?
THEY ARE **MY** MEN...
AND YES. THAT'S THE SCHEME FOR THE MOMENT.

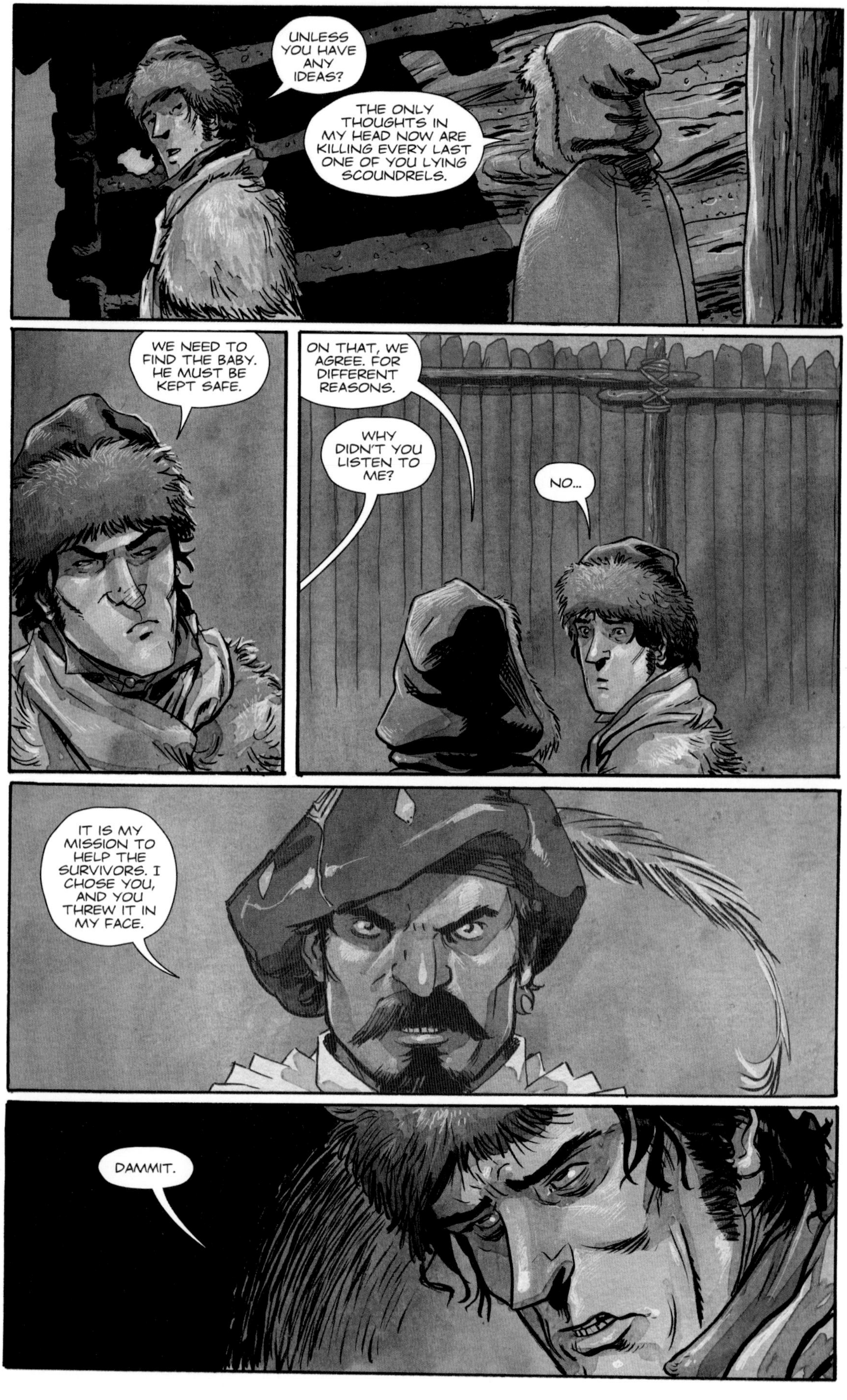
UNLESS YOU HAVE ANY IDEAS?
THE ONLY THOUGHTS IN MY HEAD NOW ARE KILLING EVERY LAST ONE OF YOU LYING SCOUNDRELS.
WE NEED TO FIND THE BABY. HE MUST BE KEPT SAFE.
ON THAT, WE AGREE. FOR DIFFERENT REASONS.
WHY DIDN'T YOU LISTEN TO ME?
NO...
IT IS MY MISSION TO HELP THE SURVIVORS. I CHOSE YOU, AND YOU THREW IT IN MY FACE.
DAMMIT.

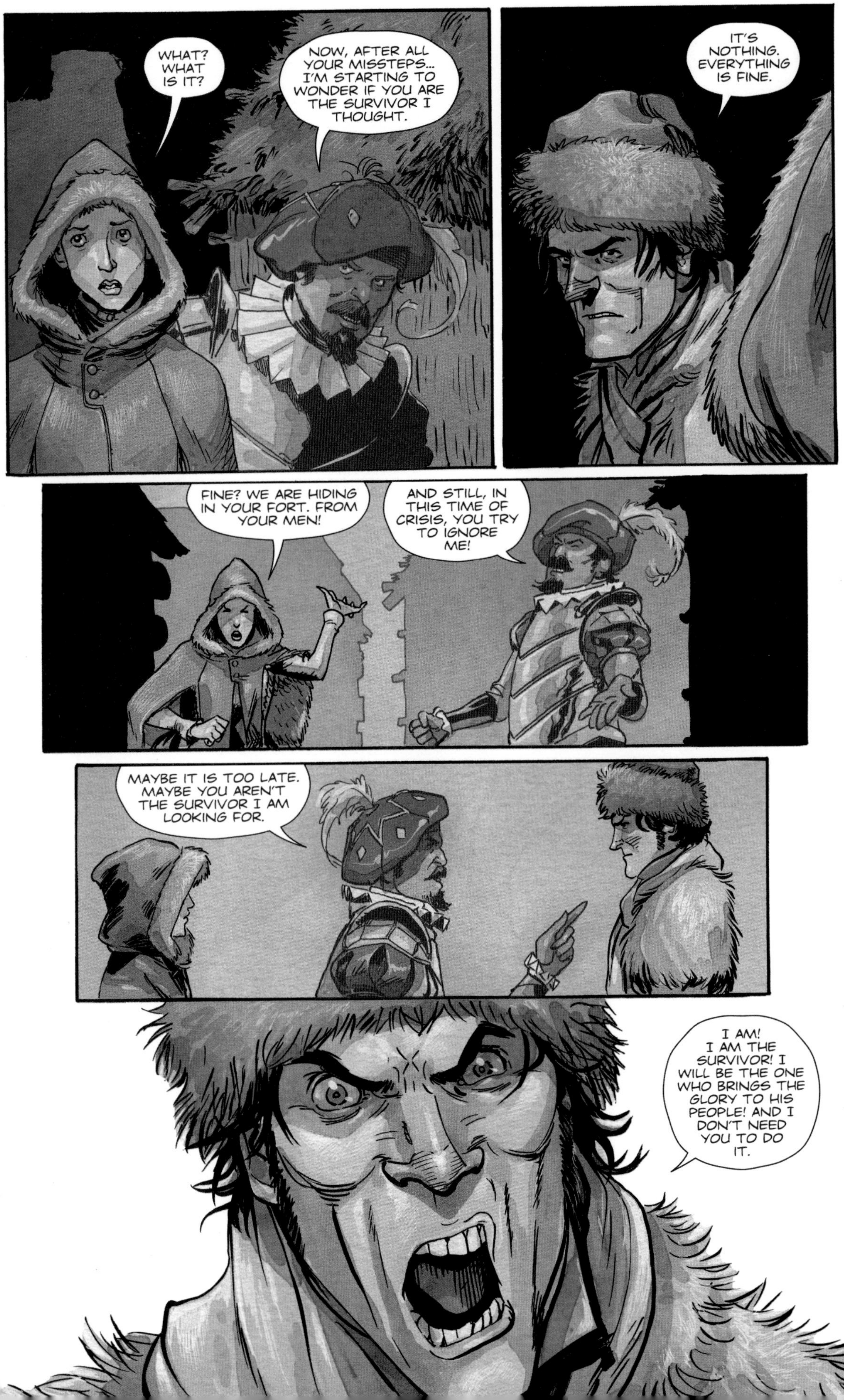
WHAT? WHAT IS IT?
NOW, AFTER ALL YOUR MISSTEPS... I'M STARTING TO WONDER IF YOU ARE THE SURVIVOR I THOUGHT.
IT'S NOTHING. EVERYTHING IS FINE.
FINE? WE ARE HIDING IN YOUR FORT. FROM YOUR MEN!
AND STILL, IN THIS TIME OF CRISIS, YOU TRY TO IGNORE ME!
MAYBE IT IS TOO LATE. MAYBE YOU AREN'T THE SURVIVOR I AM LOOKING FOR.
I AM! I AM THE SURVIVOR! I WILL BE THE ONE WHO BRINGS THE GLORY TO HIS PEOPLE! AND I DON'T NEED YOU TO DO IT.

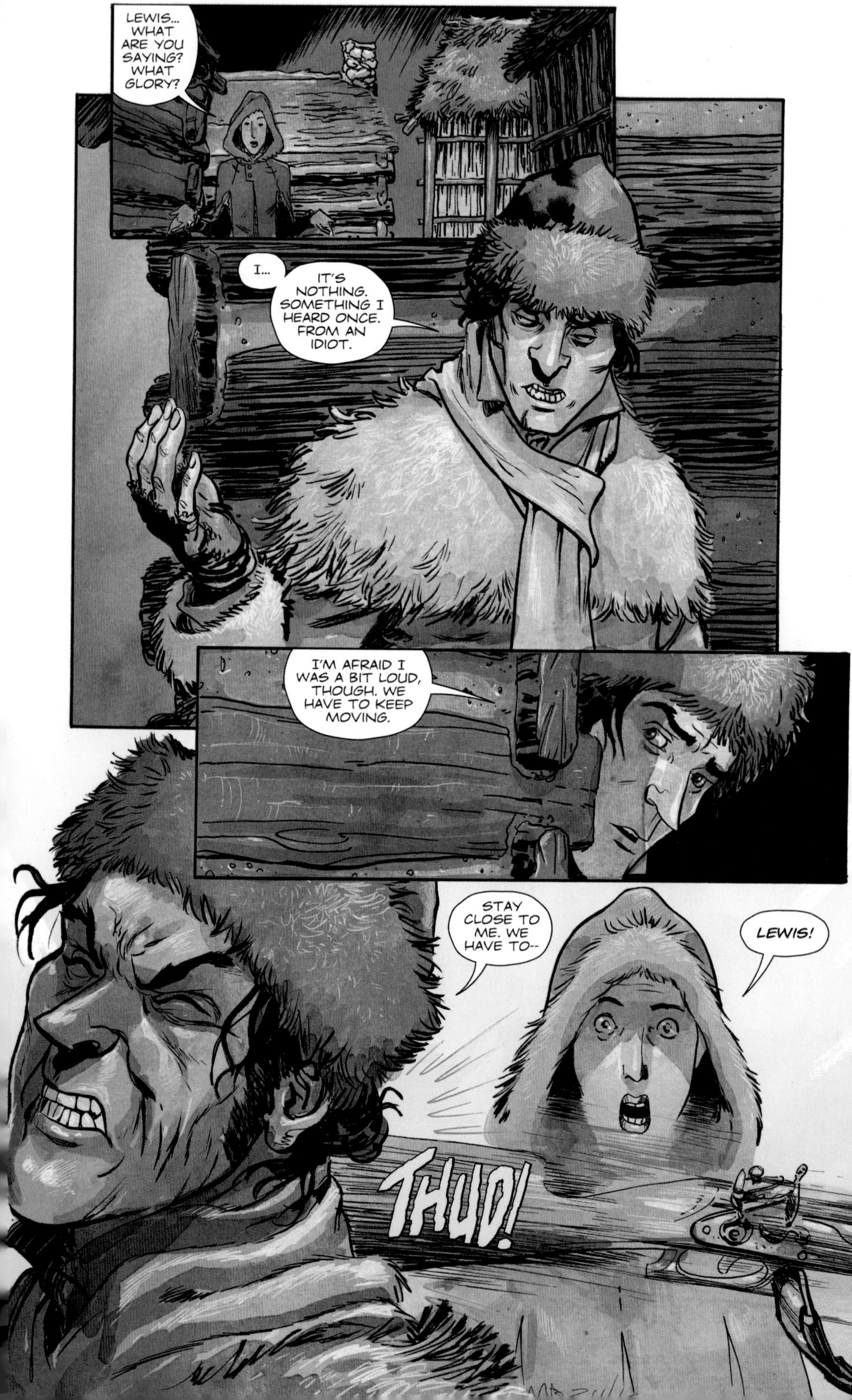
LEWIS... WHAT ARE YOU SAYING? WHAT GLORY?
I...
IT'S NOTHING. SOMETHING I HEARD ONCE. FROM AN IDIOT.
I'M AFRAID I WAS A BIT LOUD, THOUGH. WE HAVE TO KEEP MOVING.
STAY CLOSE TO ME. WE HAVE TO--
LEWIS!
THUD!

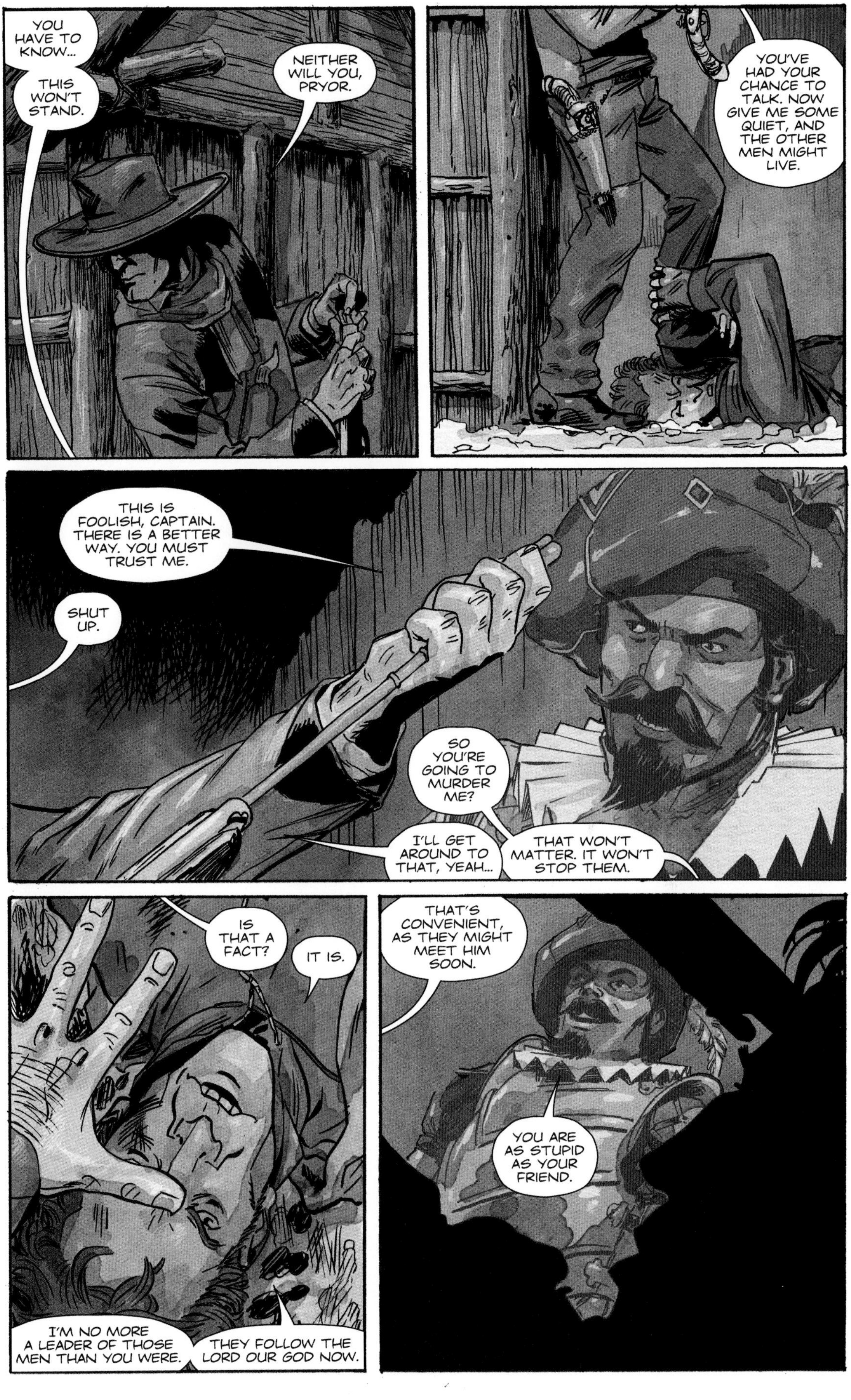
YOU HAVE TO KNOW...
THIS WON'T STAND.
NEITHER WILL YOU, PRYOR.
YOU'VE HAD YOUR CHANCE TO TALK. NOW GIVE ME SOME QUIET, AND THE OTHER MEN MIGHT LIVE.
THIS IS FOOLISH, CAPTAIN. THERE IS A BETTER WAY. YOU MUST TRUST ME.
SHUT UP.
SO YOU'RE GOING TO MURDER ME?
I'LL GET AROUND TO THAT, YEAH...
THAT WON'T MATTER. IT WON'T STOP THEM.
IS THAT A FACT?
IT IS.
I'M NO MORE A LEADER OF THOSE MEN THAN YOU WERE.
THEY FOLLOW THE LORD OUR GOD NOW.
THAT'S CONVENIENT, AS THEY MIGHT MEET HIM SOON.
YOU ARE AS STUPID AS YOUR FRIEND.

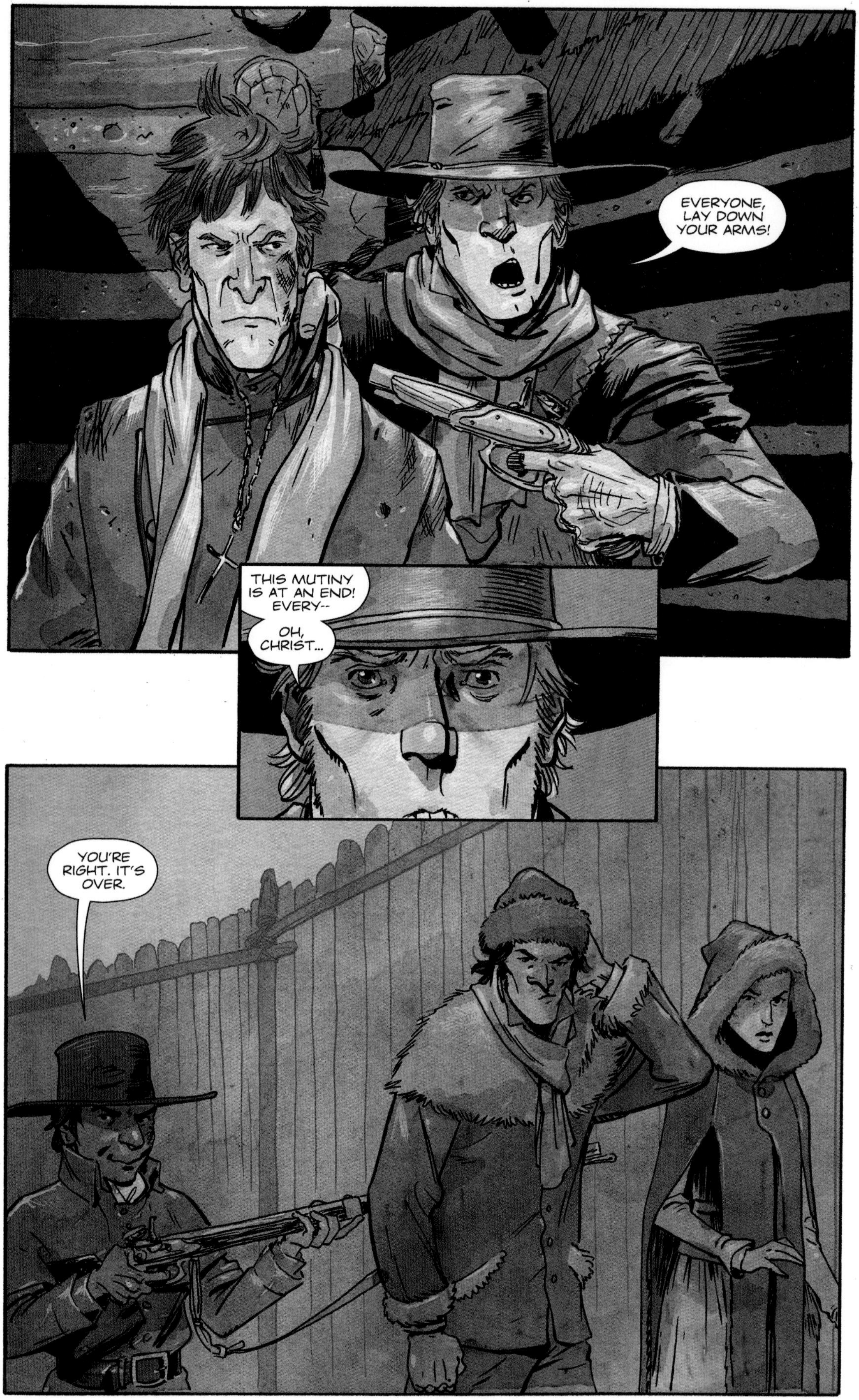
EVERYONE, LAY DOWN YOUR ARMS!
THIS MUTINY IS AT AN END! EVERY--
OH, CHRIST...
YOU'RE RIGHT. IT'S OVER.

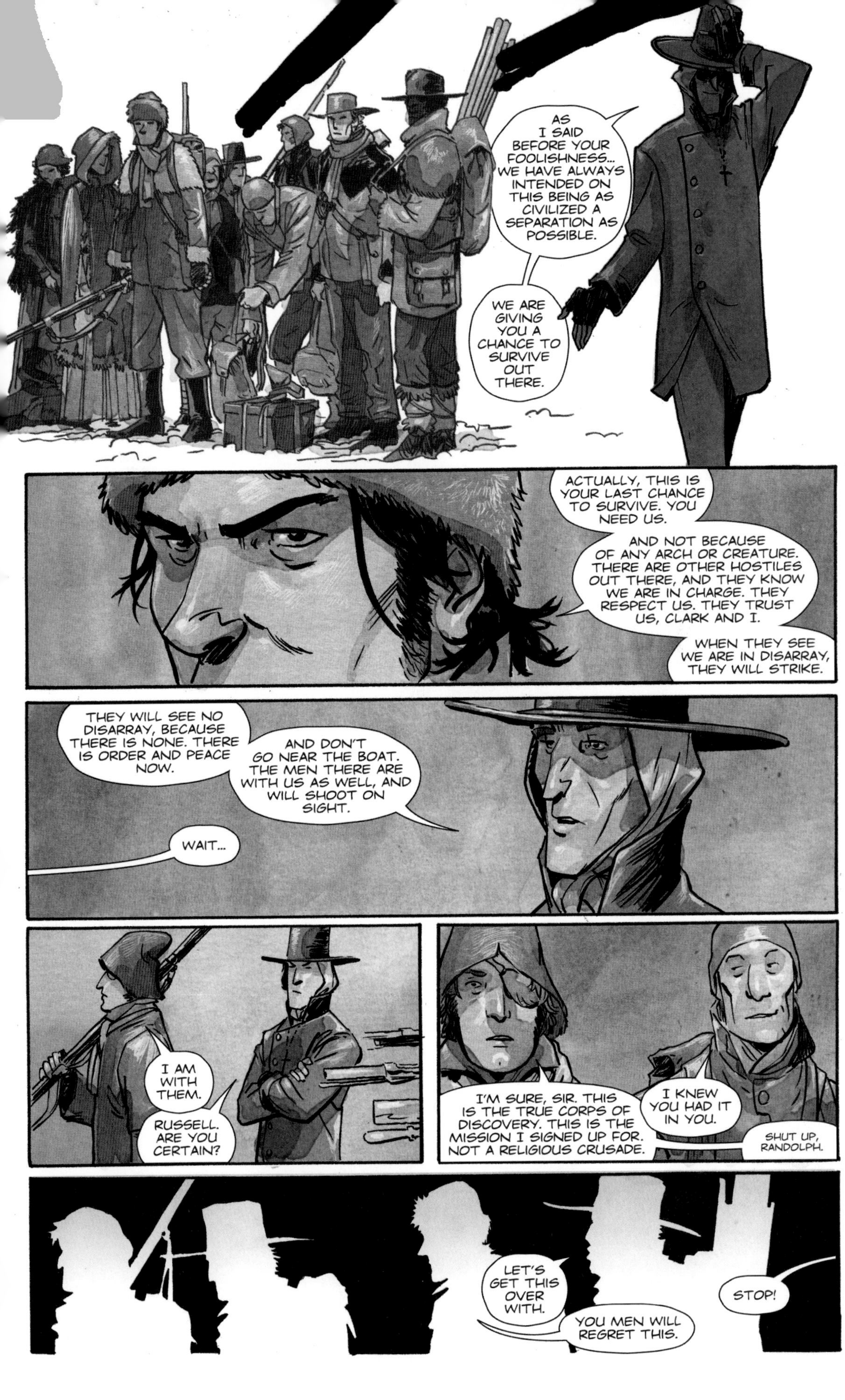
AS I SAID BEFORE YOUR FOOLISHNESS... WE HAVE ALWAYS INTENDED ON THIS BEING AS CIVILIZED A SEPARATION AS POSSIBLE.
WE ARE GIVING YOU A CHANCE TO SURVIVE OUT THERE.
ACTUALLY, THIS IS YOUR LAST CHANCE TO SURVIVE. YOU NEED US.
AND NOT BECAUSE OF ANY ARCH OR CREATURE. THERE ARE OTHER HOSTILES OUT THERE, AND THEY KNOW WE ARE IN CHARGE. THEY RESPECT US. THEY TRUST US, CLARK AND I.
WHEN THEY SEE WE ARE IN DISARRAY, THEY WILL STRIKE.
THEY WILL SEE NO DISARRAY, BECAUSE THERE IS NONE. THERE IS ORDER AND PEACE NOW.
AND DON'T GO NEAR THE BOAT. THE MEN THERE ARE WITH US AS WELL, AND WILL SHOOT ON SIGHT.
WAIT...
I AM WITH THEM.
RUSSELL. ARE YOU CERTAIN?
I'M SURE, SIR. THIS IS THE TRUE CORPS OF DISCOVERY. THIS IS THE MISSION I SIGNED UP FOR. NOT A RELIGIOUS CRUSADE.
I KNEW YOU HAD IT IN YOU.
SHUT UP, RANDOLPH.
LET'S GET THIS OVER WITH.
YOU MEN WILL REGRET THIS.
STOP!

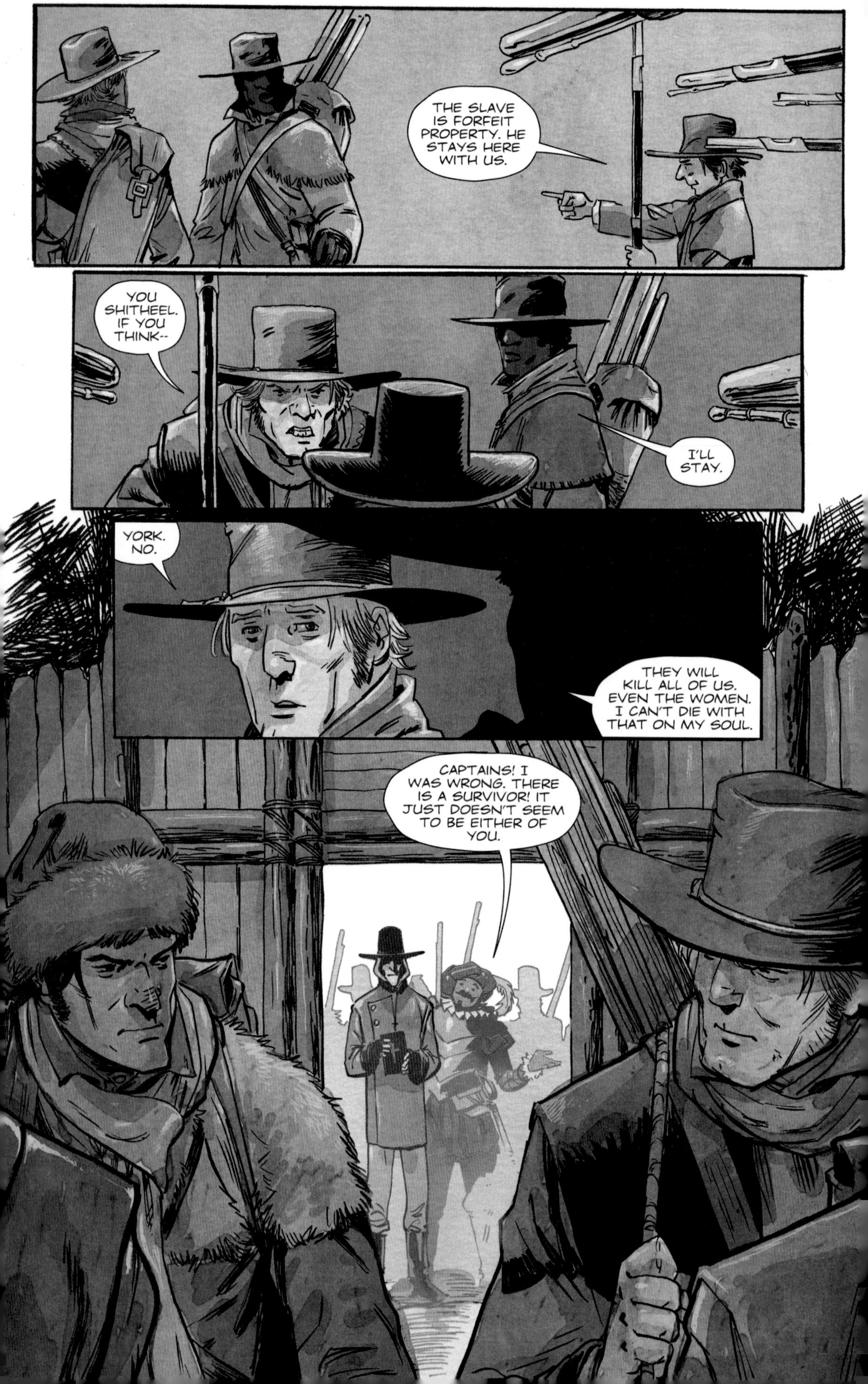
THE SLAVE IS FORFEIT PROPERTY. HE STAYS HERE WITH US.
YOU SHITHEEL. IF YOU THINK--
I'LL STAY.
YORK. NO.
THEY WILL KILL ALL OF US. EVEN THE WOMEN. I CAN'T DIE WITH THAT ON MY SOUL.
CAPTAINS! I WAS WRONG. THERE IS A SURVIVOR! IT JUST DOESN'T SEEM TO BE EITHER OF YOU.

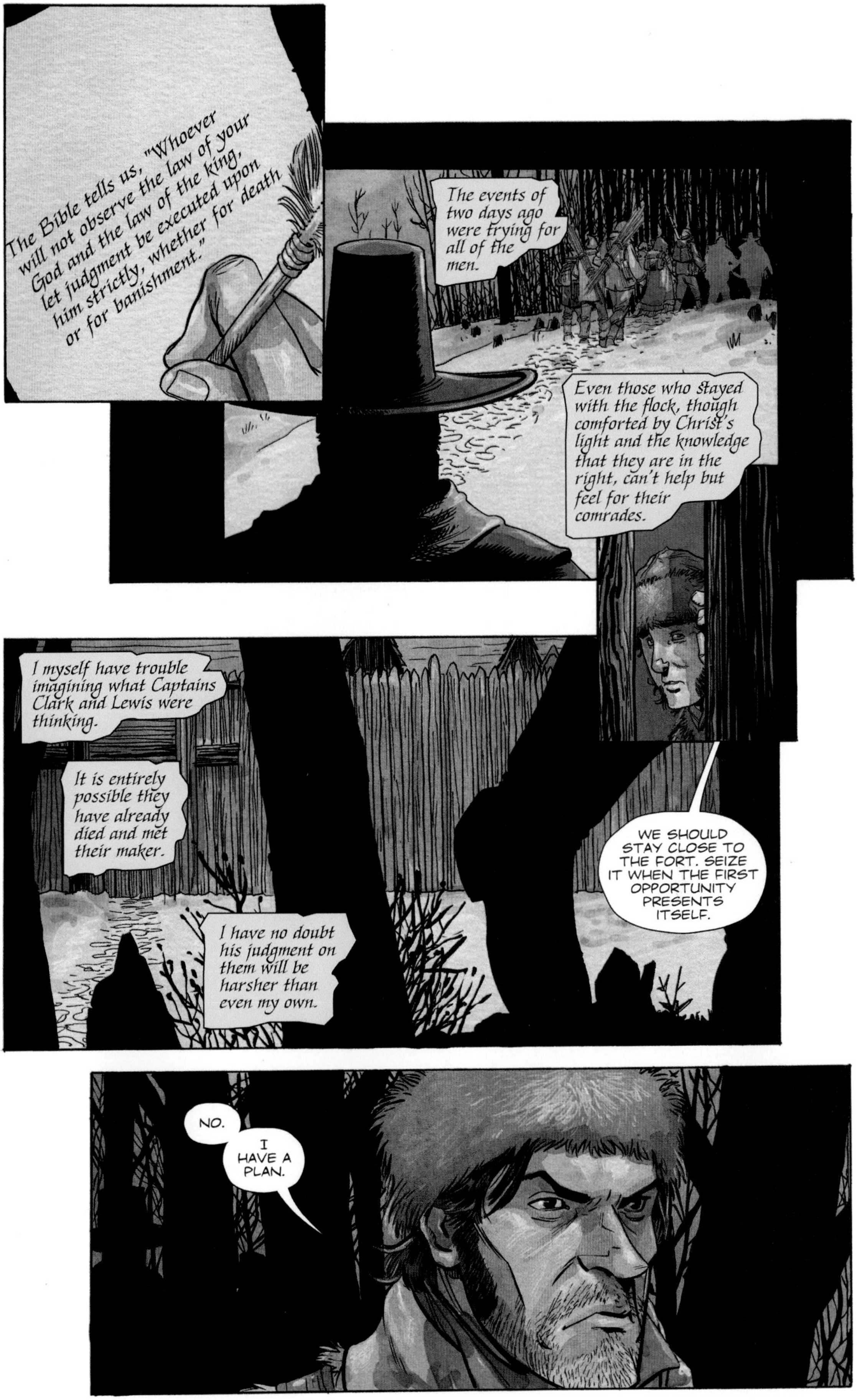
The Bible tells us, "Whoever will not observe the law of your God and the law of the king, let judgment be executed upon him strictly, whether for death or for banishment."
The events of two days ago were trying for all of the men.
Even those who stayed with the flock, though comforted by Christ's light and the knowledge that they are in the right, can't help but feel for their comrades.
I myself have trouble imagining what Captains Clark and Lewis were thinking.
It is entirely possible they have already died and met their maker.
I have no doubt his judgment on them will be harsher than even my own.
WE SHOULD STAY CLOSE TO THE FORT. SEIZE IT WHEN THE FIRST OPPORTUNITY PRESENTS ITSELF.
NO.
I HAVE A PLAN.

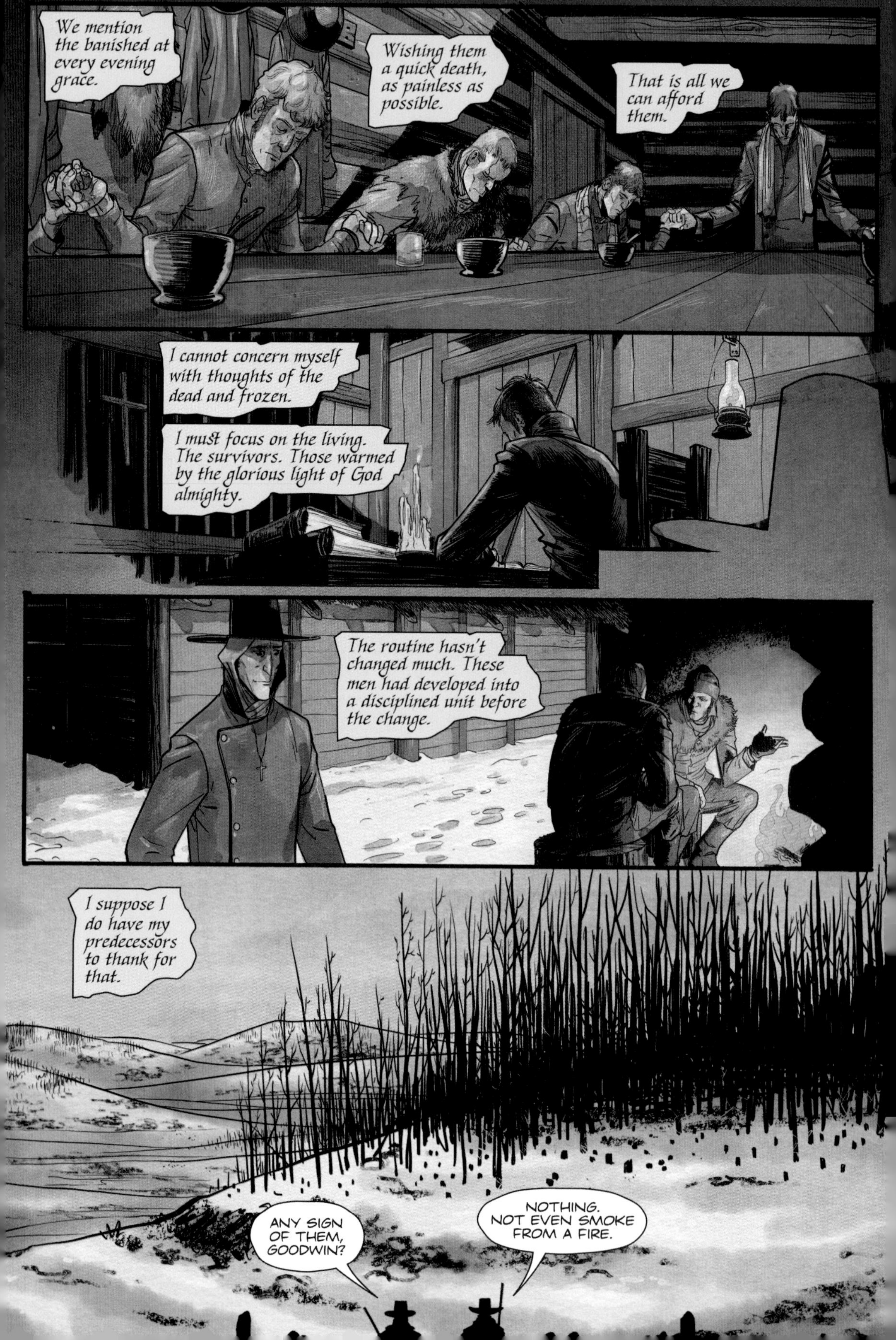
We mention the banished at every evening grace.
Wishing them a quick death, as painless as possible.
That is all we can afford them.
I cannot concern myself with thoughts of the dead and frozen.
I must focus on the living. The survivors. Those warmed by the glorious light of God almighty.
The routine hasn't changed much. These men had developed into a disciplined unit before the change.
I suppose I do have my predecessors to thank for that.
ANY SIGN OF THEM, GOODWIN?
NOTHING. NOT EVEN SMOKE FROM A FIRE.

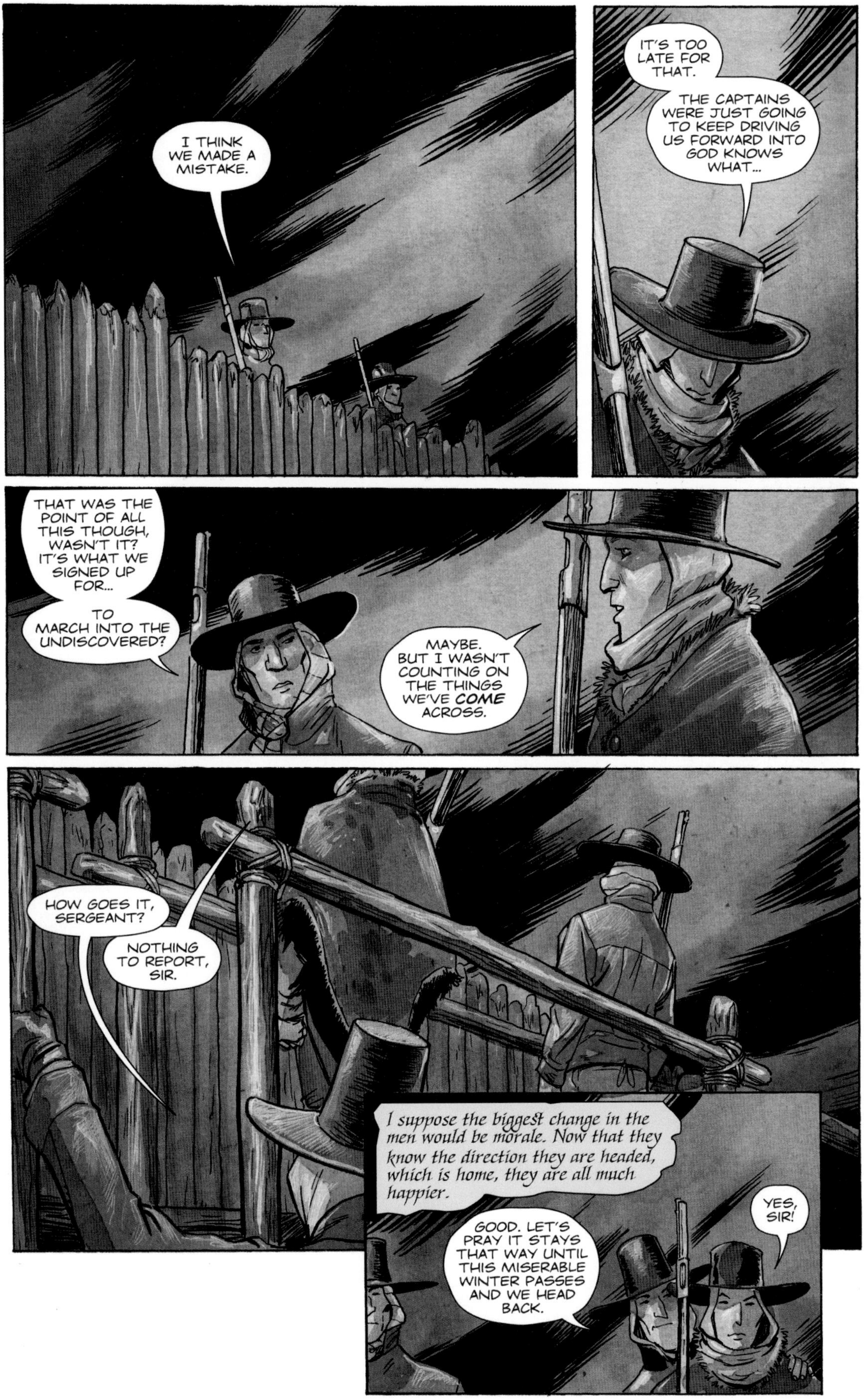
I THINK WE MADE A MISTAKE.
IT'S TOO LATE FOR THAT.
THE CAPTAINS WERE JUST GOING TO KEEP DRIVING US FORWARD INTO GOD KNOWS WHAT...
THAT WAS THE POINT OF ALL THIS THOUGH, WASN'T IT? IT'S WHAT WE SIGNED UP FOR...
TO MARCH INTO THE UNDISCOVERED?
MAYBE. BUT I WASN'T COUNTING ON THE THINGS WE'VE COME ACROSS.
HOW GOES IT, SERGEANT?
NOTHING TO REPORT, SIR.
I suppose the biggest change in the men would be morale. Now that they know the direction they are headed, which is home, they are all much happier.
GOOD. LET'S PRAY IT STAYS THAT WAY UNTIL THIS MISERABLE WINTER PASSES AND WE HEAD BACK.
YES, SIR!

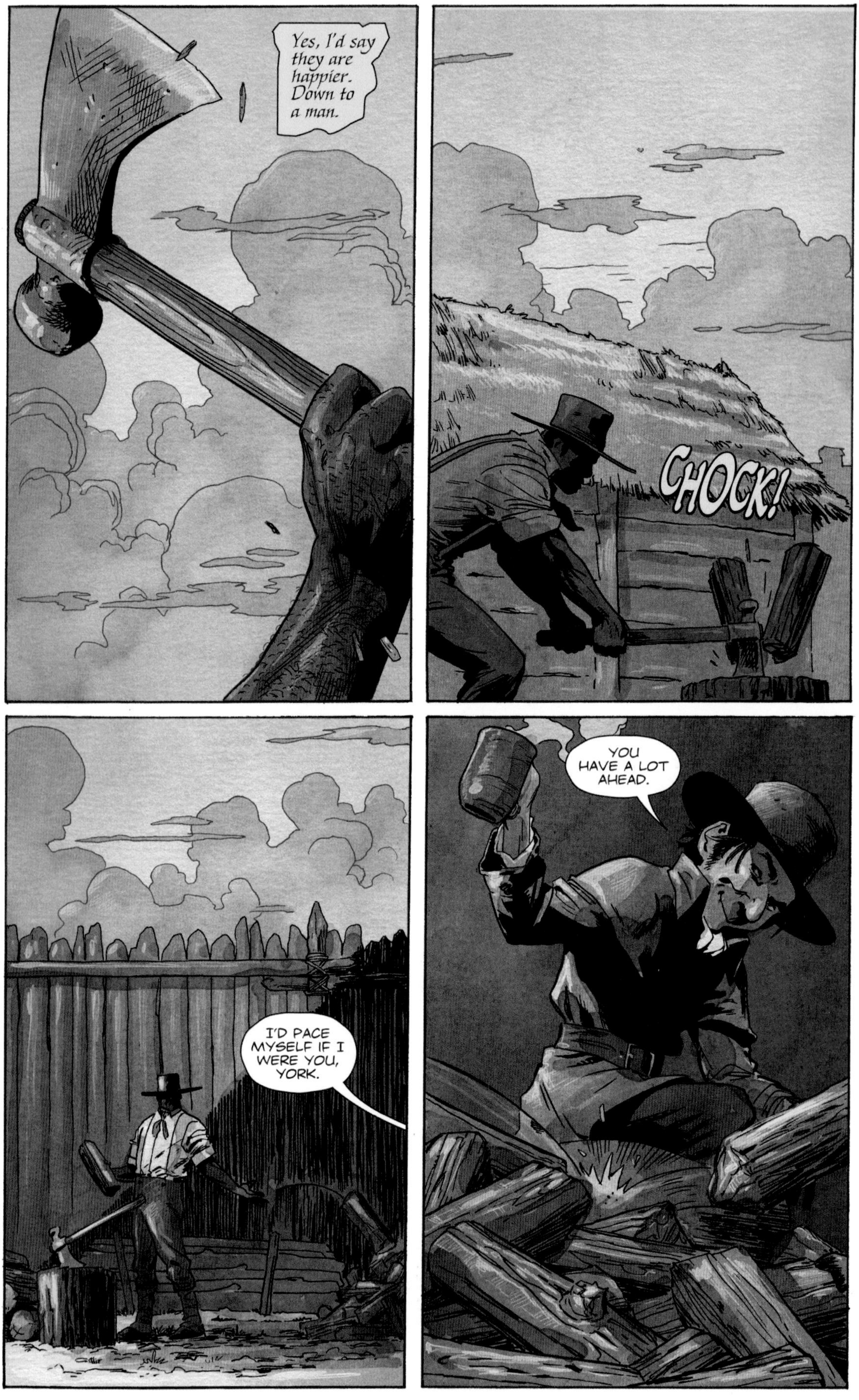
Yes, I'd say they are happier. Down to a man.
CHOCK!
I'D PACE MYSELF IF I WERE YOU, YORK.
YOU HAVE A LOT AHEAD.

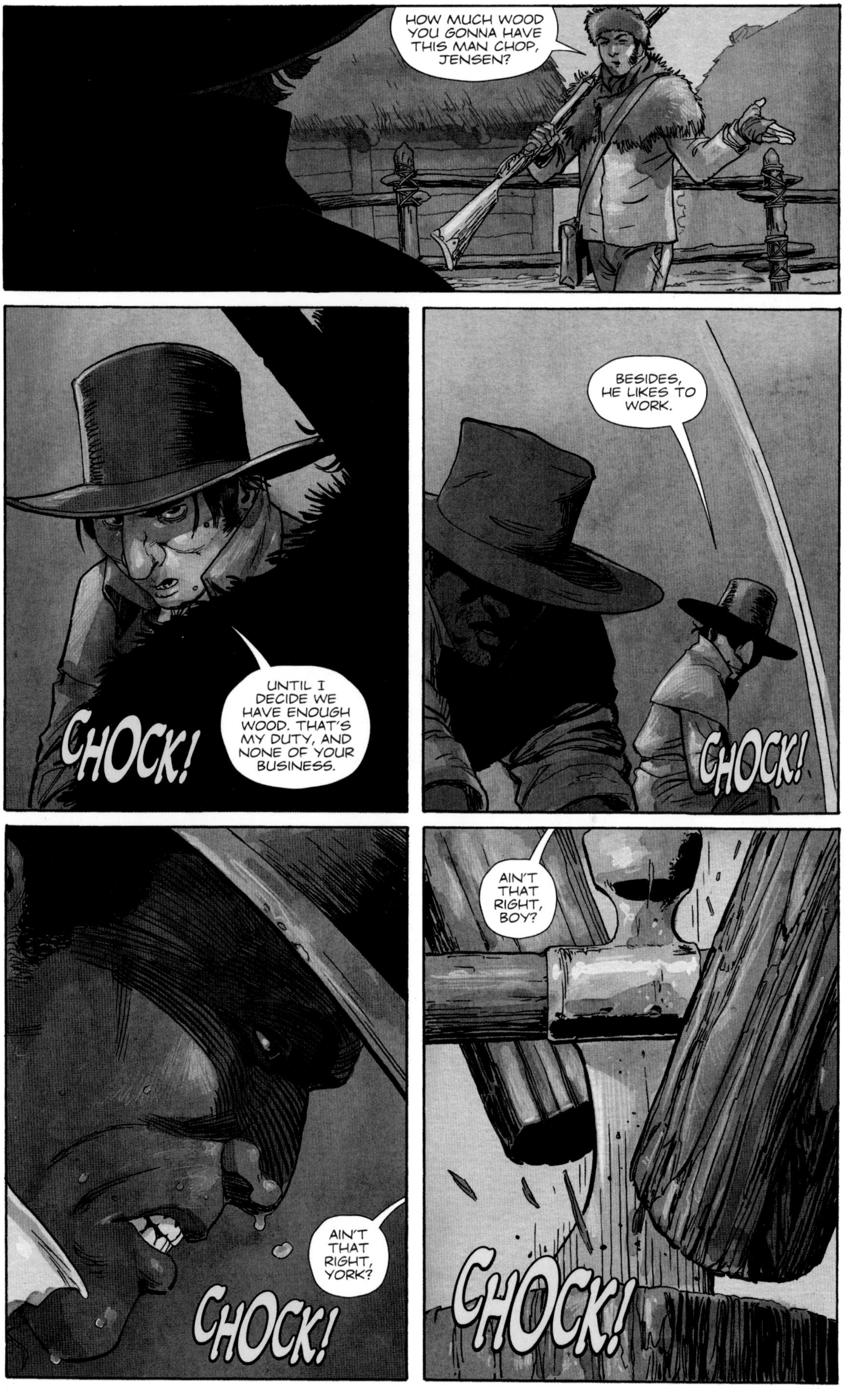
HOW MUCH WOOD YOU GONNA HAVE THIS MAN CHOP, JENSEN?
CHOCK!
UNTIL I DECIDE WE HAVE ENOUGH WOOD. THAT'S MY DUTY, AND NONE OF YOUR BUSINESS.
BESIDES, HE LIKES TO WORK.
CHOCK!
AIN'T THAT RIGHT, YORK?
CHOCK!
AIN'T THAT RIGHT, BOY?
CHOCK!

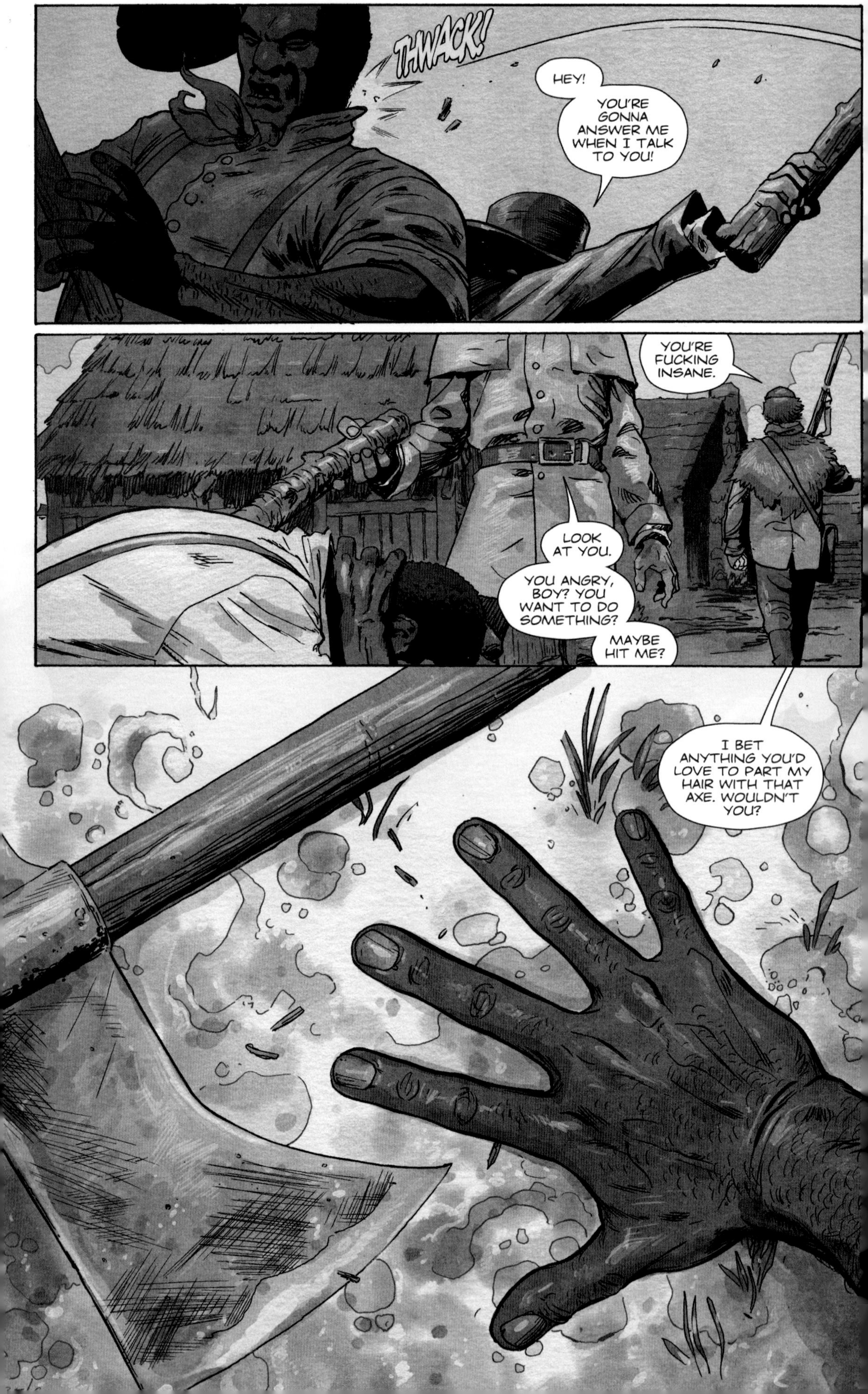
THWACK!
HEY!
YOU'RE GONNA ANSWER ME WHEN I TALK TO YOU!
YOU'RE FUCKING INSANE.
LOOK AT YOU.
YOU ANGRY, BOY? YOU WANT TO DO SOMETHING?
MAYBE HIT ME?
I BET ANYTHING YOU'D LOVE TO PART MY HAIR WITH THAT AXE. WOULDN'T YOU?

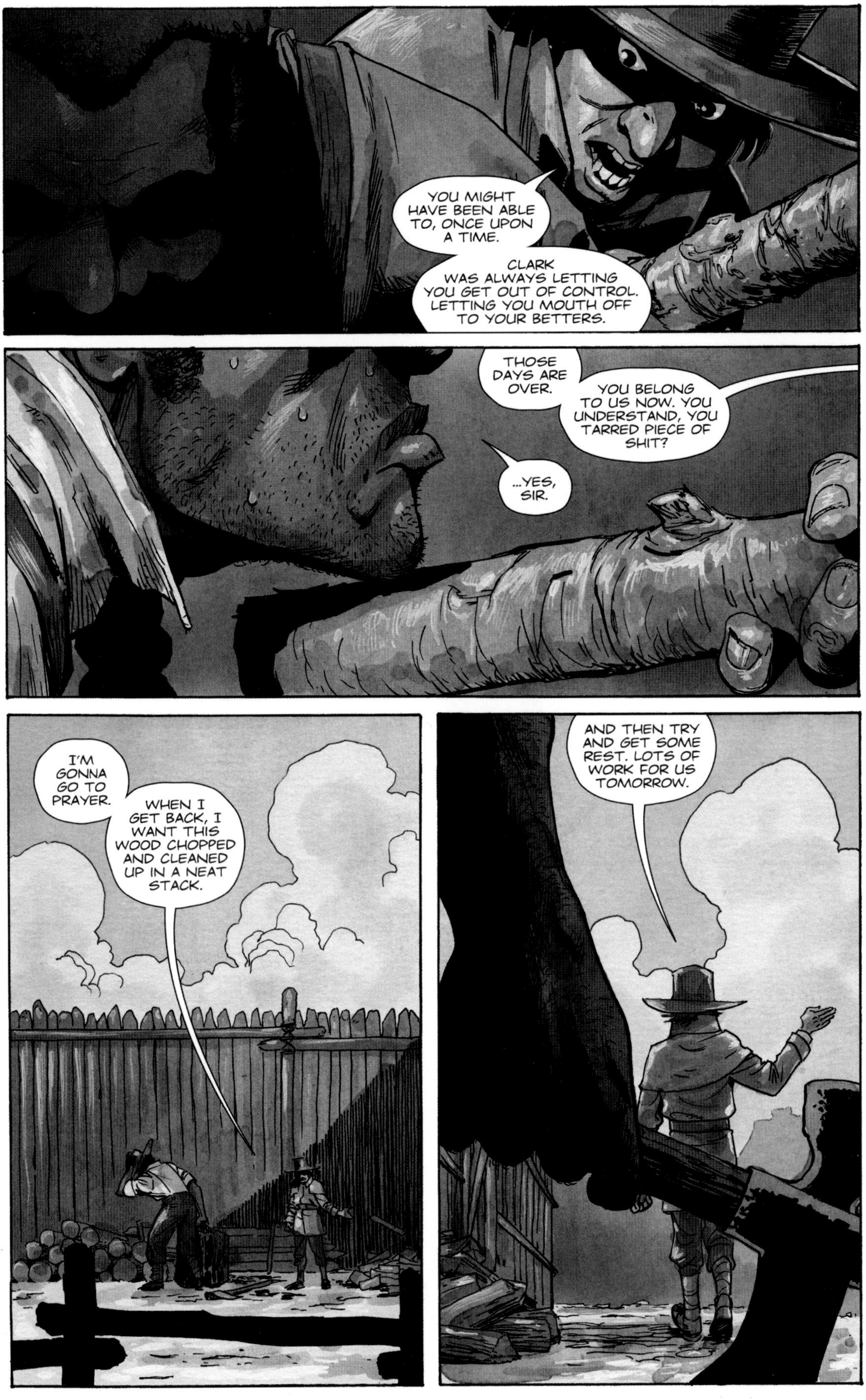
YOU MIGHT HAVE BEEN ABLE TO, ONCE UPON A TIME.
CLARK WAS ALWAYS LETTING YOU GET OUT OF CONTROL. LETTING YOU MOUTH OFF TO YOUR BETTERS.
THOSE DAYS ARE OVER.
YOU BELONG TO US NOW. YOU UNDERSTAND, YOU TARRED PIECE OF SHIT?
...YES, SIR.
I'M GONNA GO TO PRAYER.
WHEN I GET BACK, I WANT THIS WOOD CHOPPED AND CLEANED UP IN A NEAT STACK.
AND THEN TRY AND GET SOME REST. LOTS OF WORK FOR US TOMORROW.

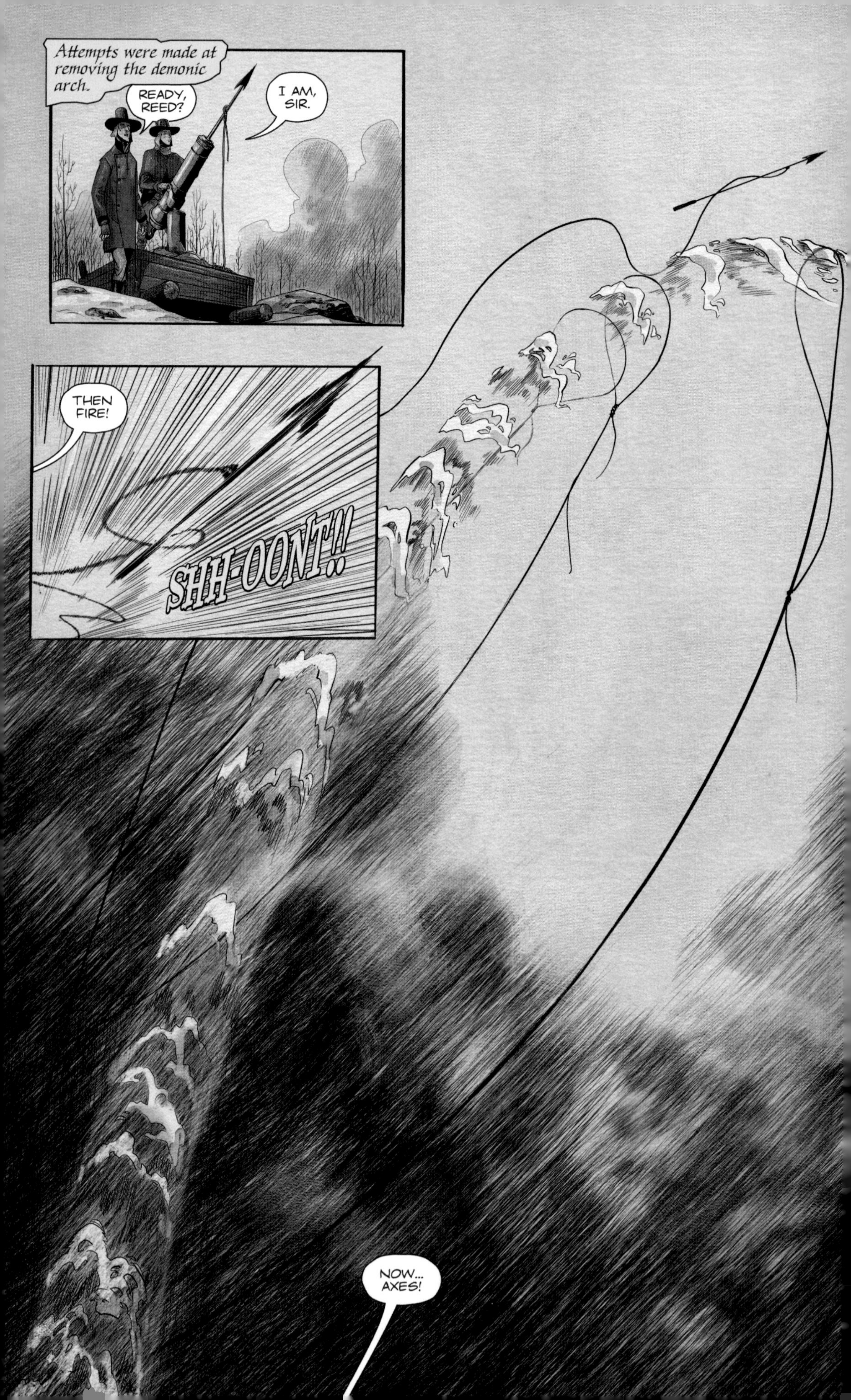
Attempts were made at removing the demonic arch.
READY, REED?
I AM, SIR.
THEN FIRE!
SHH-OONT!!
NOW... AXES!

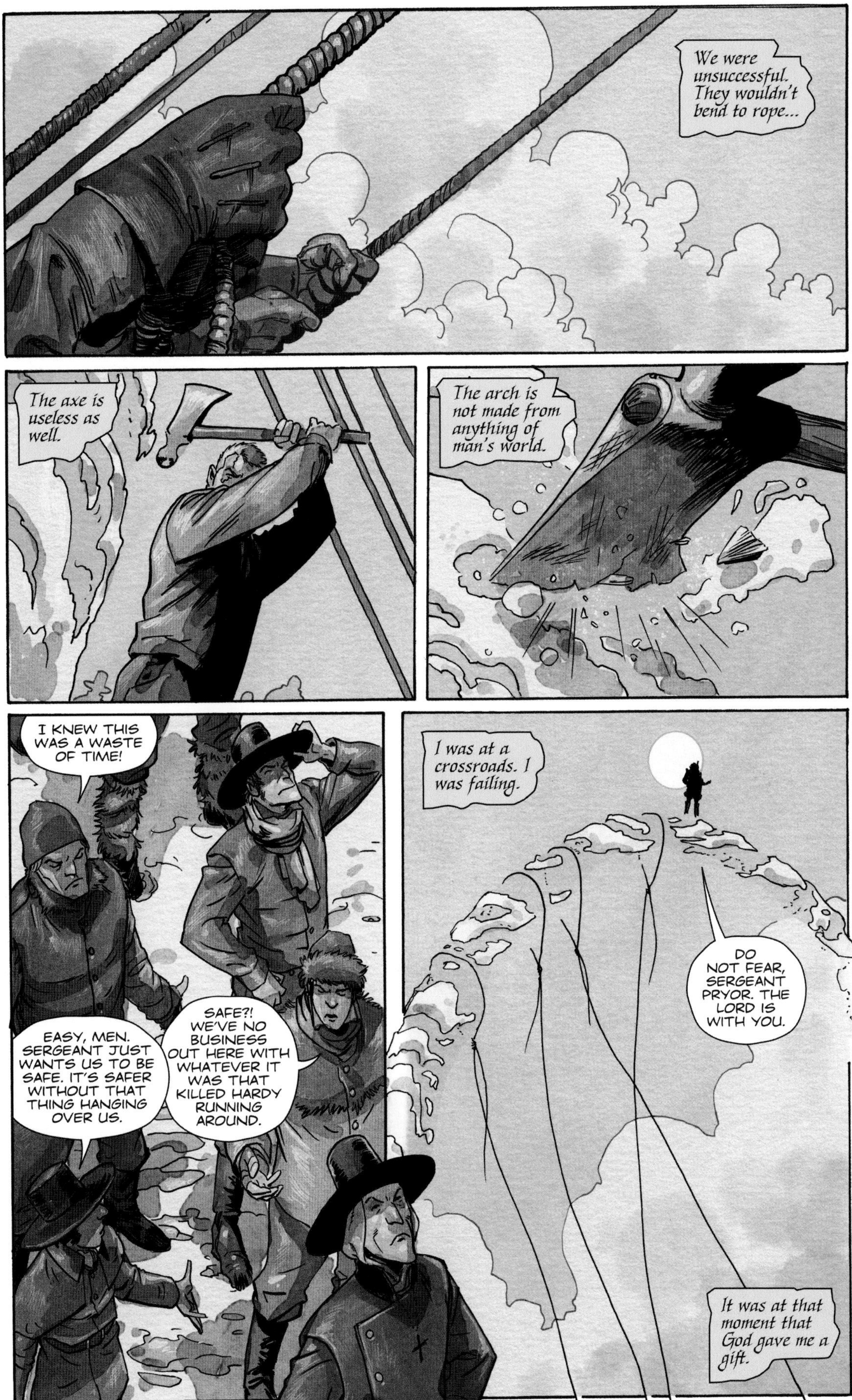
We were unsuccessful. They wouldn't bend to rope...
The axe is useless as well.
The arch is not made from anything of man's world.
I KNEW THIS WAS A WASTE OF TIME!
EASY, MEN. SERGEANT JUST WANTS US TO BE SAFE. IT'S SAFER WITHOUT THAT THING HANGING OVER US.
SAFE?! WE'VE NO BUSINESS OUT HERE WITH WHATEVER IT WAS THAT KILLED HARDY RUNNING AROUND.
I was at a crossroads. I was failing.
DO NOT FEAR, SERGEANT PRYOR. THE LORD IS WITH YOU.
It was at that moment that God gave me a gift.

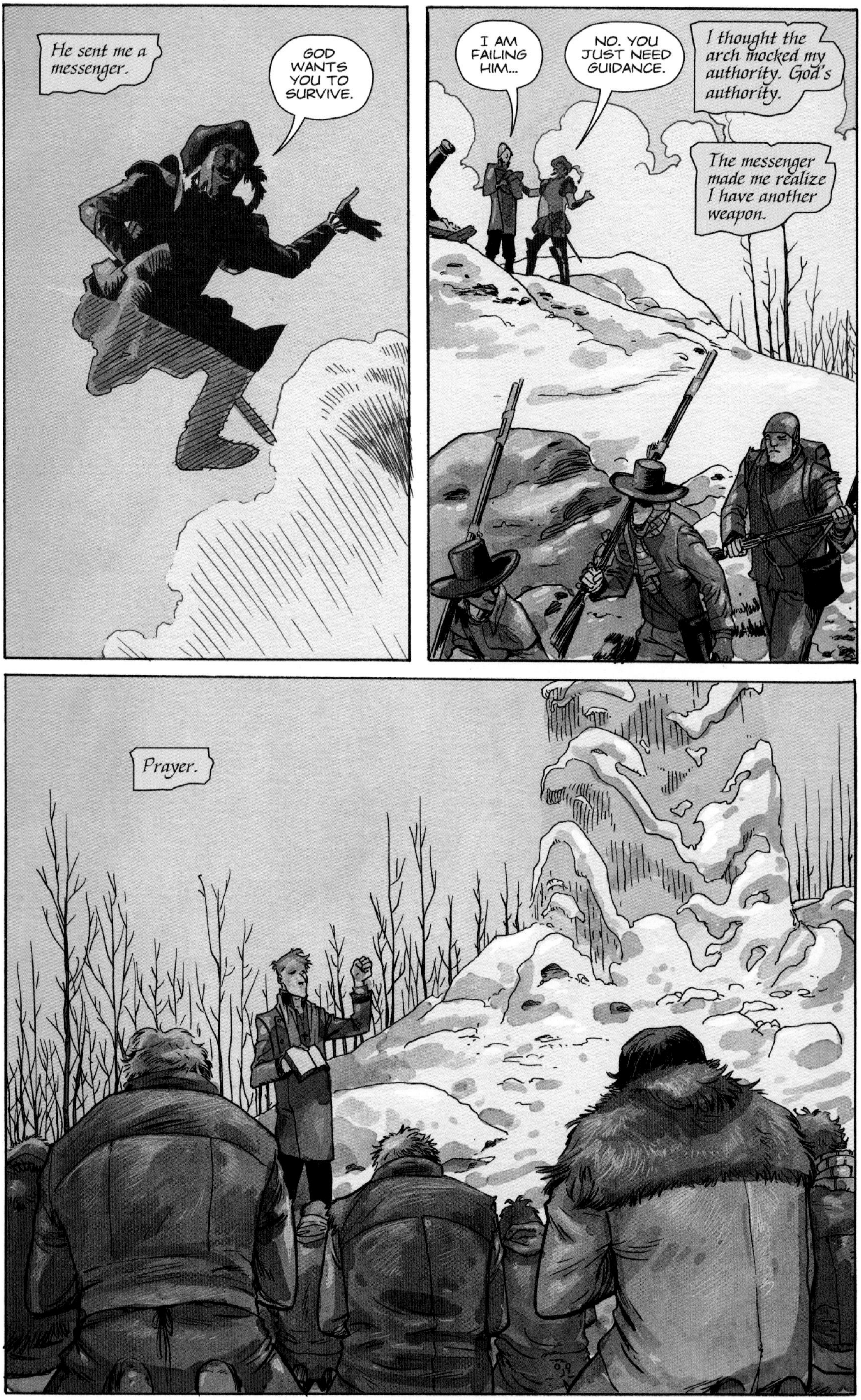
He sent me a messenger.
GOD WANTS YOU TO SURVIVE.
I AM FAILING HIM...
NO. YOU JUST NEED GUIDANCE.
I thought the arch mocked my authority. God's authority.
The messenger made me realize I have another weapon.
Prayer.

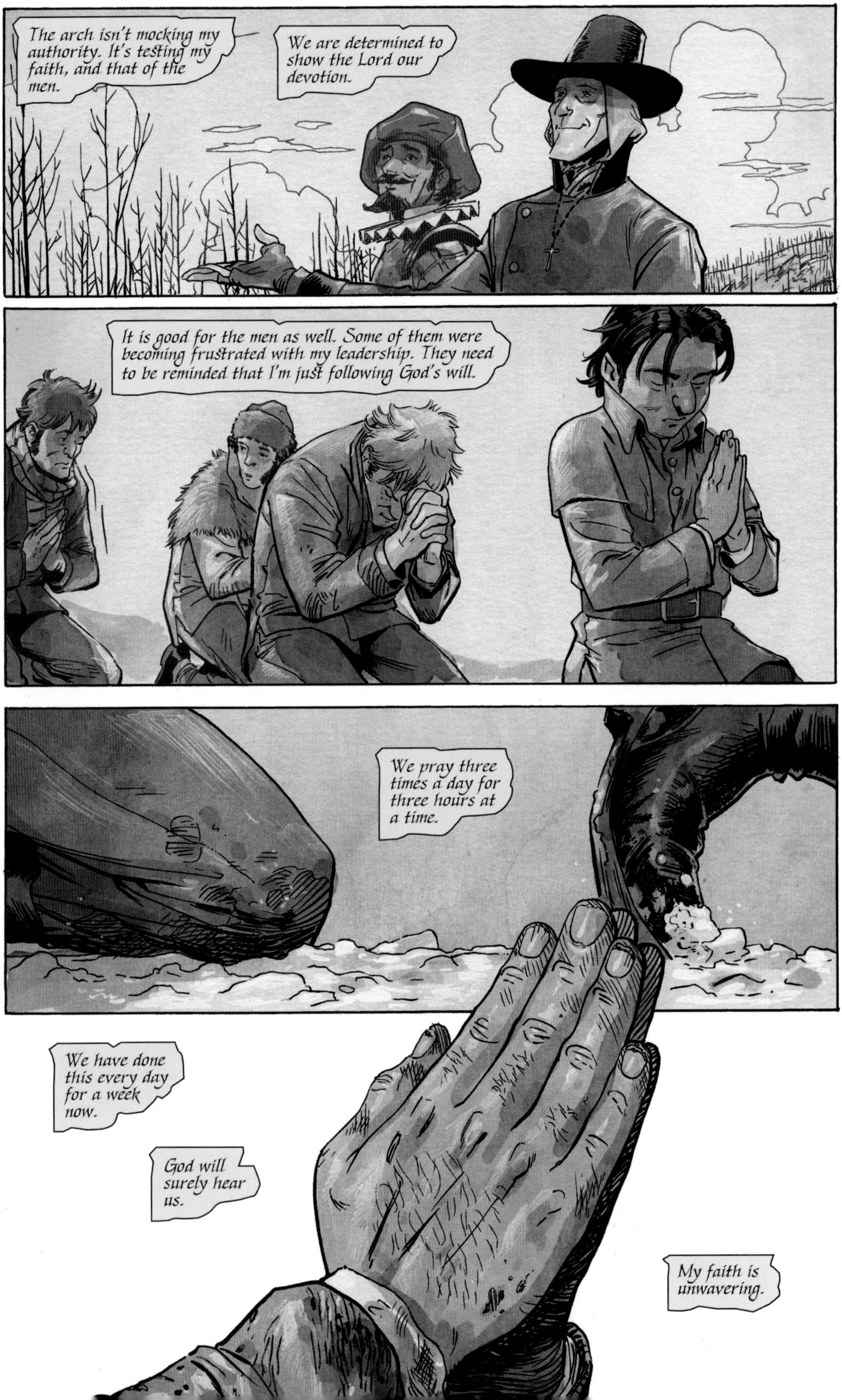
The arch isn't mocking my authority. It's testing my faith, and that of the men.
We are determined to show the Lord our devotion.
It is good for the men as well. Some of them were becoming frustrated with my leadership. They need to be reminded that I'm just following God's will.
We pray three times a day for three hours at a time.
We have done this every day for a week now.
God will surely hear us.
My faith is unwavering.

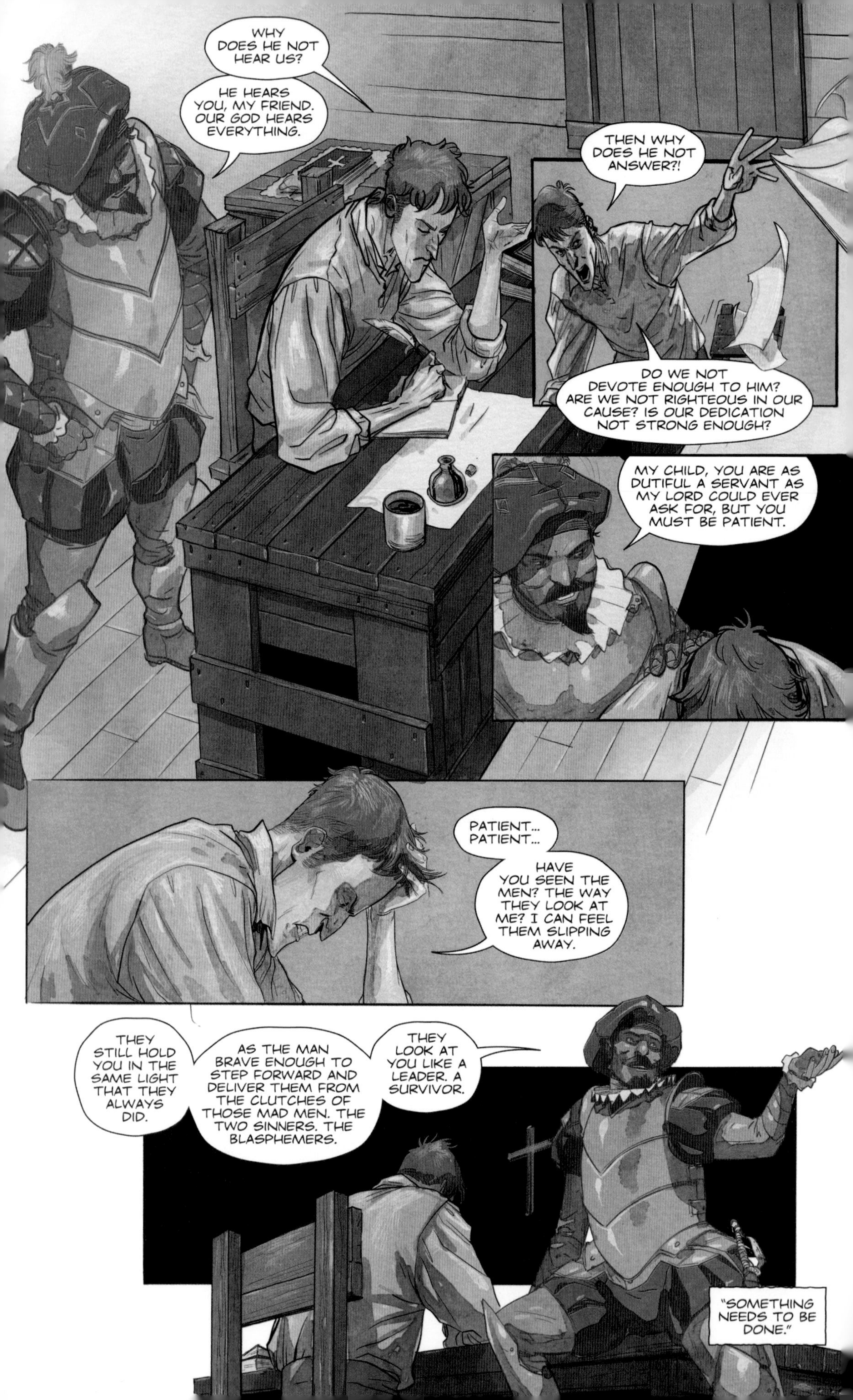
WHY DOES HE NOT HEAR US?
HE HEARS YOU, MY FRIEND. OUR GOD HEARS EVERYTHING.
THEN WHY DOES HE NOT ANSWER?!
DO WE NOT DEVOTE ENOUGH TO HIM? ARE WE NOT RIGHTEOUS IN OUR CAUSE? IS OUR DEDICATION NOT STRONG ENOUGH?
MY CHILD, YOU ARE AS DUTIFUL A SERVANT AS MY LORD COULD EVER ASK FOR, BUT YOU MUST BE PATIENT.
PATIENT... PATIENT...
HAVE YOU SEEN THE MEN? THE WAY THEY LOOK AT ME? I CAN FEEL THEM SLIPPING AWAY.
THEY LOOK AT YOU LIKE A LEADER. A SURVIVOR.
AS THE MAN BRAVE ENOUGH TO STEP FORWARD AND DELIVER THEM FROM THE CLUTCHES OF THOSE MAD MEN. THE TWO SINNERS. THE BLASPHEMERS.
THEY STILL HOLD YOU IN THE SAME LIGHT THAT THEY ALWAYS DID.
"SOMETHING NEEDS TO BE DONE."

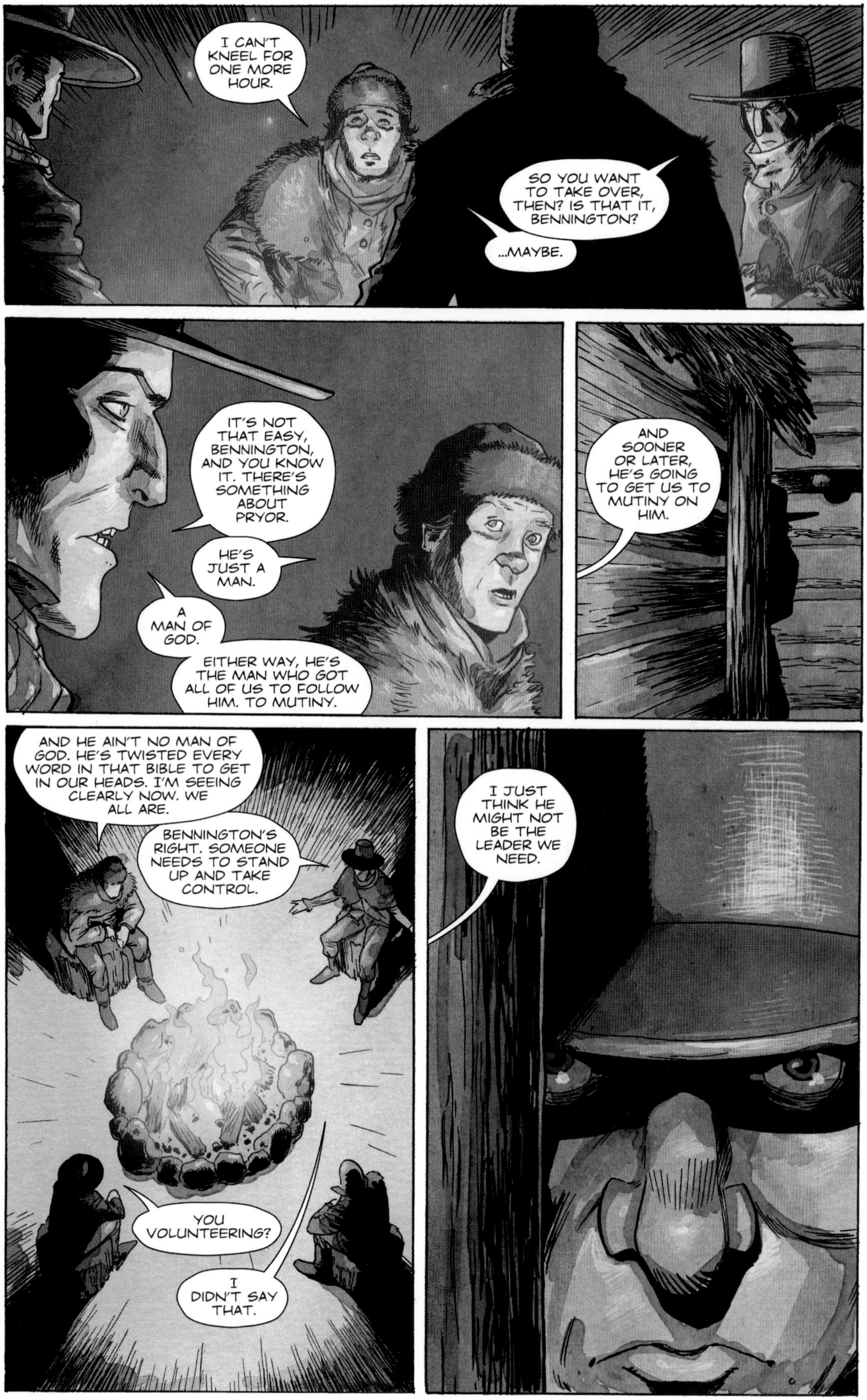
I CAN'T KNEEL FOR ONE MORE HOUR.
SO YOU WANT TO TAKE OVER, THEN? IS THAT IT, BENNINGTON?
...MAYBE.
IT'S NOT THAT EASY, BENNINGTON, AND YOU KNOW IT. THERE'S SOMETHING ABOUT PRYOR.
HE'S JUST A MAN.
A MAN OF GOD.
EITHER WAY, HE'S THE MAN WHO GOT ALL OF US TO FOLLOW HIM. TO MUTINY.
AND SOONER OR LATER, HE'S GOING TO GET US TO MUTINY ON HIM.
AND HE AIN'T NO MAN OF GOD. HE'S TWISTED EVERY WORD IN THAT BIBLE TO GET IN OUR HEADS. I'M SEEING CLEARLY NOW. WE ALL ARE.
BENNINGTON'S RIGHT. SOMEONE NEEDS TO STAND UP AND TAKE CONTROL.
YOU VOLUNTEERING?
I DIDN'T SAY THAT.
I JUST THINK HE MIGHT NOT BE THE LEADER WE NEED.

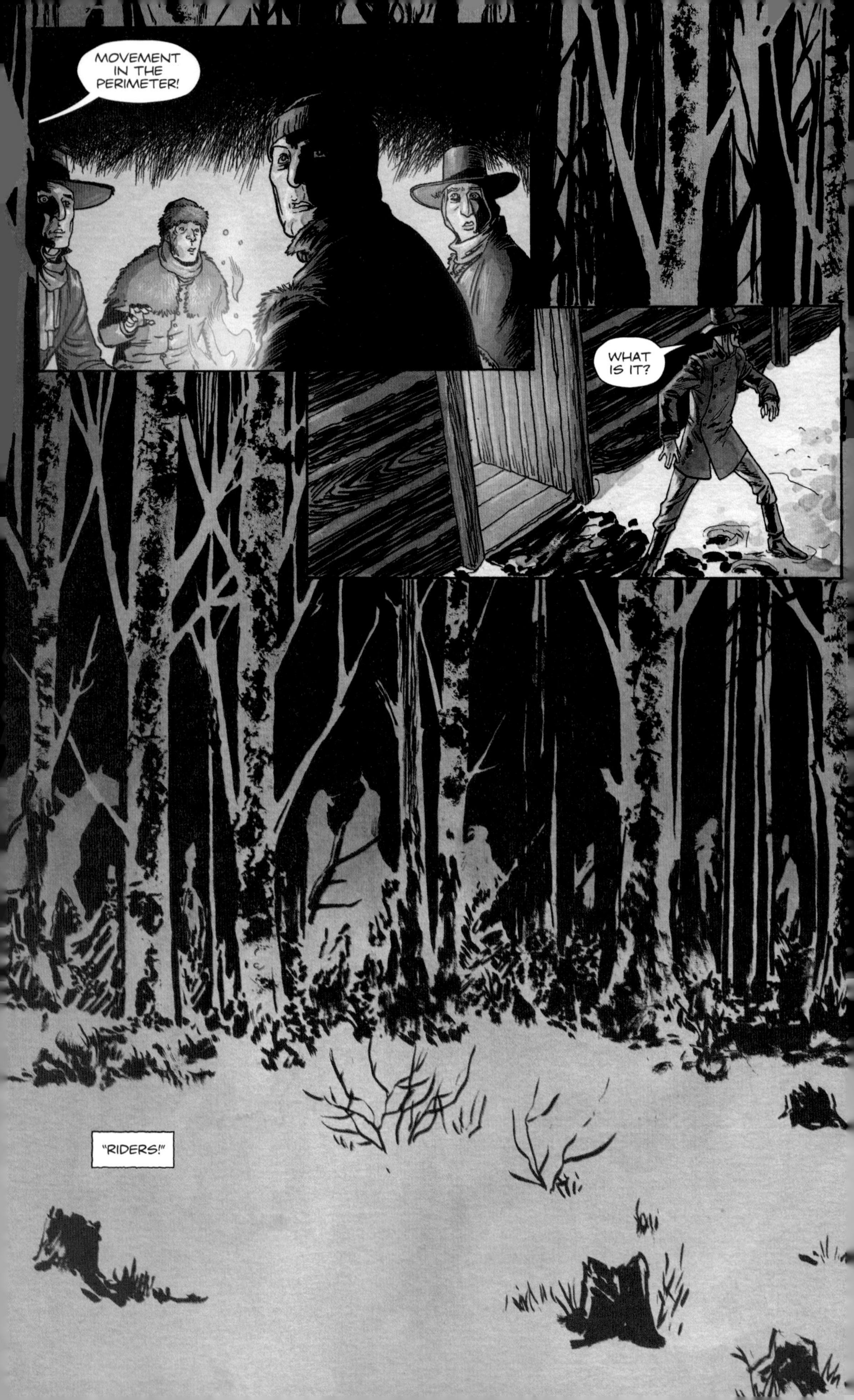
MOVEMENT IN THE PERIMETER!
WHAT IS IT?
"RIDERS!"

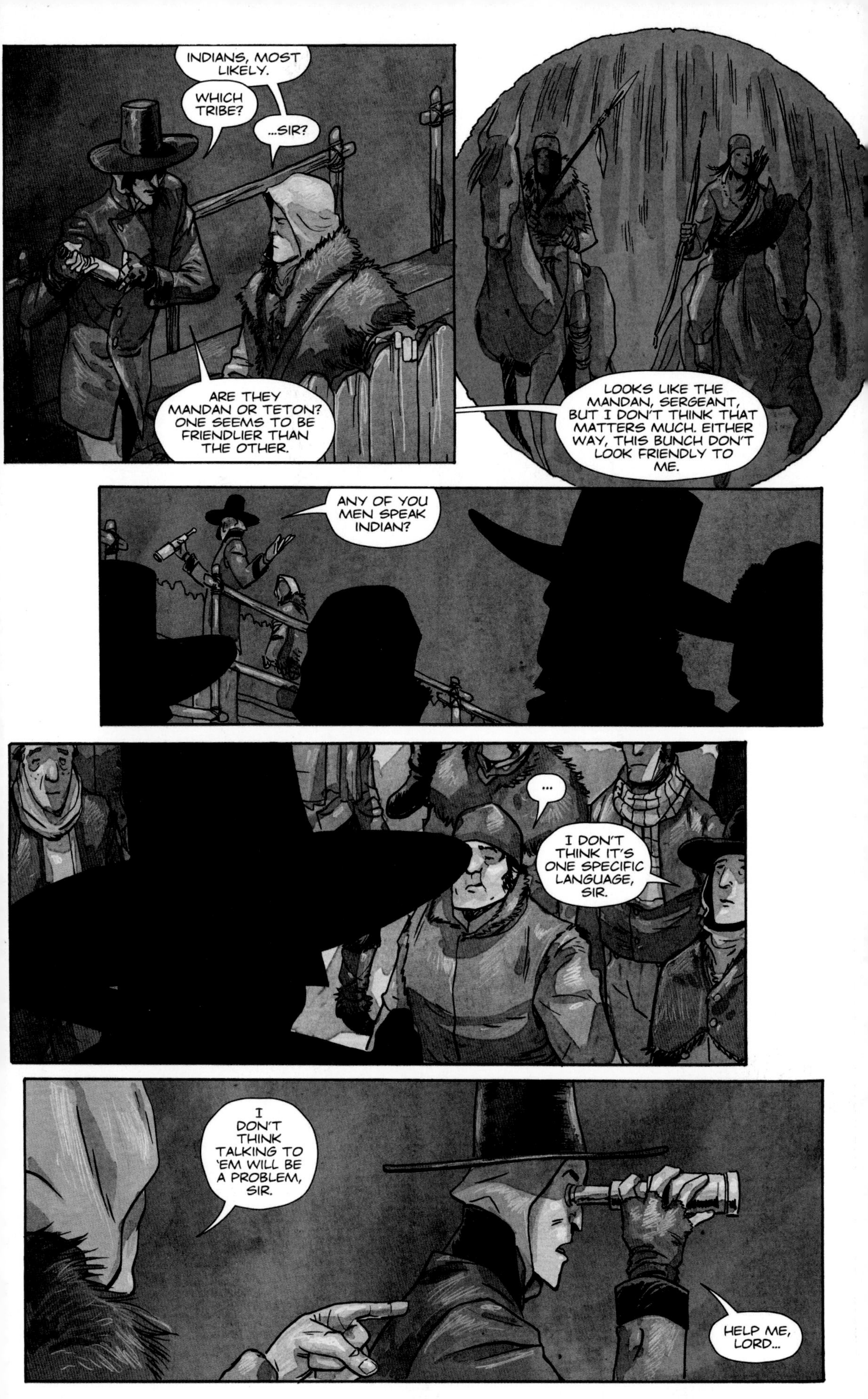
INDIANS, MOST LIKELY.
WHICH TRIBE?
...SIR?
ARE THEY MANDAN OR TETON? ONE SEEMS TO BE FRIENDLIER THAN THE OTHER.
LOOKS LIKE THE MANDAN, SERGEANT, BUT I DON'T THINK THAT MATTERS MUCH. EITHER WAY, THIS BUNCH DON'T LOOK FRIENDLY TO ME.
ANY OF YOU MEN SPEAK INDIAN?
...
I DON'T THINK IT'S ONE SPECIFIC LANGUAGE, SIR.
I DON'T THINK TALKING TO 'EM WILL BE A PROBLEM, SIR.
HELP ME, LORD...

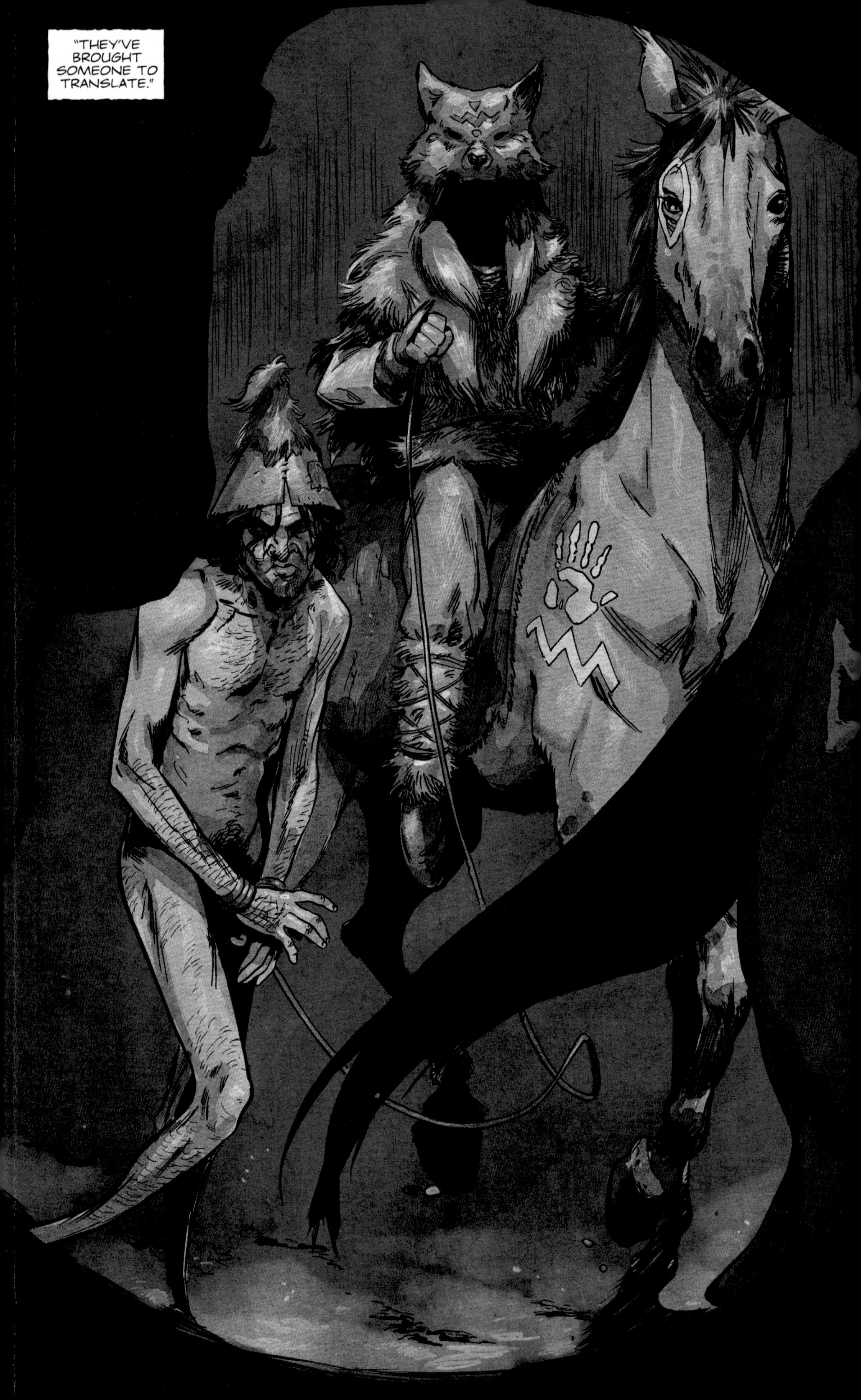
"THEY'VE BROUGHT SOMEONE TO TRANSLATE."

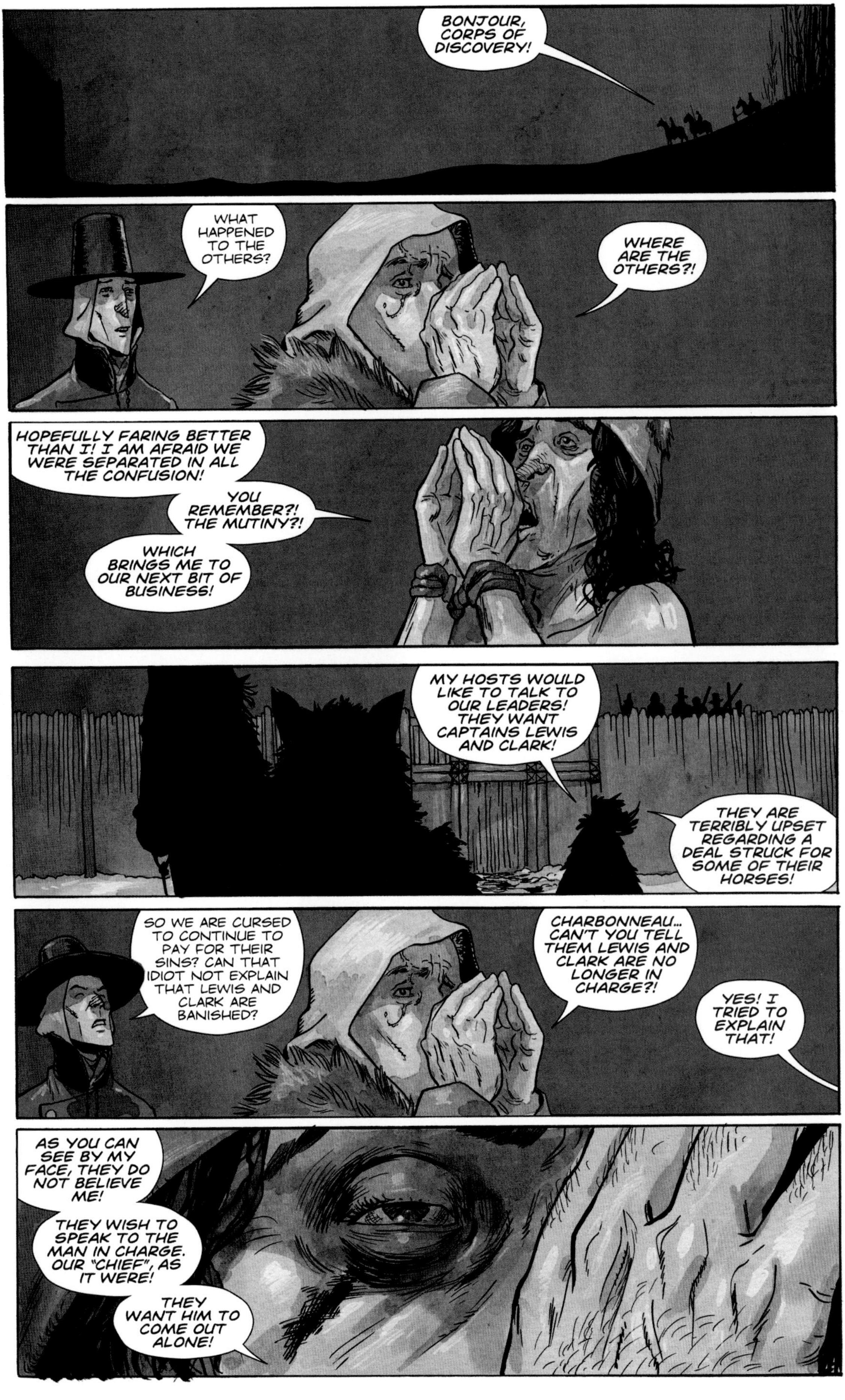

BONJOUR, CORPS OF DISCOVERY!
WHAT HAPPENED TO THE OTHERS?
WHERE ARE THE OTHERS?!
HOPEFULLY FARING BETTER THAN I! I AM AFRAID WE WERE SEPARATED IN ALL THE CONFUSION!
YOU REMEMBER?! THE MUTINY?!
WHICH BRINGS ME TO OUR NEXT BIT OF BUSINESS!
MY HOSTS WOULD LIKE TO TALK TO OUR LEADERS! THEY WANT CAPTAINS LEWIS AND CLARK!
THEY ARE TERRIBLY UPSET REGARDING A DEAL STRUCK FOR SOME OF THEIR HORSES!
SO WE ARE CURSED TO CONTINUE TO PAY FOR THEIR SINS? CAN THAT IDIOT NOT EXPLAIN THAT LEWIS AND CLARK ARE BANISHED?
CHARBONNEAU... CAN'T YOU TELL THEM LEWIS AND CLARK ARE NO LONGER IN CHARGE?!
YES! I TRIED TO EXPLAIN THAT!
AS YOU CAN SEE BY MY FACE, THEY DO NOT BELIEVE ME!
THEY WISH TO SPEAK TO THE MAN IN CHARGE. OUR "CHIEF", AS IT WERE!
THEY WANT HIM TO COME OUT ALONE!

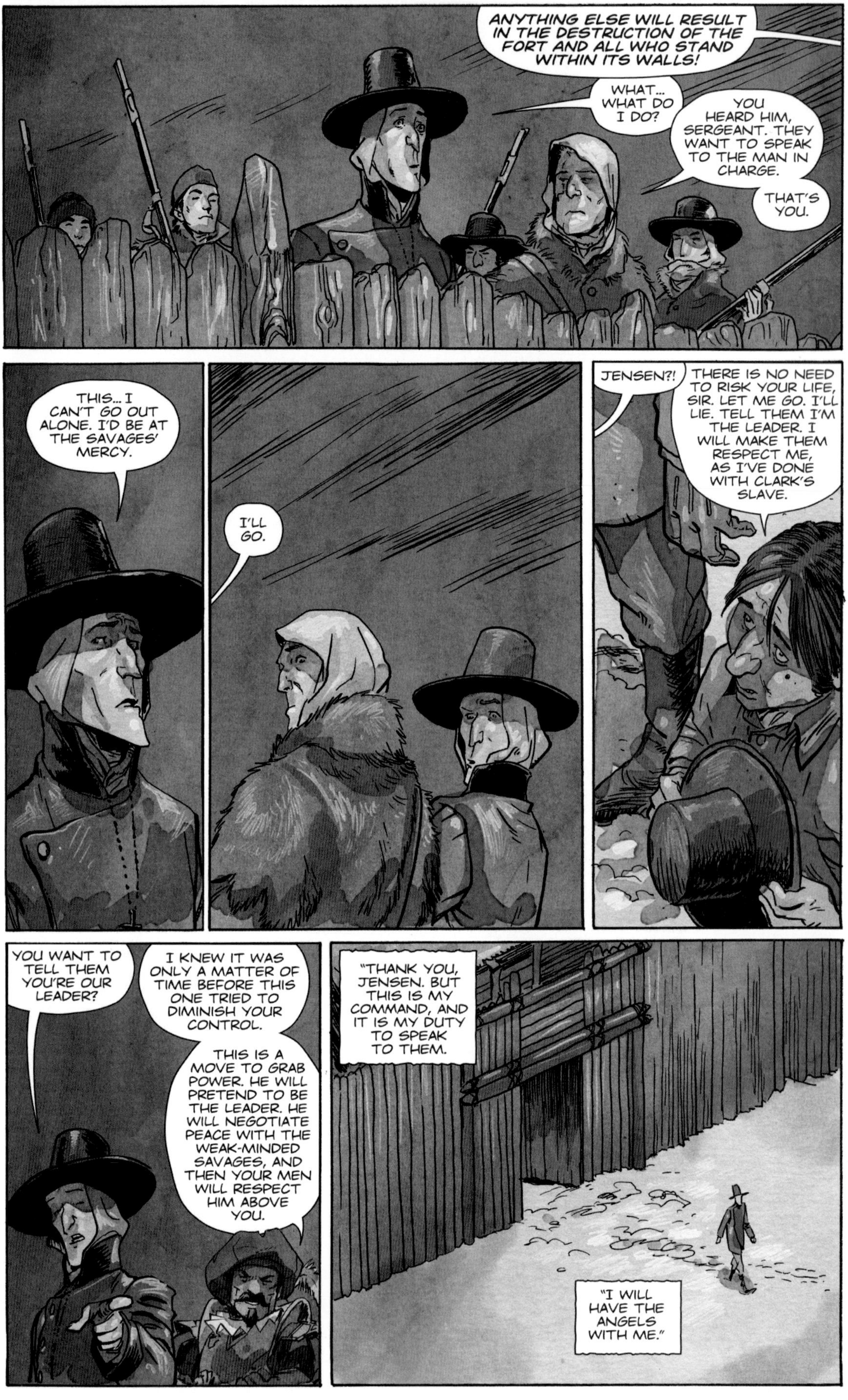
ANYTHING ELSE WILL RESULT IN THE DESTRUCTION OF THE FORT AND ALL WHO STAND WITHIN ITS WALLS!
WHAT... WHAT DO I DO?
YOU HEARD HIM, SERGEANT. THEY WANT TO SPEAK TO THE MAN IN CHARGE.
THAT'S YOU.
THIS... I CAN'T GO OUT ALONE. I'D BE AT THE SAVAGES' MERCY.
I'LL GO.
JENSEN?!
THERE IS NO NEED TO RISK YOUR LIFE, SIR. LET ME GO. I'LL LIE. TELL THEM I'M THE LEADER. I WILL MAKE THEM RESPECT ME, AS I'VE DONE WITH CLARK'S SLAVE.
YOU WANT TO TELL THEM YOU'RE OUR LEADER?
I KNEW IT WAS ONLY A MATTER OF TIME BEFORE THIS ONE TRIED TO DIMINISH YOUR CONTROL.
THIS IS A MOVE TO GRAB POWER. HE WILL PRETEND TO BE THE LEADER. HE WILL NEGOTIATE PEACE WITH THE WEAK-MINDED SAVAGES, AND THEN YOUR MEN WILL RESPECT HIM ABOVE YOU.
"THANK YOU, JENSEN. BUT THIS IS MY COMMAND, AND IT IS MY DUTY TO SPEAK TO THEM.
"I WILL HAVE THE ANGELS WITH ME."

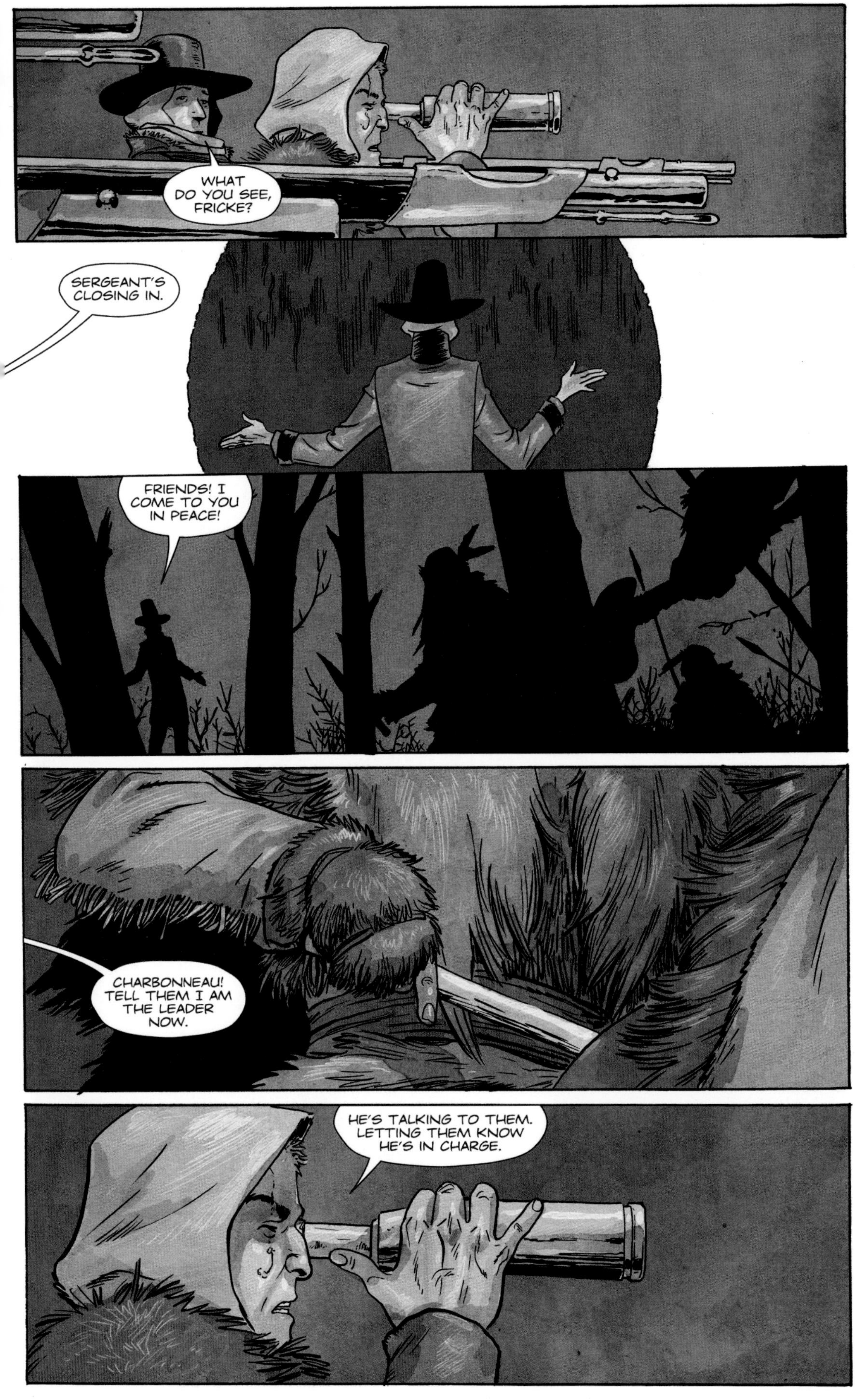
WHAT DO YOU SEE, FRICKE?
SERGEANT'S CLOSING IN.
FRIENDS! I COME TO YOU IN PEACE!
CHARBONNEAU! TELL THEM I AM THE LEADER NOW.
HE'S TALKING TO THEM. LETTING THEM KNOW HE'S IN CHARGE.

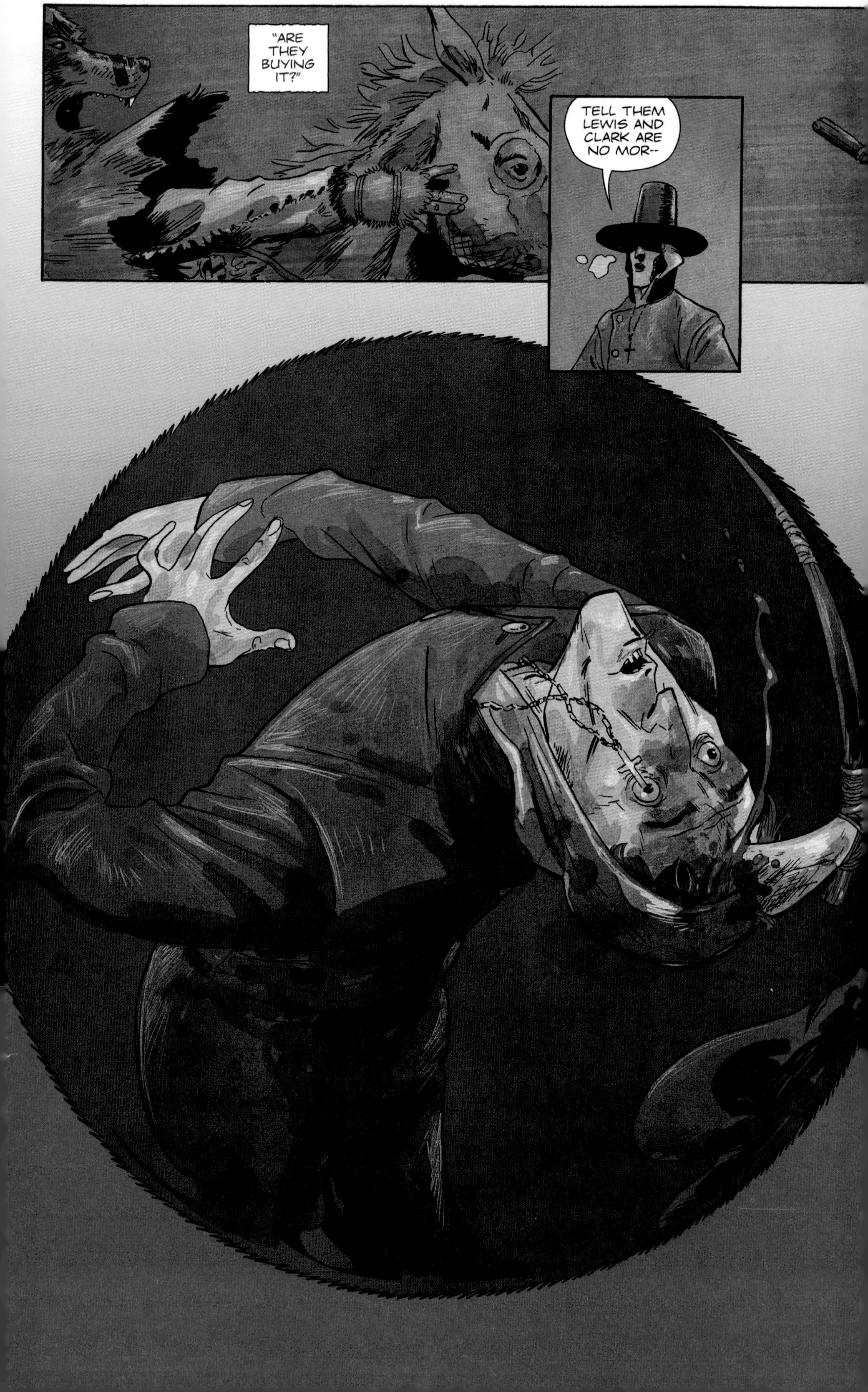
"ARE THEY BUYING IT?"
TELL THEM LEWIS AND CLARK ARE NO MOR--

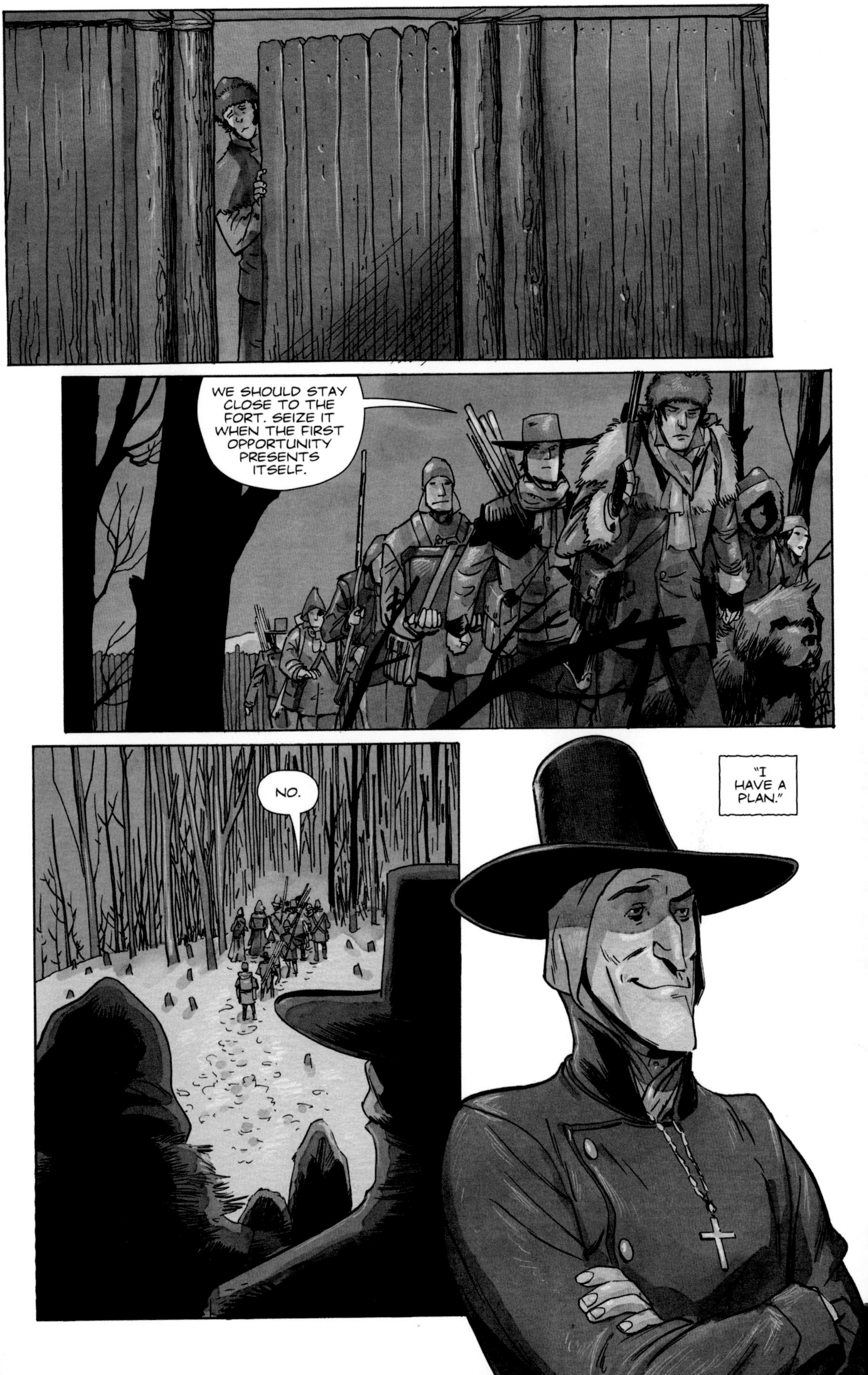
WE SHOULD STAY CLOSE TO THE FORT. SEIZE IT WHEN THE FIRST OPPORTUNITY PRESENTS ITSELF.
NO.
"I HAVE A PLAN."

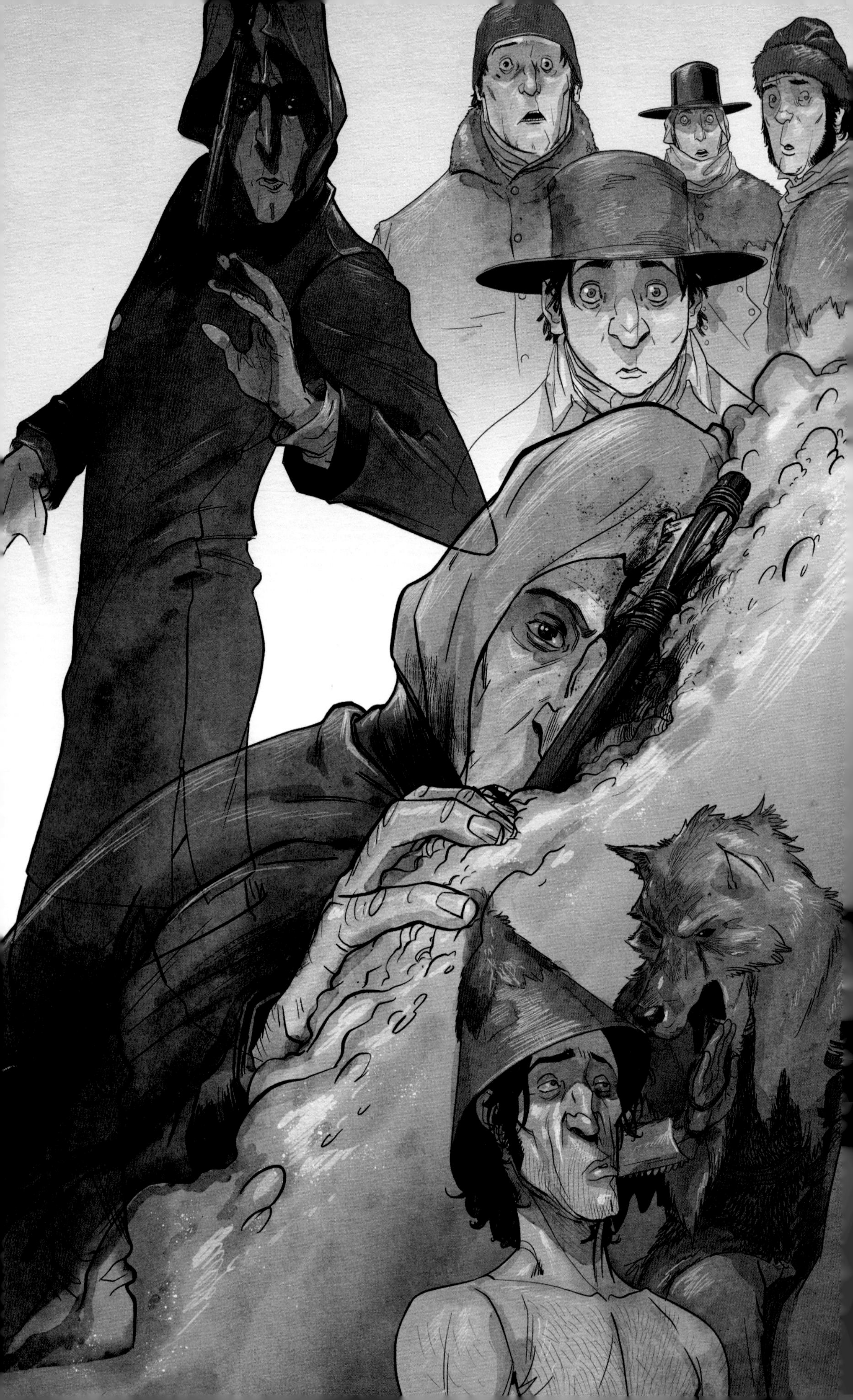

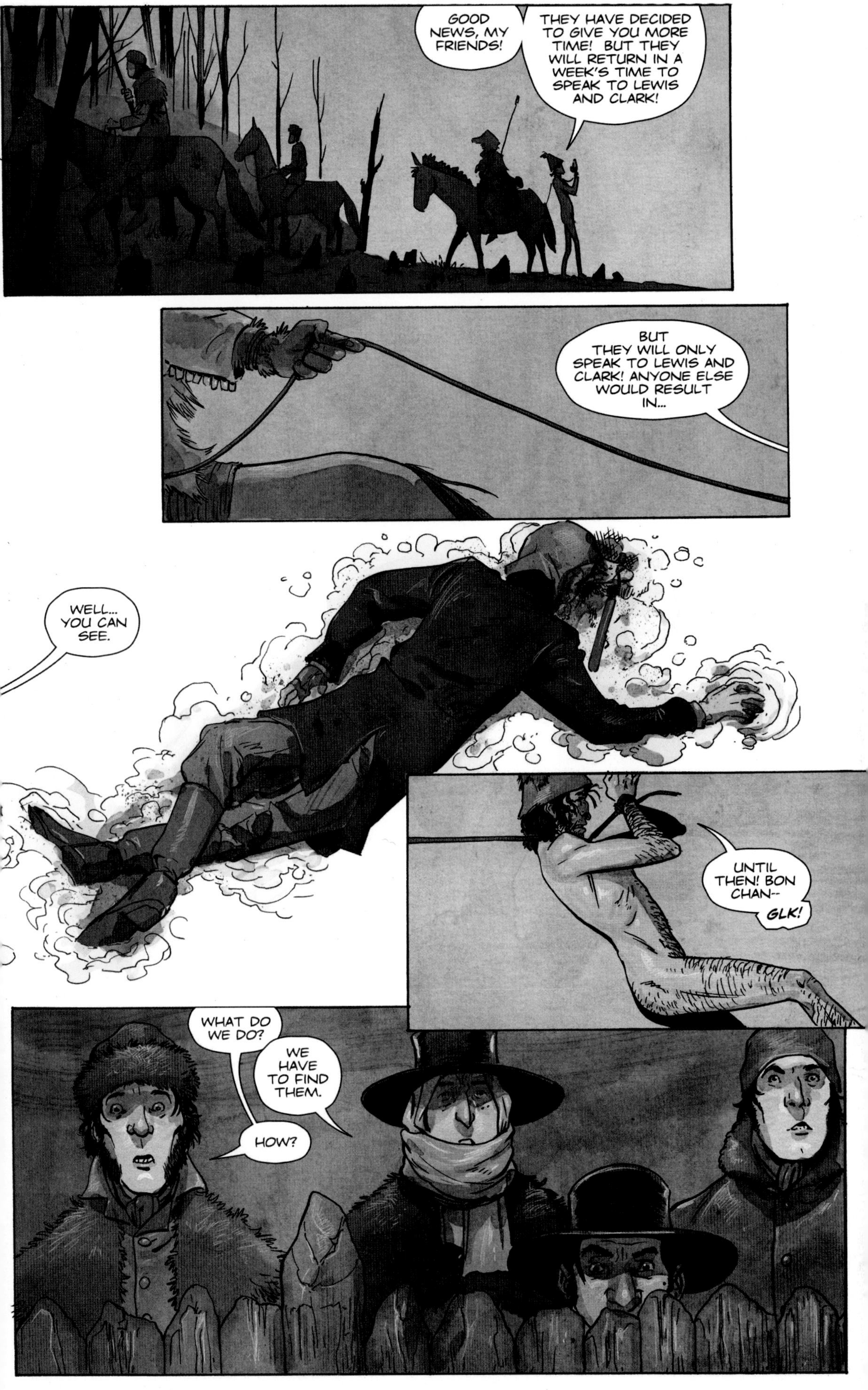
GOOD NEWS, MY FRIENDS!
THEY HAVE DECIDED TO GIVE YOU MORE TIME! BUT THEY WILL RETURN IN A WEEK'S TIME TO SPEAK TO LEWIS AND CLARK!
BUT THEY WILL ONLY SPEAK TO LEWIS AND CLARK! ANYONE ELSE WOULD RESULT IN...
WELL... YOU CAN SEE.
UNTIL THEN! BON CHAN--
GLK!
WHAT DO WE DO?
WE HAVE TO FIND THEM.
HOW?

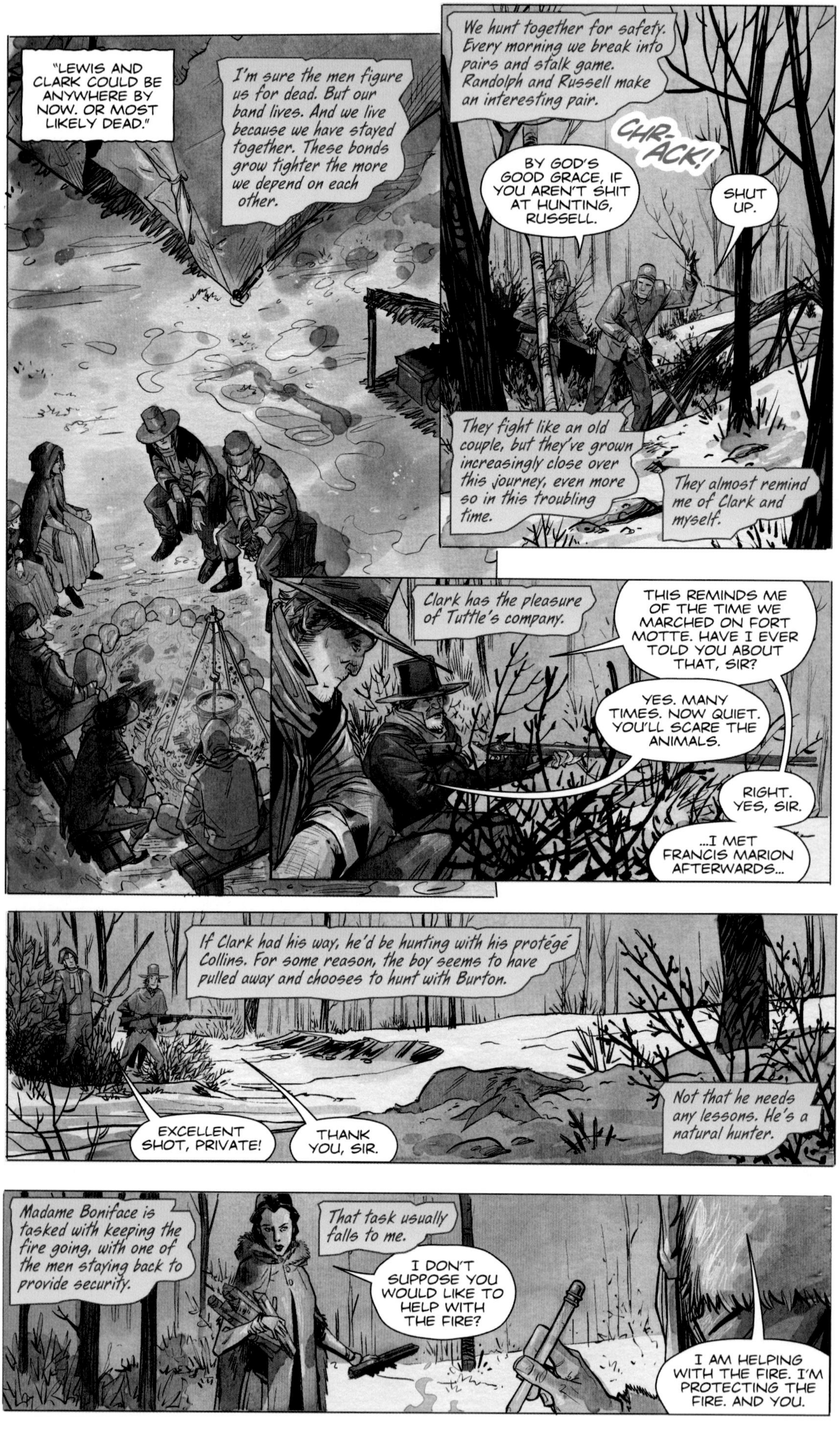
"LEWIS AND CLARK COULD BE ANYWHERE BY NOW. OR MOST LIKELY DEAD."
I'm sure the men figure us for dead. But our band lives. And we live because we have stayed together. These bonds grow tighter the more we depend on each other.
We hunt together for safety. Every morning we break into pairs and stalk game. Randolph and Russell make an interesting pair.
CHR-ACK!
BY GOD'S GOOD GRACE, IF YOU AREN'T SHIT AT HUNTING, RUSSELL.
SHUT UP.
They fight like an old couple, but they've grown increasingly close over this journey, even more so in this troubling time.
They almost remind me of Clark and myself.
Clark has the pleasure of Tuttle's company.
THIS REMINDS ME OF THE TIME WE MARCHED ON FORT MOTTE. HAVE I EVER TOLD YOU ABOUT THAT, SIR?
YES. MANY TIMES. NOW QUIET. YOU'LL SCARE THE ANIMALS.
RIGHT. YES, SIR.
...I MET FRANCIS MARION AFTERWARDS...
If Clark had his way, he'd be hunting with his protégé Collins. For some reason, the boy seems to have pulled away and chooses to hunt with Burton.
EXCELLENT SHOT, PRIVATE!
THANK YOU, SIR.
Not that he needs any lessons. He's a natural hunter.
Madame Boniface is tasked with keeping the fire going, with one of the men staying back to provide security.
That task usually falls to me.
I DON'T SUPPOSE YOU WOULD LIKE TO HELP WITH THE FIRE?
I AM HELPING WITH THE FIRE. I'M PROTECTING THE FIRE. AND YOU.

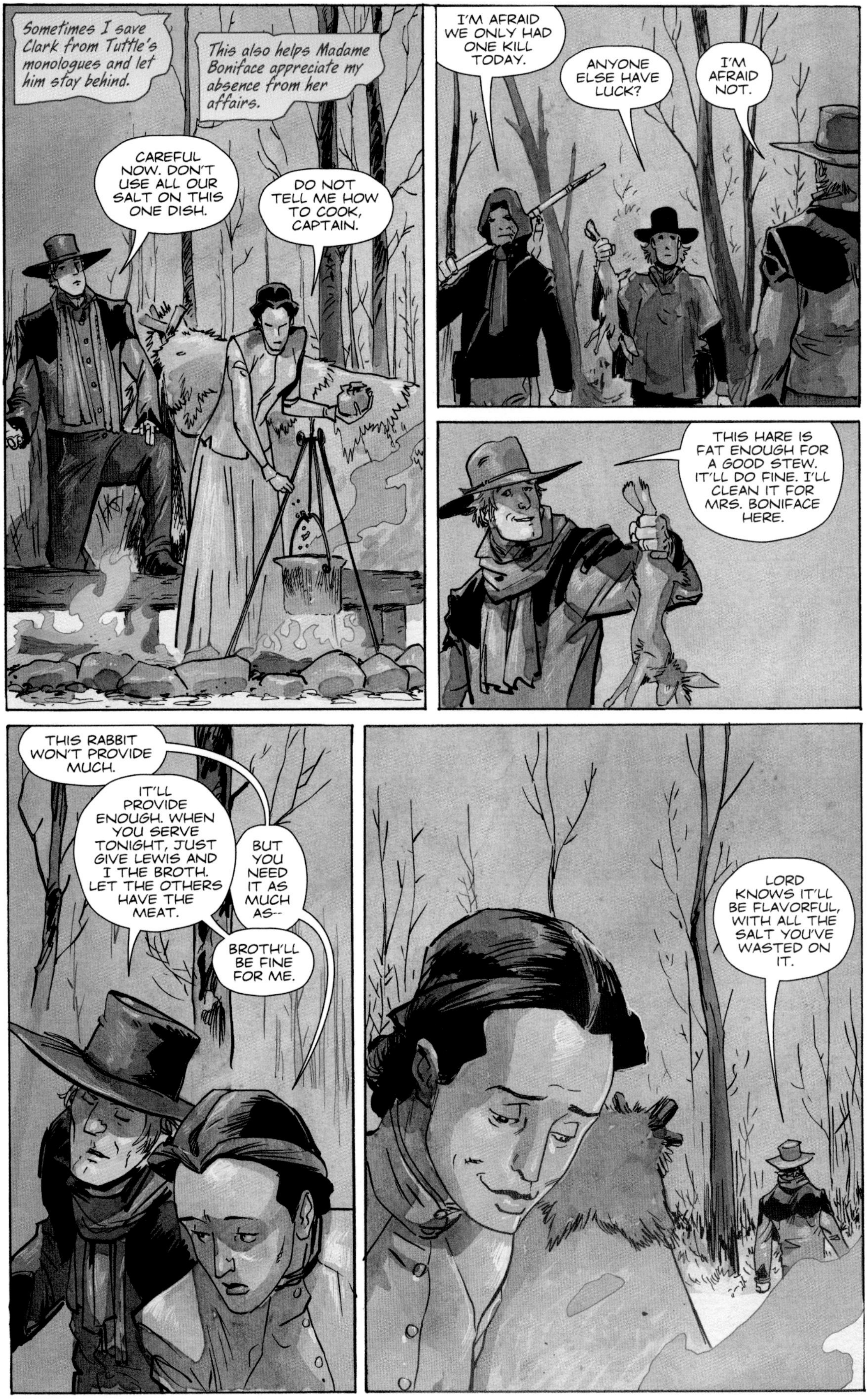
Sometimes I save Clark from Tuttle's monologues and let him stay behind.
This also helps Madame Boniface appreciate my absence from her affairs.
CAREFUL NOW. DON'T USE ALL OUR SALT ON THIS ONE DISH.
DO NOT TELL ME HOW TO COOK, CAPTAIN.
I'M AFRAID WE ONLY HAD ONE KILL TODAY.
ANYONE ELSE HAVE LUCK?
I'M AFRAID NOT.
THIS HARE IS FAT ENOUGH FOR A GOOD STEW. IT'LL DO FINE. I'LL CLEAN IT FOR MRS. BONIFACE HERE.
THIS RABBIT WON'T PROVIDE MUCH.
IT'LL PROVIDE ENOUGH. WHEN YOU SERVE TONIGHT, JUST GIVE LEWIS AND I THE BROTH. LET THE OTHERS HAVE THE MEAT.
BUT YOU NEED IT AS MUCH AS--
BROTH'LL BE FINE FOR ME.
LORD KNOWS IT'LL BE FLAVORFUL, WITH ALL THE SALT YOU'VE WASTED ON IT.

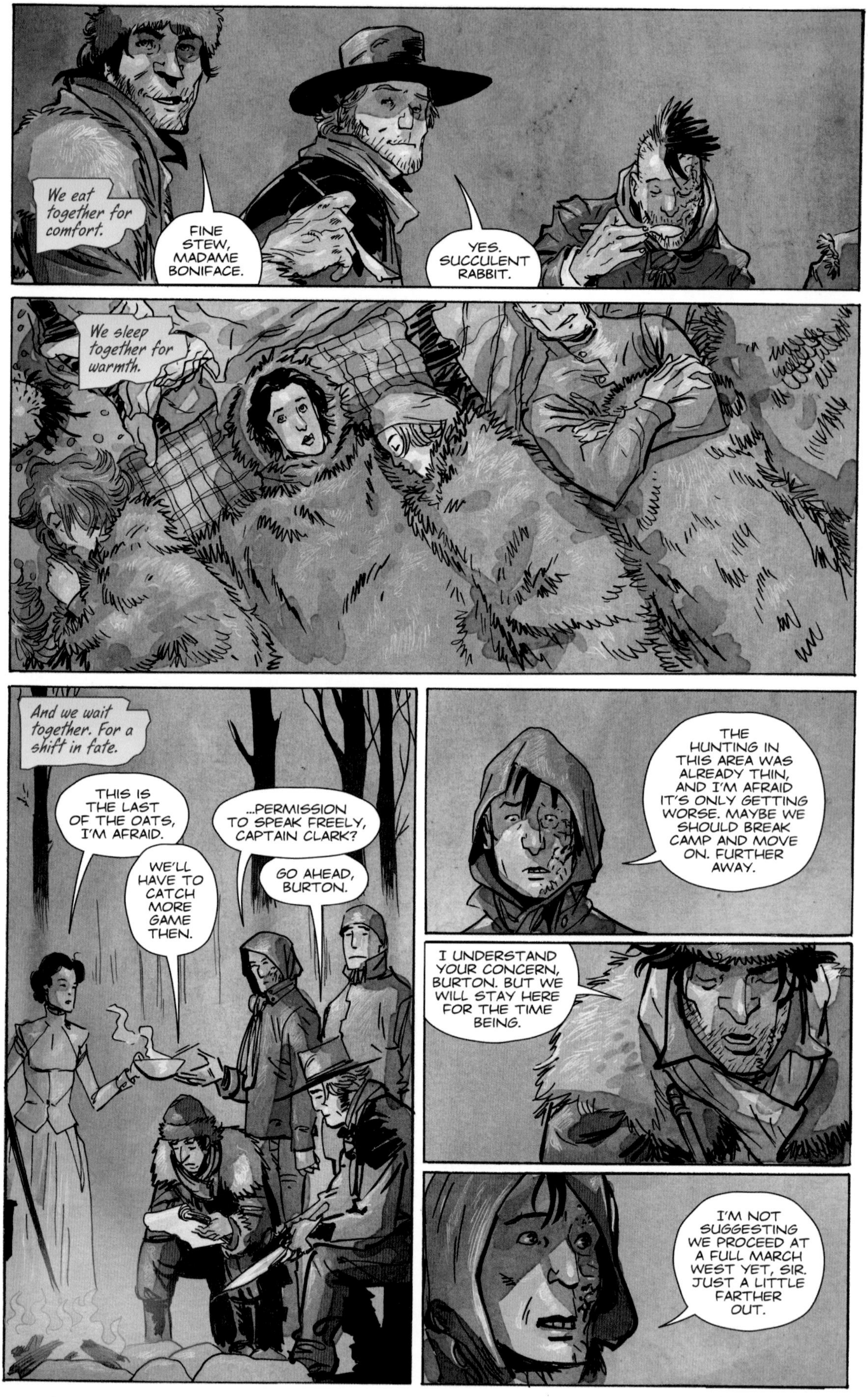

We eat together for comfort.
FINE STEW, MADAME BONIFACE.
YES. SUCCULENT RABBIT.
We sleep together for warmth.
And we wait together. For a shift in fate.
THIS IS THE LAST OF THE OATS, I'M AFRAID.
WE'LL HAVE TO CATCH MORE GAME THEN.
...PERMISSION TO SPEAK FREELY, CAPTAIN CLARK?
GO AHEAD, BURTON.
THE HUNTING IN THIS AREA WAS ALREADY THIN, AND I'M AFRAID IT'S ONLY GETTING WORSE. MAYBE WE SHOULD BREAK CAMP AND MOVE ON. FURTHER AWAY.
I UNDERSTAND YOUR CONCERN, BURTON. BUT WE WILL STAY HERE FOR THE TIME BEING.
I'M NOT SUGGESTING WE PROCEED AT A FULL MARCH WEST YET, SIR. JUST A LITTLE FARTHER OUT.

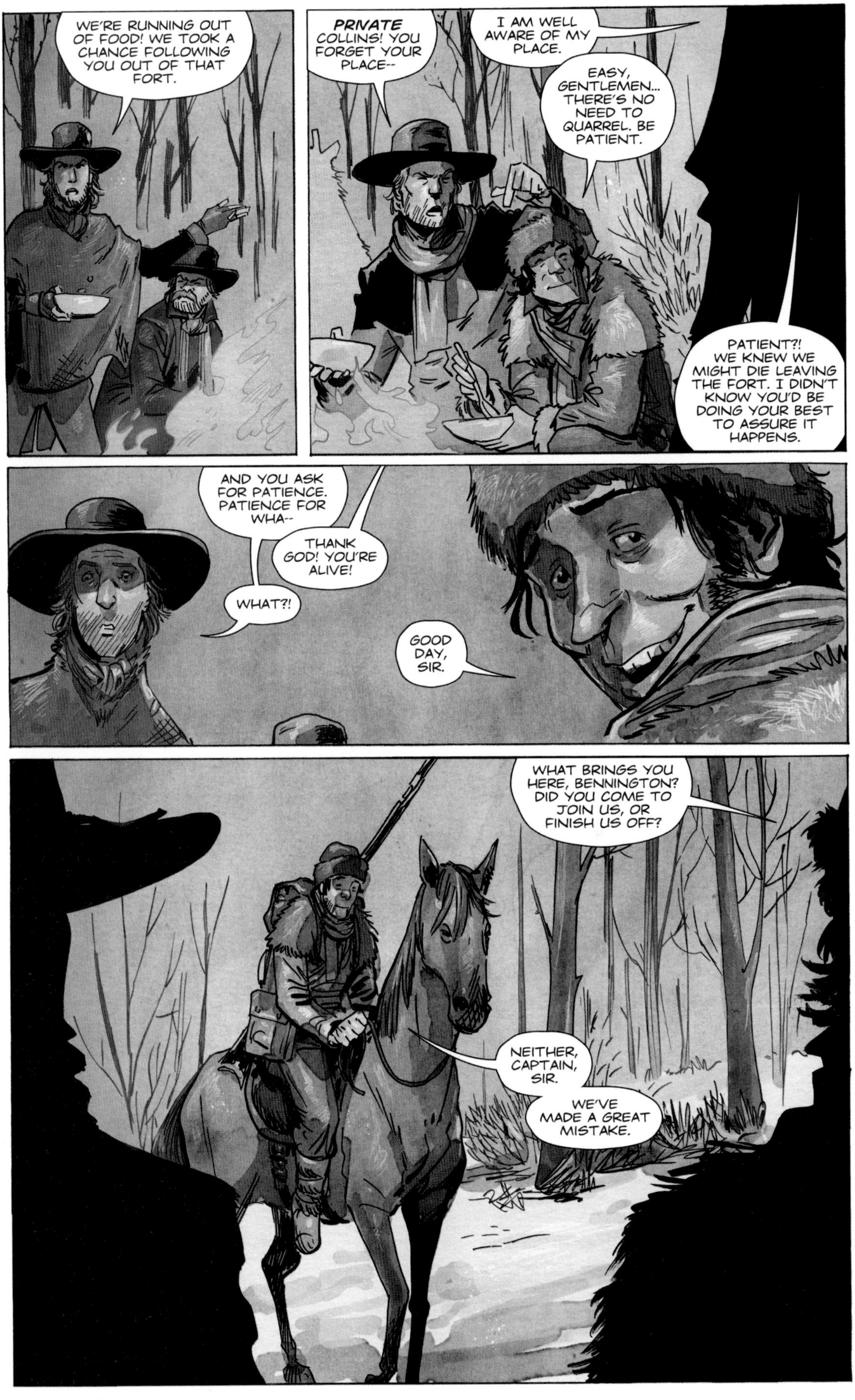
WE'RE RUNNING OUT OF FOOD! WE TOOK A CHANCE FOLLOWING YOU OUT OF THAT FORT.
PRIVATE COLLINS! YOU FORGET YOUR PLACE--
I AM WELL AWARE OF MY PLACE.
EASY, GENTLEMEN... THERE'S NO NEED TO QUARREL. BE PATIENT.
PATIENT?! WE KNEW WE MIGHT DIE LEAVING THE FORT. I DIDN'T KNOW YOU'D BE DOING YOUR BEST TO ASSURE IT HAPPENS.
AND YOU ASK FOR PATIENCE. PATIENCE FOR WHA--
THANK GOD! YOU'RE ALIVE!
WHAT?!
GOOD DAY, SIR.
WHAT BRINGS YOU HERE, BENNINGTON? DID YOU COME TO JOIN US, OR FINISH US OFF?
NEITHER, CAPTAIN, SIR.
WE'VE MADE A GREAT MISTAKE.

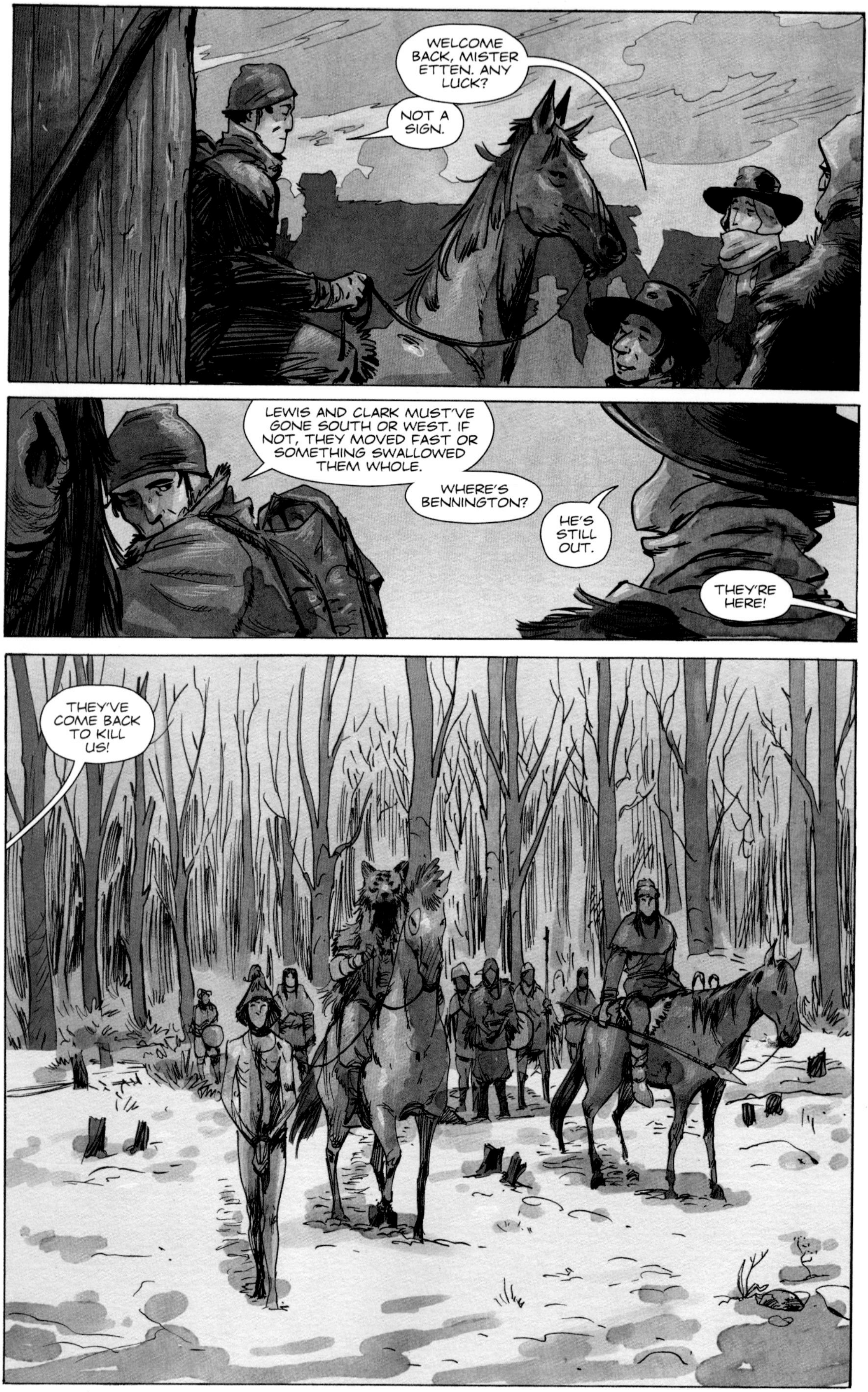
WELCOME BACK, MISTER ETTEN. ANY LUCK?
NOT A SIGN.
LEWIS AND CLARK MUST'VE GONE SOUTH OR WEST. IF NOT, THEY MOVED FAST OR SOMETHING SWALLOWED THEM WHOLE.
WHERE'S BENNINGTON?
HE'S STILL OUT.
THEY'RE HERE!
THEY'VE COME BACK TO KILL US!

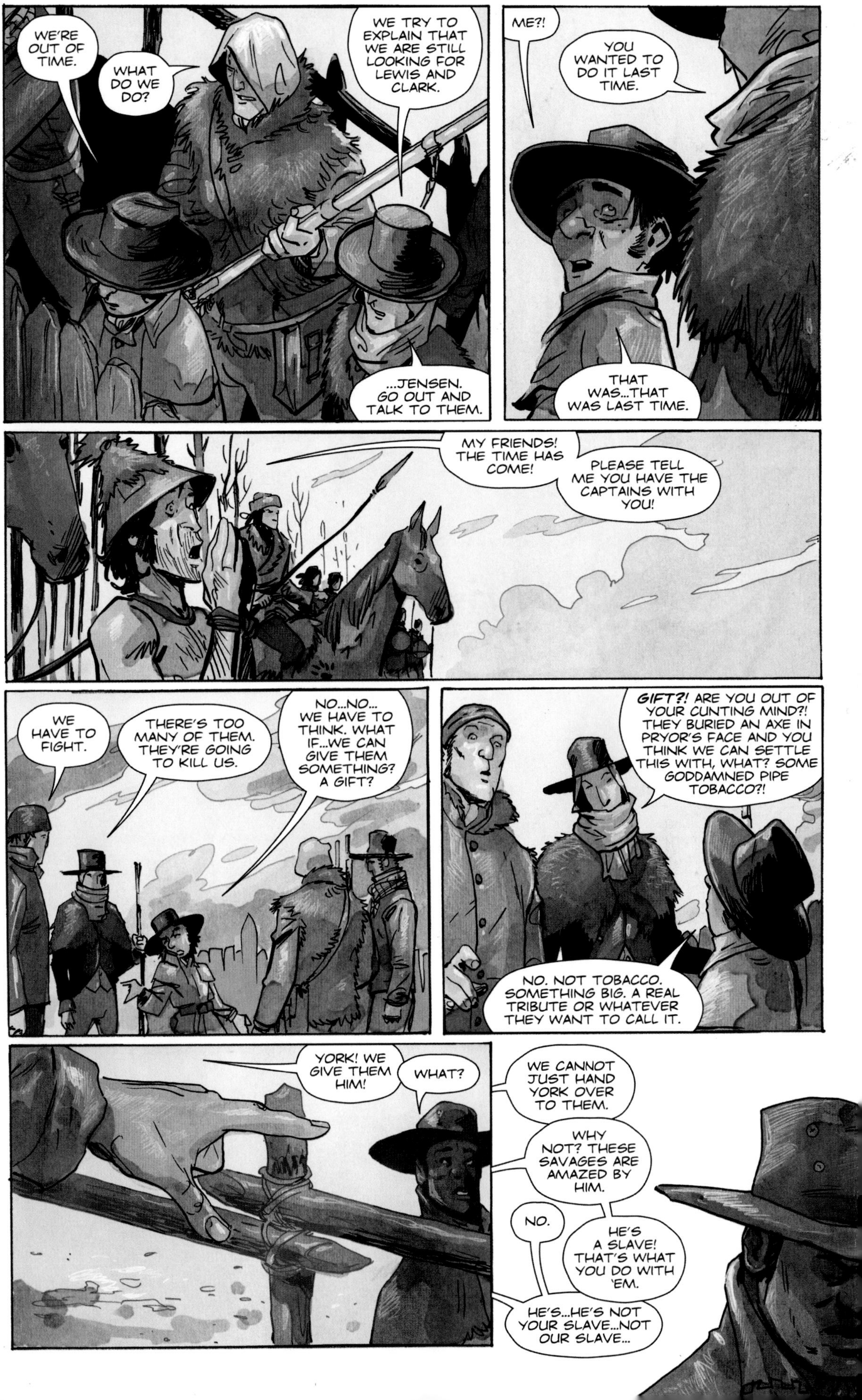
WE'RE OUT OF TIME.
WHAT DO WE DO?
WE TRY TO EXPLAIN THAT WE ARE STILL LOOKING FOR LEWIS AND CLARK.
...JENSEN. GO OUT AND TALK TO THEM.
ME?!
YOU WANTED TO DO IT LAST TIME.
THAT WAS...THAT WAS LAST TIME.
MY FRIENDS! THE TIME HAS COME!
PLEASE TELL ME YOU HAVE THE CAPTAINS WITH YOU!
WE HAVE TO FIGHT.
THERE'S TOO MANY OF THEM. THEY'RE GOING TO KILL US.
NO...NO... WE HAVE TO THINK. WHAT IF...WE CAN GIVE THEM SOMETHING? A GIFT?
GIFT?! ARE YOU OUT OF YOUR CUNTING MIND?! THEY BURIED AN AXE IN PRYOR'S FACE AND YOU THINK WE CAN SETTLE THIS WITH, WHAT? SOME GODDAMNED PIPE TOBACCO?!
NO. NOT TOBACCO. SOMETHING BIG. A REAL TRIBUTE OR WHATEVER THEY WANT TO CALL IT.
YORK! WE GIVE THEM HIM!
WHAT?
WE CANNOT JUST HAND YORK OVER TO THEM.
WHY NOT? THESE SAVAGES ARE AMAZED BY HIM.
NO.
HE'S A SLAVE! THAT'S WHAT YOU DO WITH 'EM.
HE'S...HE'S NOT YOUR SLAVE...NOT OUR SLAVE...

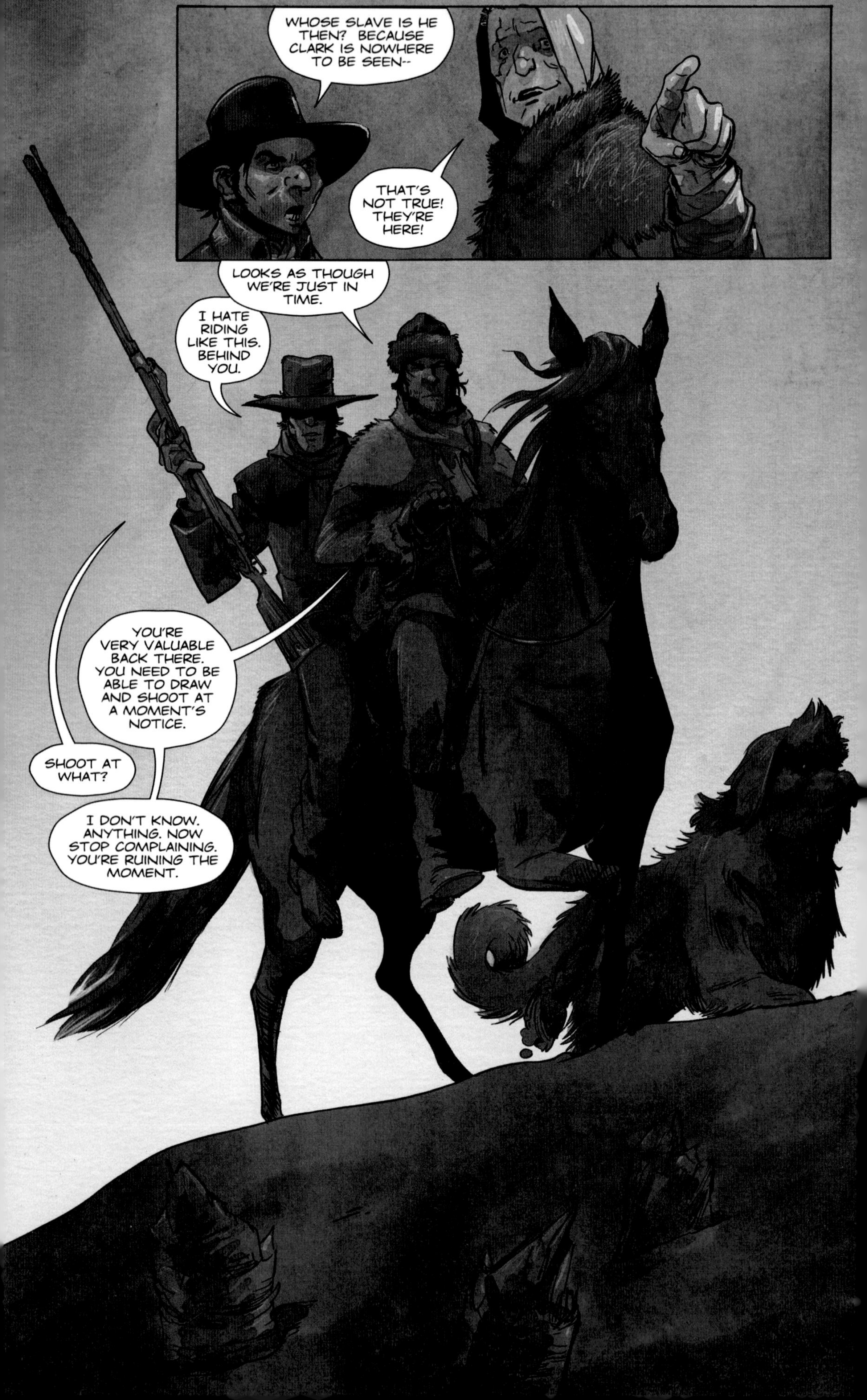
WHOSE SLAVE IS HE THEN? BECAUSE CLARK IS NOWHERE TO BE SEEN--
THAT'S NOT TRUE! THEY'RE HERE!
LOOKS AS THOUGH WE'RE JUST IN TIME.
I HATE RIDING LIKE THIS. BEHIND YOU.
YOU'RE VERY VALUABLE BACK THERE. YOU NEED TO BE ABLE TO DRAW AND SHOOT AT A MOMENT'S NOTICE.
SHOOT AT WHAT?
I DON'T KNOW. ANYTHING. NOW STOP COMPLAINING. YOU'RE RUINING THE MOMENT.

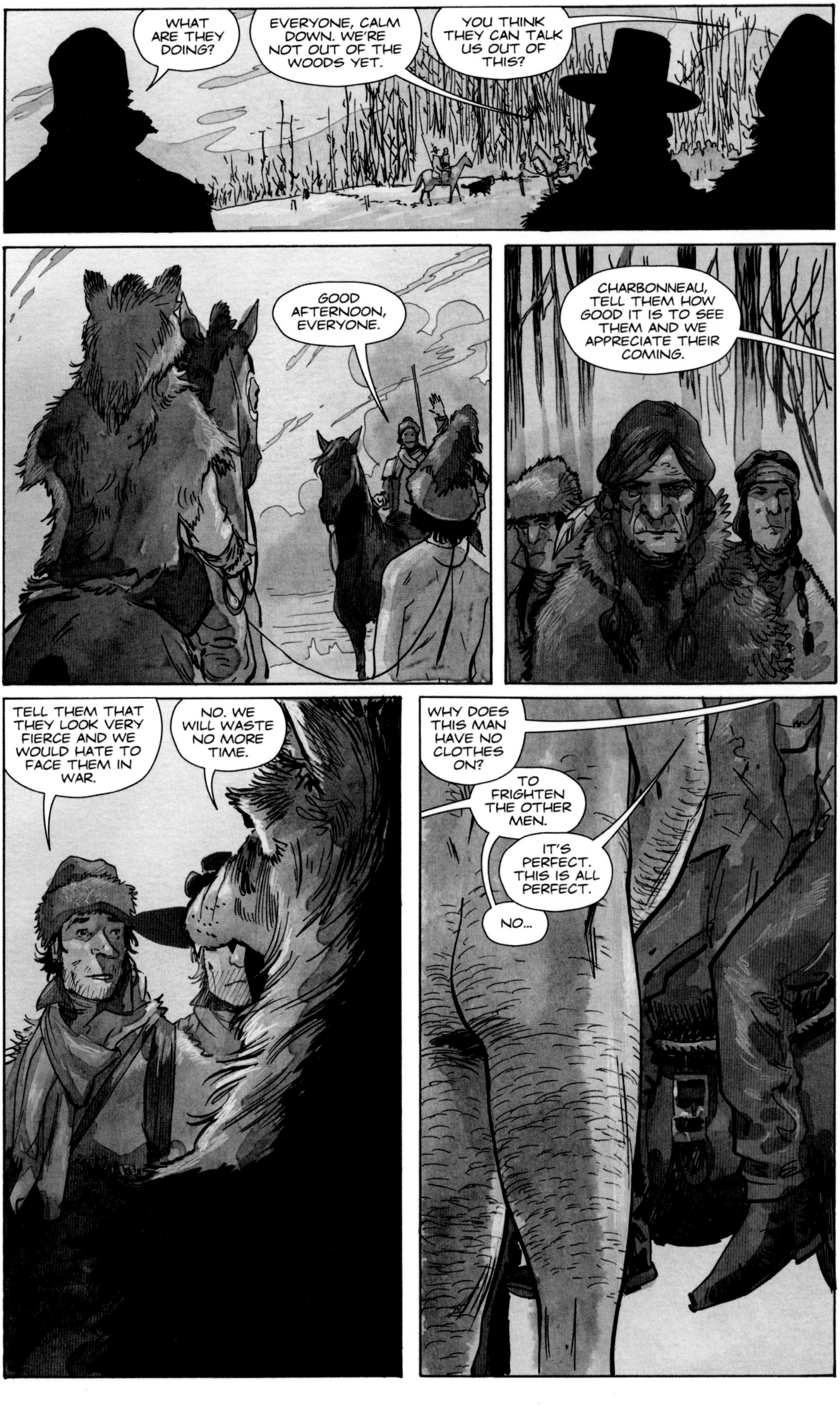

WHAT ARE THEY DOING?
EVERYONE, CALM DOWN. WE'RE NOT OUT OF THE WOODS YET.
YOU THINK THEY CAN TALK US OUT OF THIS?
GOOD AFTERNOON, EVERYONE.
CHARBONNEAU, TELL THEM HOW GOOD IT IS TO SEE THEM AND WE APPRECIATE THEIR COMING.
TELL THEM THAT THEY LOOK VERY FIERCE AND WE WOULD HATE TO FACE THEM IN WAR.
NO. WE WILL WASTE NO MORE TIME.
WHY DOES THIS MAN HAVE NO CLOTHES ON?
TO FRIGHTEN THE OTHER MEN.
IT'S PERFECT. THIS IS ALL PERFECT.
NO...

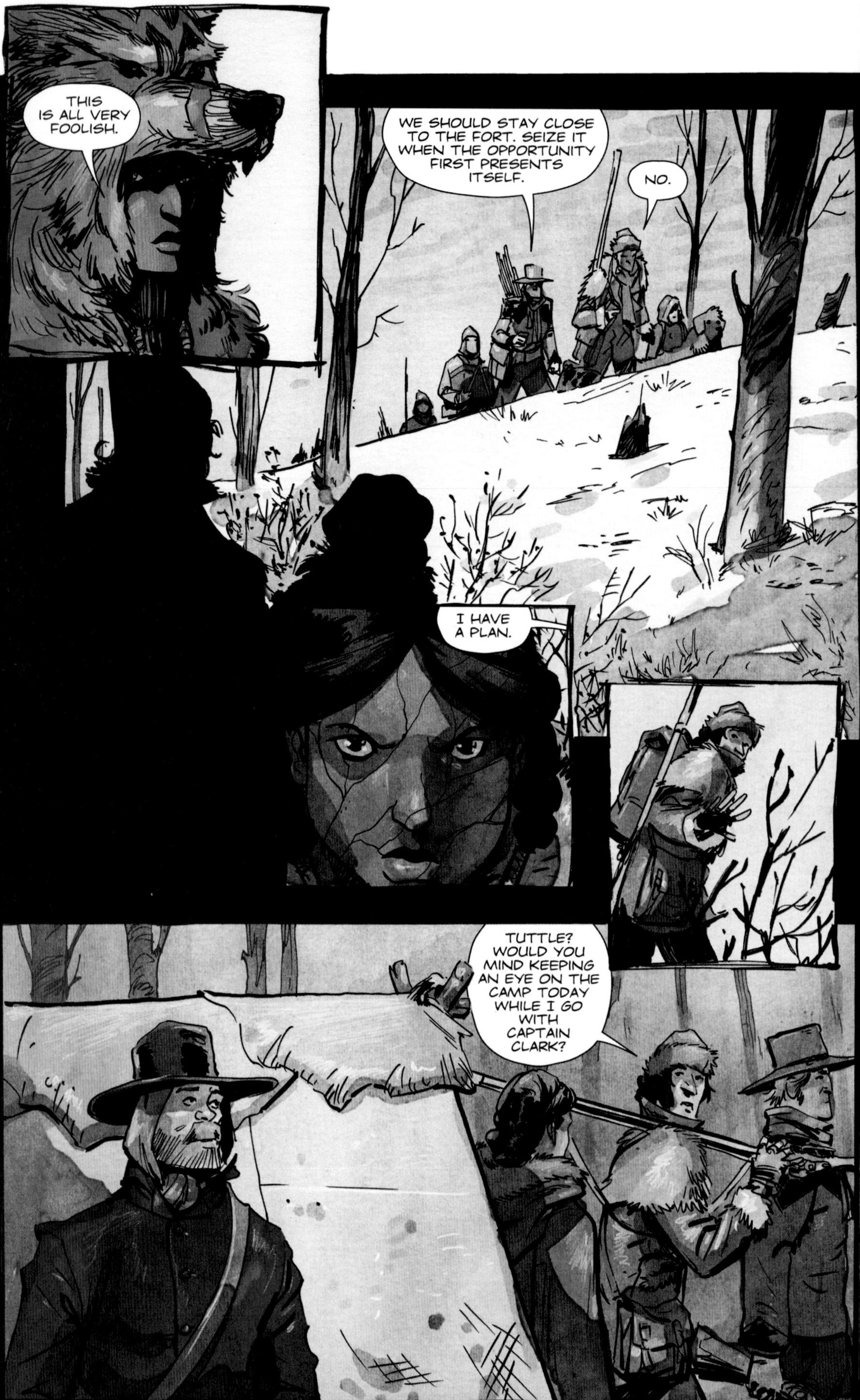
THIS IS ALL VERY FOOLISH.
WE SHOULD STAY CLOSE TO THE FORT. SEIZE IT WHEN THE OPPORTUNITY FIRST PRESENTS ITSELF.
NO.
I HAVE A PLAN.
TUTTLE? WOULD YOU MIND KEEPING AN EYE ON THE CAMP TODAY WHILE I GO WITH CAPTAIN CLARK?

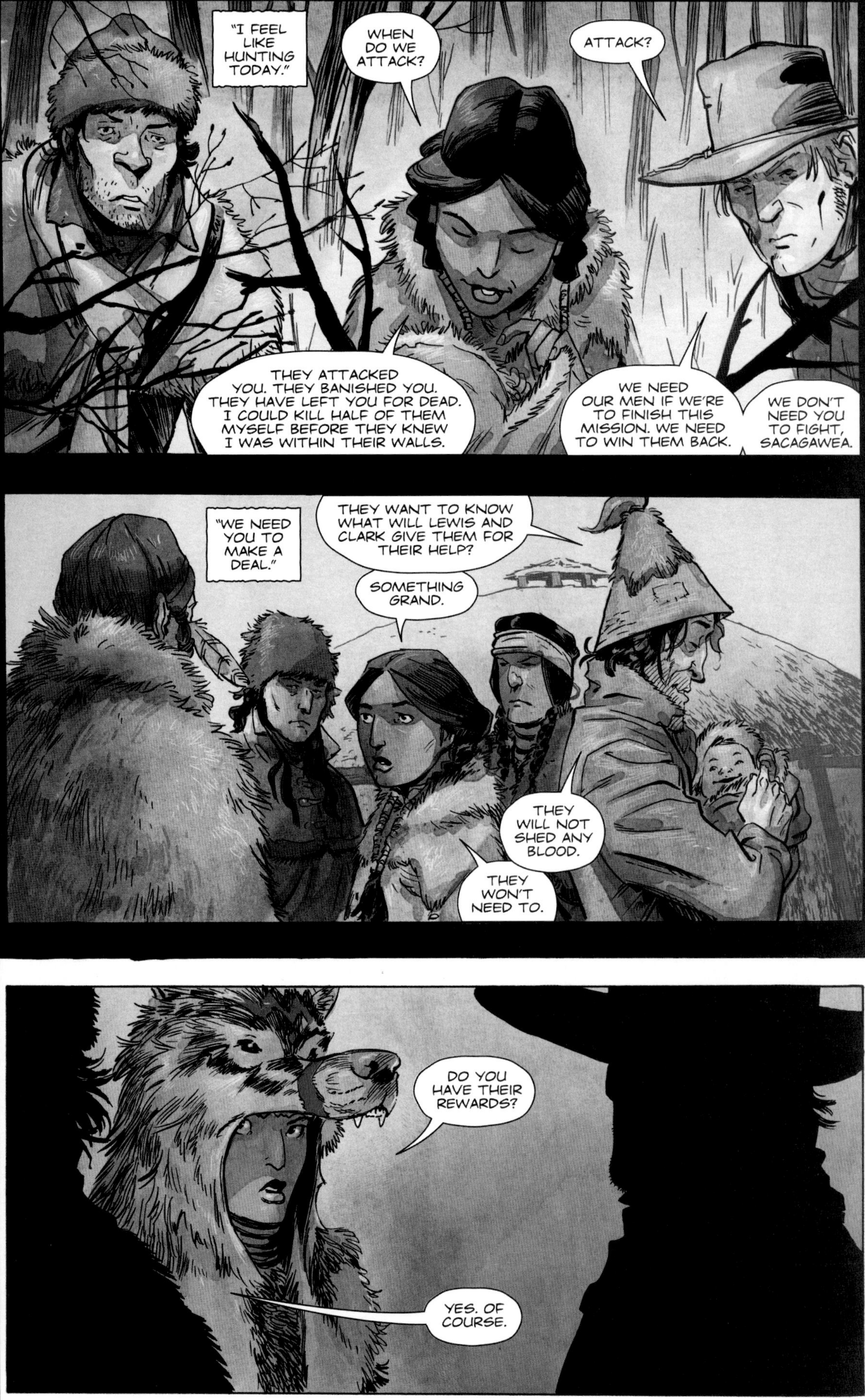

"I FEEL LIKE HUNTING TODAY."
WHEN DO WE ATTACK?
ATTACK?
THEY ATTACKED YOU. THEY BANISHED YOU. THEY HAVE LEFT YOU FOR DEAD. I COULD KILL HALF OF THEM MYSELF BEFORE THEY KNEW I WAS WITHIN THEIR WALLS.
WE NEED OUR MEN IF WE'RE TO FINISH THIS MISSION. WE NEED TO WIN THEM BACK.
WE DON'T NEED YOU TO FIGHT, SACAGAWEA.
"WE NEED YOU TO MAKE A DEAL."
THEY WANT TO KNOW WHAT WILL LEWIS AND CLARK GIVE THEM FOR THEIR HELP?
SOMETHING GRAND.
THEY WILL NOT SHED ANY BLOOD.
THEY WON'T NEED TO.
DO YOU HAVE THEIR REWARDS?
YES. OF COURSE.

WHAT ARE THEY DOING?

"LOOKS LIKE THEY'RE GIVIN' THEM THEIR HORSE BACK."

YOU PROMISED MORE THAN THIS HORSE.

I'M WELL AWARE OF THAT.

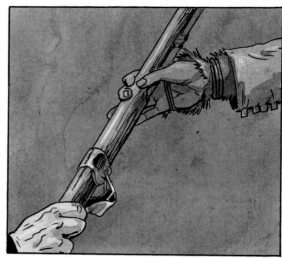

I THINK HE JUST GAVE THEM A RIFLE, TOO.

A RIFLE? CHRIST.

WHO CARES, AS LONG AS WE DON'T DIE IN THIS FORT.

LOOKS LIKE...IT LOOKS LIKE...

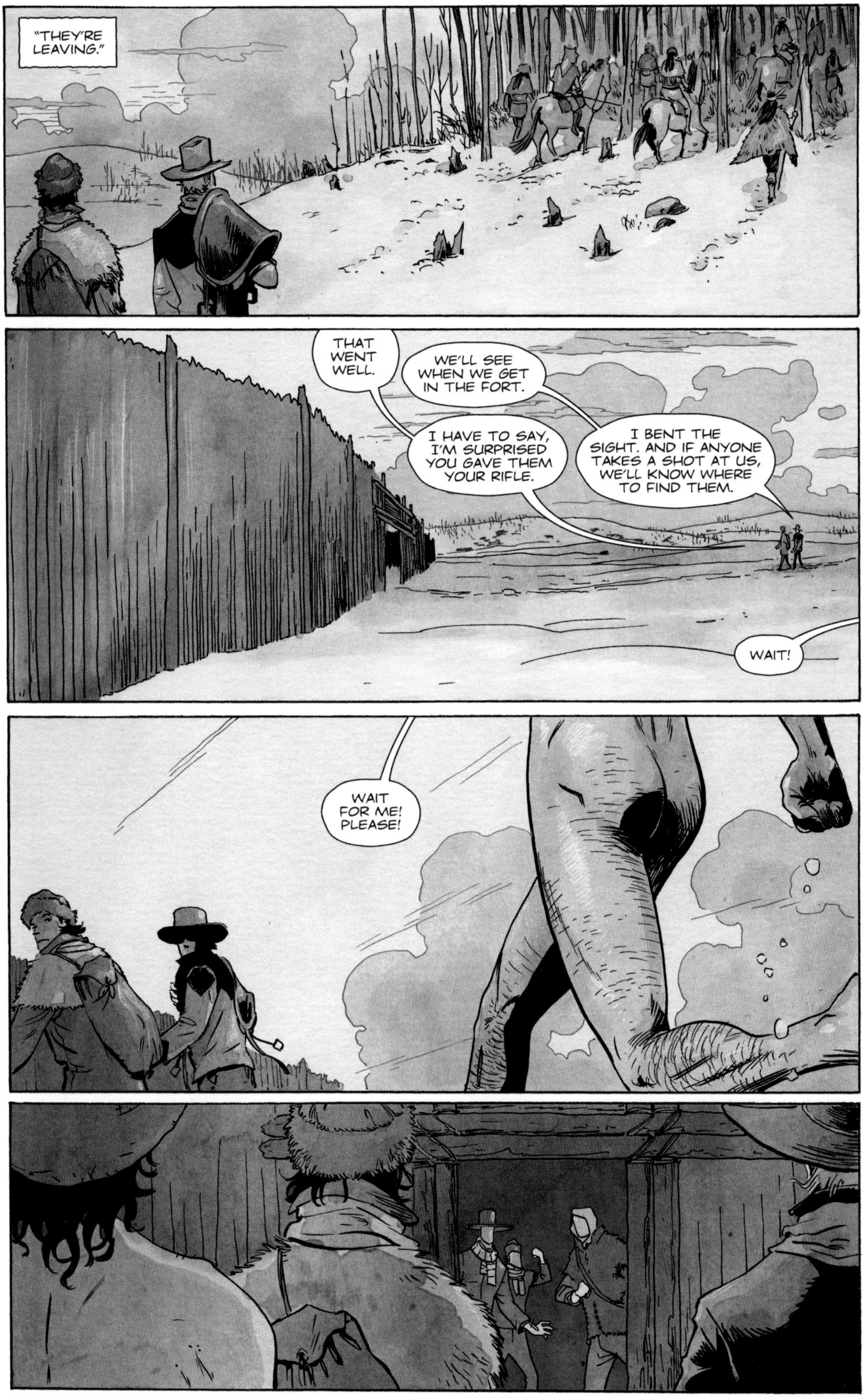
"THEY'RE LEAVING."
THAT WENT WELL.
WE'LL SEE WHEN WE GET IN THE FORT.
I HAVE TO SAY, I'M SURPRISED YOU GAVE THEM YOUR RIFLE.
I BENT THE SIGHT. AND IF ANYONE TAKES A SHOT AT US, WE'LL KNOW WHERE TO FIND THEM.
WAIT!
WAIT FOR ME! PLEASE!

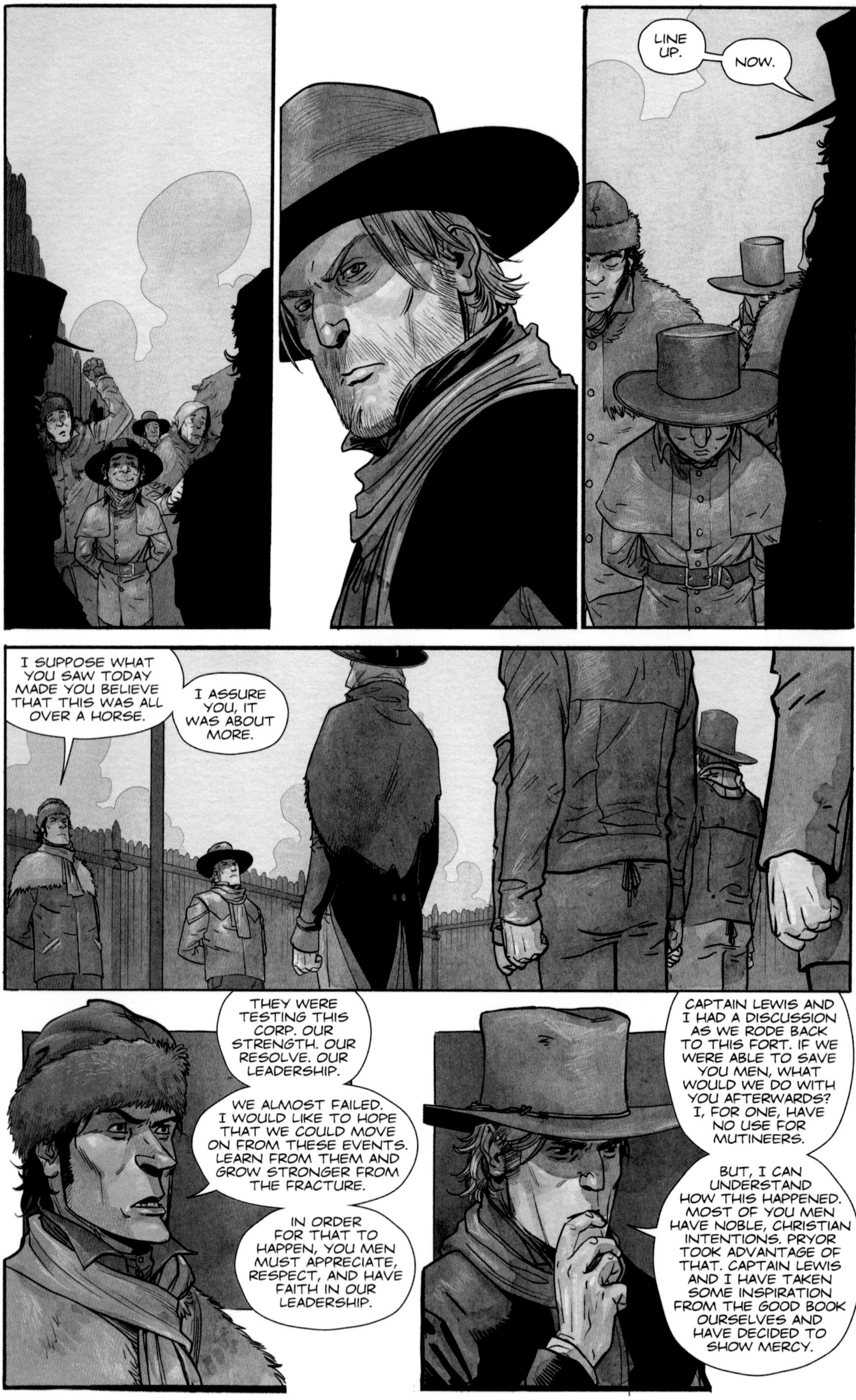
LINE UP.
NOW.
I SUPPOSE WHAT YOU SAW TODAY MADE YOU BELIEVE THAT THIS WAS ALL OVER A HORSE.
I ASSURE YOU, IT WAS ABOUT MORE.
THEY WERE TESTING THIS CORP. OUR STRENGTH. OUR RESOLVE. OUR LEADERSHIP.
WE ALMOST FAILED. I WOULD LIKE TO HOPE THAT WE COULD MOVE ON FROM THESE EVENTS. LEARN FROM THEM AND GROW STRONGER FROM THE FRACTURE.
IN ORDER FOR THAT TO HAPPEN, YOU MEN MUST APPRECIATE, RESPECT, AND HAVE FAITH IN OUR LEADERSHIP.
CAPTAIN LEWIS AND I HAD A DISCUSSION AS WE RODE BACK TO THIS FORT. IF WE WERE ABLE TO SAVE YOU MEN, WHAT WOULD WE DO WITH YOU AFTERWARDS? I, FOR ONE, HAVE NO USE FOR MUTINEERS.
BUT, I CAN UNDERSTAND HOW THIS HAPPENED. MOST OF YOU MEN HAVE NOBLE, CHRISTIAN INTENTIONS. PRYOR TOOK ADVANTAGE OF THAT. CAPTAIN LEWIS AND I HAVE TAKEN SOME INSPIRATION FROM THE GOOD BOOK OURSELVES AND HAVE DECIDED TO SHOW MERCY.

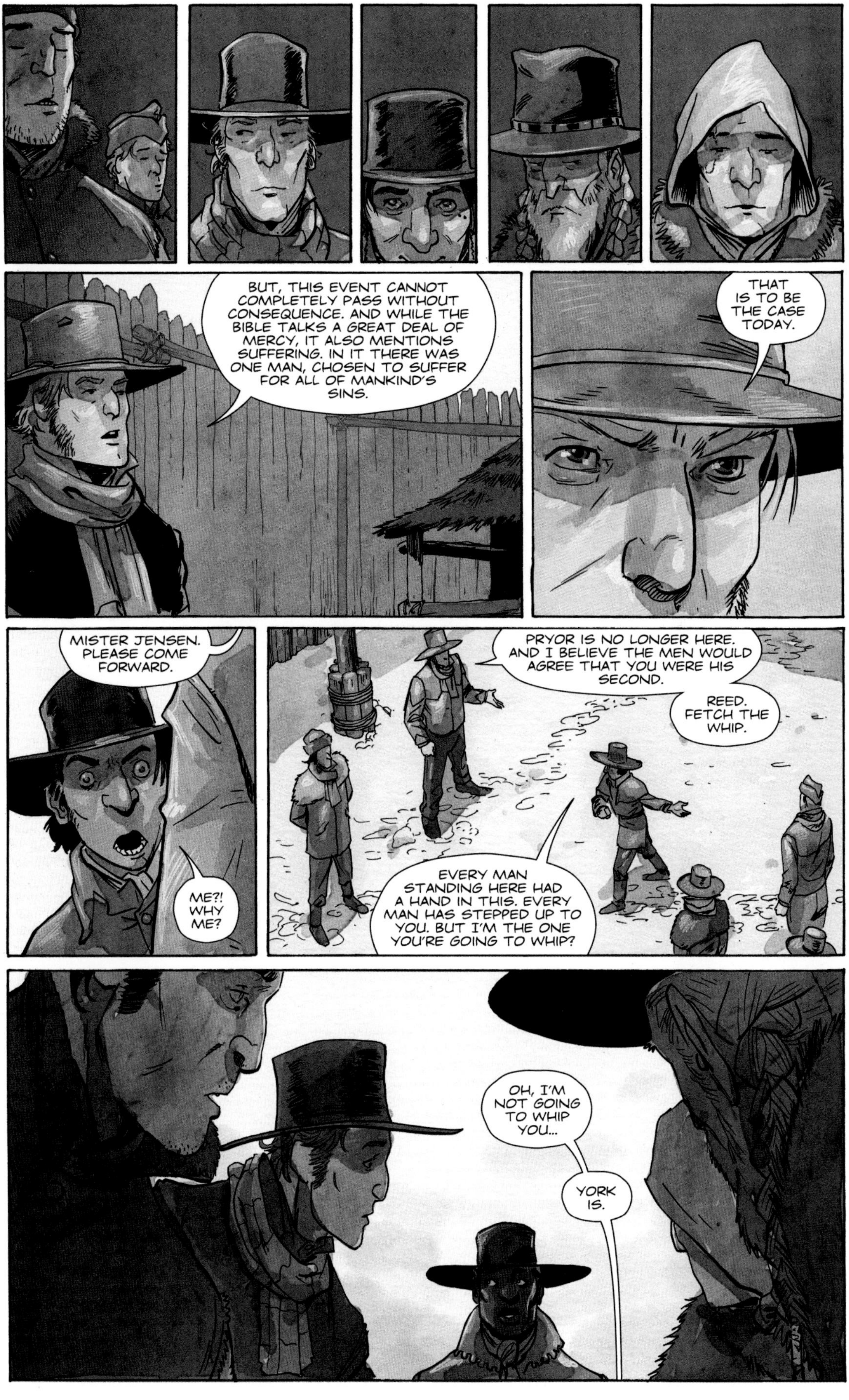
BUT, THIS EVENT CANNOT COMPLETELY PASS WITHOUT CONSEQUENCE. AND WHILE THE BIBLE TALKS A GREAT DEAL OF MERCY, IT ALSO MENTIONS SUFFERING. IN IT THERE WAS ONE MAN, CHOSEN TO SUFFER FOR ALL OF MANKIND'S SINS.
THAT IS TO BE THE CASE TODAY.
MISTER JENSEN. PLEASE COME FORWARD.
ME?! WHY ME?
PRYOR IS NO LONGER HERE. AND I BELIEVE THE MEN WOULD AGREE THAT YOU WERE HIS SECOND.
REED. FETCH THE WHIP.
EVERY MAN STANDING HERE HAD A HAND IN THIS. EVERY MAN HAS STEPPED UP TO YOU. BUT I'M THE ONE YOU'RE GOING TO WHIP?
OH, I'M NOT GOING TO WHIP YOU...
YORK IS.

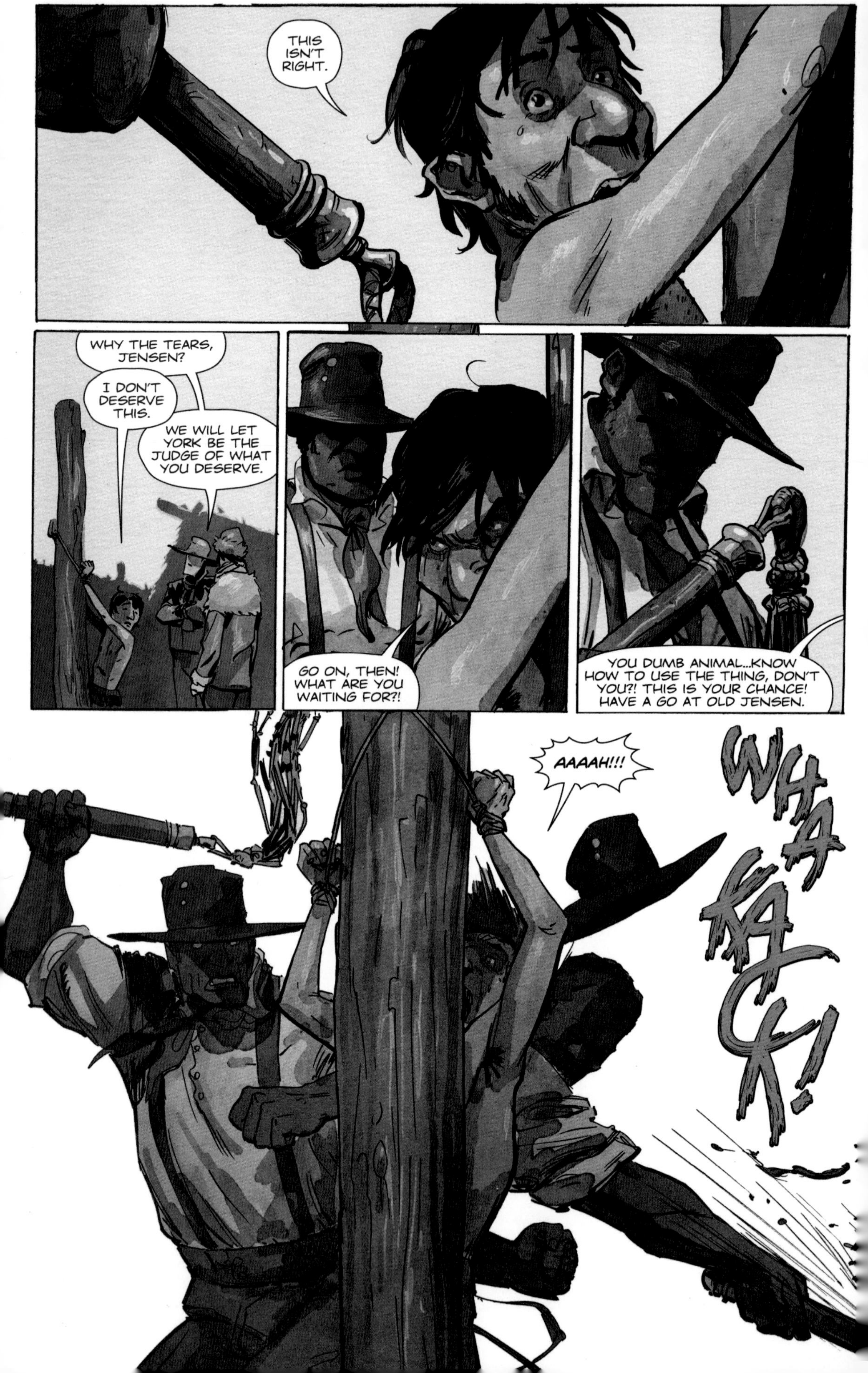
THIS ISN'T RIGHT.
WHY THE TEARS, JENSEN?
I DON'T DESERVE THIS.
WE WILL LET YORK BE THE JUDGE OF WHAT YOU DESERVE.
GO ON, THEN! WHAT ARE YOU WAITING FOR?!
YOU DUMB ANIMAL...KNOW HOW TO USE THE THING, DON'T YOU?! THIS IS YOUR CHANCE! HAVE A GO AT OLD JENSEN.
AAAAH!!!
WHAKACK!

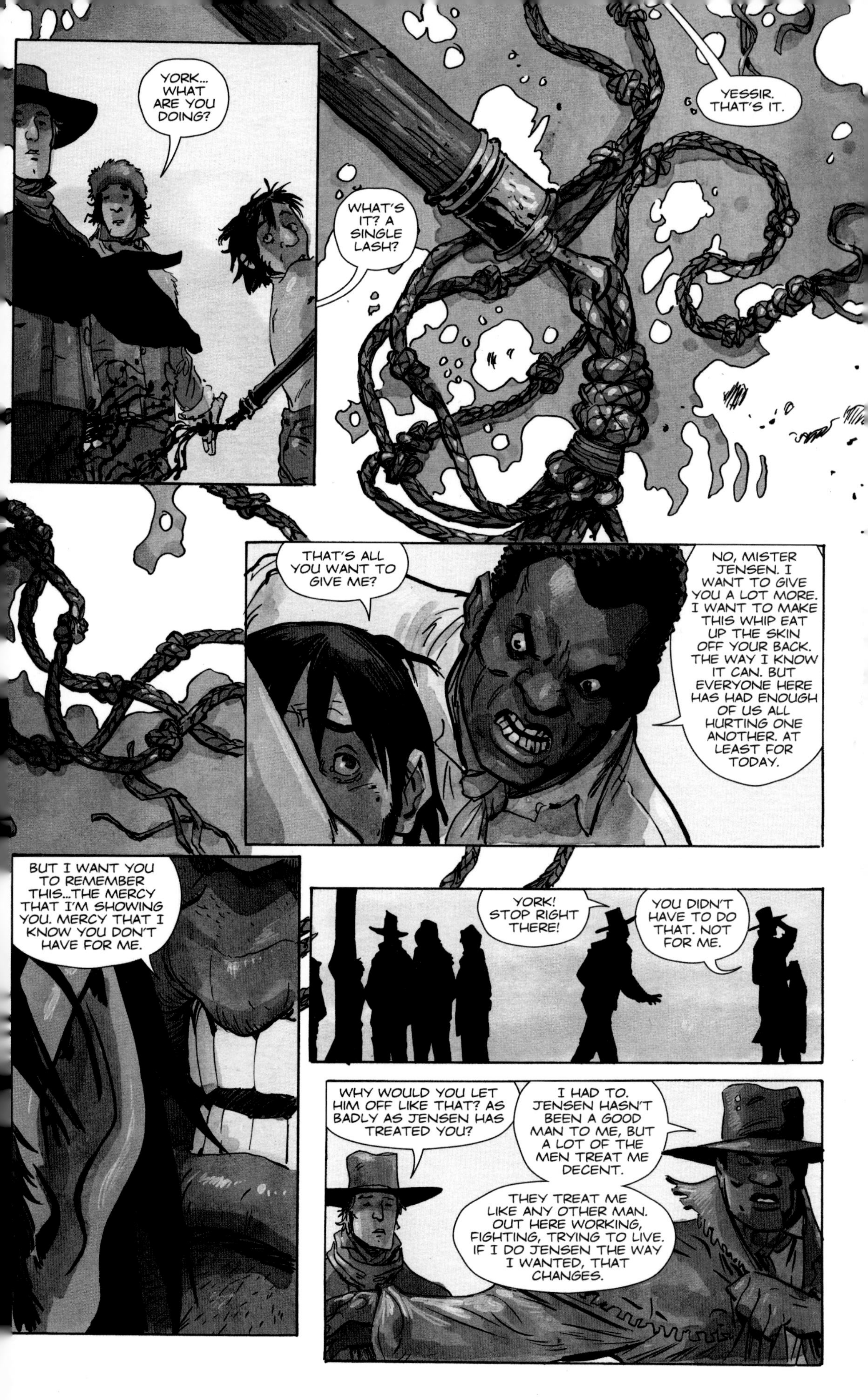
YORK... WHAT ARE YOU DOING?
YESSIR. THAT'S IT.
WHAT'S IT? A SINGLE LASH?
THAT'S ALL YOU WANT TO GIVE ME?
NO, MISTER JENSEN. I WANT TO GIVE YOU A LOT MORE. I WANT TO MAKE THIS WHIP EAT UP THE SKIN OFF YOUR BACK. THE WAY I KNOW IT CAN. BUT EVERYONE HERE HAS HAD ENOUGH OF US ALL HURTING ONE ANOTHER. AT LEAST FOR TODAY.
BUT I WANT YOU TO REMEMBER THIS...THE MERCY THAT I'M SHOWING YOU. MERCY THAT I KNOW YOU DON'T HAVE FOR ME.
YORK! STOP RIGHT THERE!
YOU DIDN'T HAVE TO DO THAT. NOT FOR ME.
WHY WOULD YOU LET HIM OFF LIKE THAT? AS BADLY AS JENSEN HAS TREATED YOU?
I HAD TO. JENSEN HASN'T BEEN A GOOD MAN TO ME, BUT A LOT OF THE MEN TREAT ME DECENT.
THEY TREAT ME LIKE ANY OTHER MAN. OUT HERE WORKING, FIGHTING, TRYING TO LIVE. IF I DO JENSEN THE WAY I WANTED, THAT CHANGES.

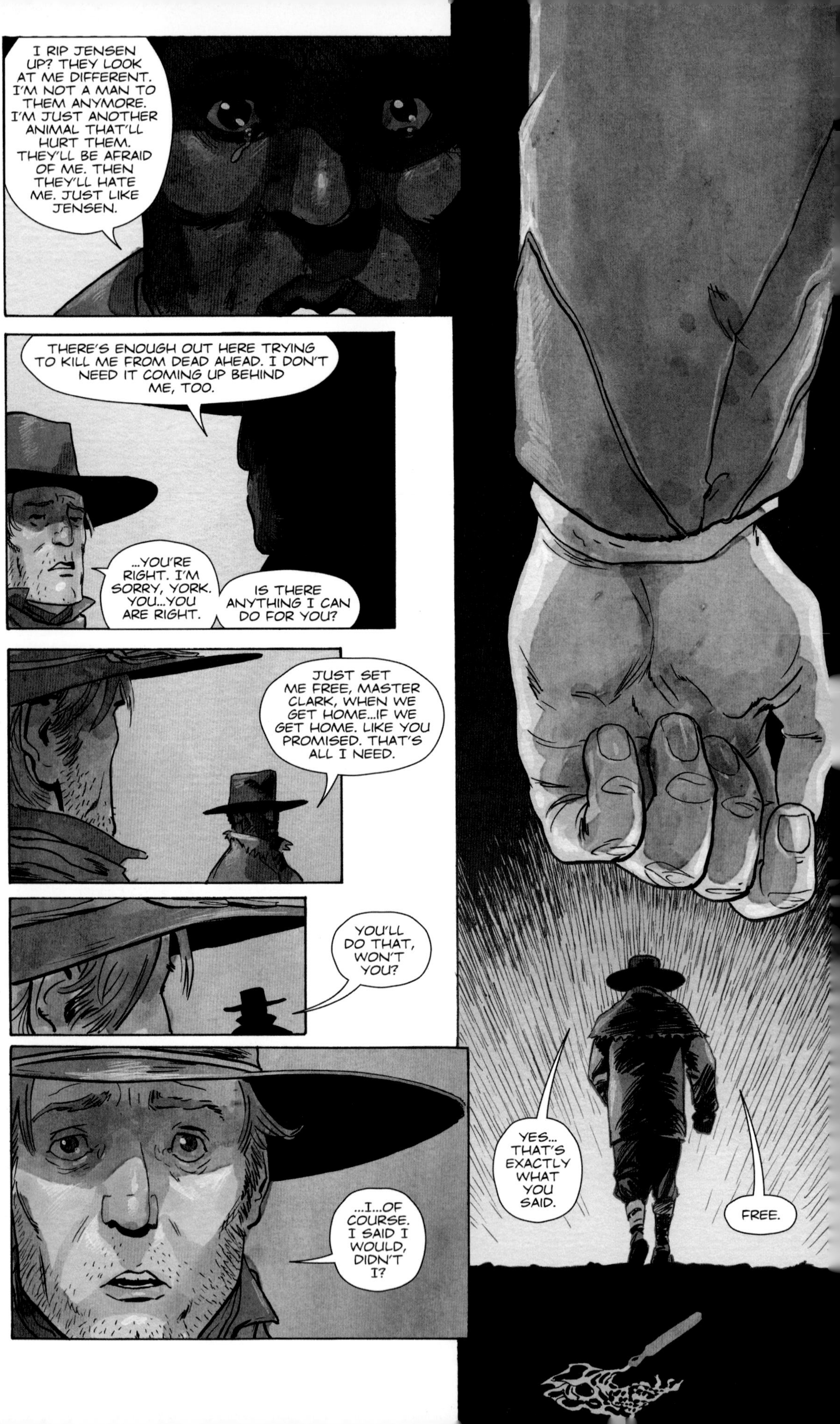
I RIP JENSEN UP? THEY LOOK AT ME DIFFERENT. I'M NOT A MAN TO THEM ANYMORE. I'M JUST ANOTHER ANIMAL THAT'LL HURT THEM. THEY'LL BE AFRAID OF ME. THEN THEY'LL HATE ME. JUST LIKE JENSEN.
THERE'S ENOUGH OUT HERE TRYING TO KILL ME FROM DEAD AHEAD. I DON'T NEED IT COMING UP BEHIND ME, TOO.
...YOU'RE RIGHT. I'M SORRY, YORK. YOU...YOU ARE RIGHT.
IS THERE ANYTHING I CAN DO FOR YOU?
JUST SET ME FREE, MASTER CLARK, WHEN WE GET HOME...IF WE GET HOME. LIKE YOU PROMISED. THAT'S ALL I NEED.
YOU'LL DO THAT, WON'T YOU?
...I...OF COURSE. I SAID I WOULD, DIDN'T I?
YES... THAT'S EXACTLY WHAT YOU SAID.
FREE.

To be continued...

❖ TRANSLATION ❖
GUIDE

Page 23

Quand ils travaillent...

Ils me regardent.

Pendant qu'ils mangent...

Ils me regardent.

Written in pencil:
Ils se croient malins. Ils croient que je ne les vois pas.

~~~~~~~~~~~~~~~~~~~~~~~~~~~

Page 24

Mais je sais.

Je sens leurs regards

Je voudrais me cacher. Leur échapper. Mais c'est impossible. Et je dois faire semblant de les ignorer. Alors, je tente de m'occuper.

Si j'ai l'air occupé, peut-être qu'ils ne m'adresseront pas la parole.

Quand ils me parlent, ils s'approchent de moi.

~~~~~~~~~~~~~~~~~~~~~~~~~~~

Page 25

C'est pour ça que je trouve chaque jour quelque chose à faire.

Tous les matins, je prépare le petit déjeuner avec Madame Grenier.

Page 23

When they work...

They watch me.

When they eat...

They watch me.

Written in pencil:
They think they are clever. They think I don't see.

~~~~~~~~~~~~~~~~~~~~~~~~~~~

Page 24

But I know.

I can feel their eyes.

I would hide from them. But that is impossible. And so I must try to ignore them. I try to keep occupied.

If I appear busy. They might not speak to me.

When they speak to me, they get close.

~~~~~~~~~~~~~~~~~~~~~~~~~~~

Page 25

And so, I keep every day filled with activity.

I start the breakfast every morning with Madame Grenier.

J'amène son petit déjeuner au Capitaine Lewis.

Madame Boniface a insisté pour que je poursuive mes études. C'est elle qui me fait écrire cela.

Avant, je détestais écrire. Maintenant, j'aime le temps que cela prend. Je peux me cacher et m'évader grâce aux mots.

~~~~~~~~~~~~~~~~~~~~~~~~~~~~

Page 26

Une fois que j'ai terminé d'étudier, j'accompagne Madame Boniface et nous nous occupons de l'indienne et de son bébé.

J'adore ce bébé. C'est lui qui m'apporte le plus de joie chaque jour.

Le soir, j'aide à nouveau Madame Grenier à tout ranger. Je me débrouille bien avec un couteau.

Ensuite, je vais au lit. Mais je ne dors pas beaucoup. Mes rêves sont pleins de choses terrifiantes.

Pour un temps, j'ai été capable de garder toutes ces horreurs tapies au fond de moi, pendant que je dormais.

~~~~~~~~~~~~~~~~~~~~~~~~~~~~

Page 27

Mais le brouillard est venu. Et avec lui, les cauchemars qui assaillent dorénavant aussi mes heures d'éveil.

Je savais que c'était dingue. Je savais qu'il ne pouvait me pourchasser. Qu'il n'avait qu'une seule jambe.

I bring Captain Lewis his breakfast.

Madame Boniface has insisted that I continue my studies. She is the one making me write this.

I used to hate writing. But now I enjoy the time it takes. I can hide in writing.

~~~~~~~~~~~~~~~~~~~~~~~~~~~~

Page 26

After my studies, I go with Madame Boniface to tend the Indian girl and her baby.

I love the baby. He gives me the most happiness of the day.

At night. I help Madame Grenier again with evening mess. I am good with the knife now.

And then, bed. But I do not sleep much. My dreams are filled with a terror.

For a long time, I was able to keep the horror confined to sleeping hours.

~~~~~~~~~~~~~~~~~~~~~~~~~~~~

Page 27

The fog came. It brought the nightmare to my waking life.

Hardy. I knew it was insane. I knew he cannot chase me. That he had only one leg.

Mais peu importait. La peur avait pris le dessus.

Je m'étais cachée. Dans les latrines.

C'est là que les hommes m'ont trouvée au petit matin.

~~~~~~~~~~~~~~~~~~~~~~~~~~~~

Page 28

Je ne peux même pas imaginer à quoi je devais ressembler pour eux. Un animal. Ils étaient tous très gentils.

Mais ce n'est pas de la gentillesse que j'ai vue.

Je ne voyais que lui. Le brouillard fait voir des monstres. Et Hardy est mon monstre.

~~~~~~~~~~~~~~~~~~~~~~~~~~~~

Page 29

Les autres ont de la chance.

Lorsque le brouillard s'est levé, leurs cauchemars s'en sont allés avec lui.

Le mien est toujours là.

Et il est de plus en plus intense.

Comment puis-je m'enfuir?

~~~~~~~~~~~~~~~~~~~~~~~~~~~~

Page 31

J'aimerais tellement croire à ce que dit Madame Boniface.

Mais nous connaissons la vérité. Nous connaissons ces hommes.

I did not care. Fear was in control.

I hid. In the privet of all places.

That is where the men found me in the morning.

~~~~~~~~~~~~~~~~~~~~~~~~~~~~

Page 28

I cannot image what I looked like to them. An animal. They were all kind.

But I did not see kindness.

I only saw him. The fog made the men see monsters. And Hardy is mine.

~~~~~~~~~~~~~~~~~~~~~~~~~~~~

Page 29

The others here are fortunate.

When the fog left, so did their nightmares.

Mine is still here.

And he is getting stronger.

How long can I run?

~~~~~~~~~~~~~~~~~~~~~~~~~~~~

Page 31

I wish I could believe Madame Boniface.

But we know the truth. We know these men.

Ils n'en ont rien à faire de moi. Je ne suis pas des leurs. Je ne sais pas me battre. Et ils n'ont même pas le droit de me baiser. Je ne leur suis d'aucune utilité.

They do not care about me. I am an outsider. I am not a fighter. And they are not allowed to fuck me. To them I am useless.

Mais Hardy était l'un d'entre eux. Il était fort. Il savait se battre. Il savait tirer. Il était utile.

But Hardy was one of them. He was strong. He could fight. He could shoot. He was useful.

Il est en train de guérir. Il pourrait à nouveau leur être utile. Et redevenir dangereux.

He is healing. He will be useful again. And dangerous.

Moi aussi j'ai envie de guérir. Pour ça, je sais ce qu'il me reste à faire.

I want to heal. I know what I must do.

~~~~~~~~~~~~~~~~~~~~~~~

~~~~~~~~~~~~~~~~~~~~~~~

Page 34

Page 34

Je sais ce que je dois faire. Je sais comment le faire. Mais pas quand.

I know what I must do. And I know how. But when?

Je dois être patiente. Il est déterminé. Mais moi aussi.

I will wait. He is determined. But I am determined now as well.

Il travaille. Il devient plus fort. Certains hommes l'encouragent, même.

He keeps working. Getting stronger. Some of the men even cheer him on.

Les hommes accueillent un autre soldat.

The men welcome another soldier.

Il veut se prouver à lui-même qu'il est utile, et avec le temps, ils lui redonneront sa chance. Ça commence avec des tâches simples. Ils lui permettent de monter la garde. Mais Clark refuse de lui confier une arme.

He wants to prove himself, and in time they give him the chance. It starts with light duty. He is allowed to keep watch, but Clark refuses to give him a gun.

Clark sait ce que je sais.

Clark knows what I know.

Written in pencil:
Le moment est venu.

Written in pencil:
The time has come.

For more tales from Robert Kirkman and Skybound

ROBERT KIRKMAN
LORENZO DE FELICI
ANNALISA LEONI
OBLIVION SONG
CHAPTER ONE

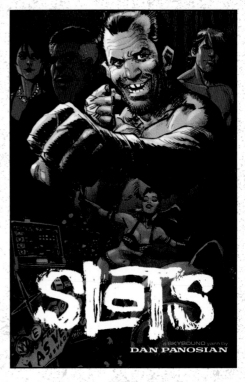

CHAPTER ONE TP
ISBN: 978-1-5343-0642-4
$ 9.99

SLOTS
a SKYBOUND yarn by
DAN PANOSIAN

SLOTS TP
ISBN: 978-1-5343-0655-4
$16.99

BIRTHRIGHT

VOL. 1: HOMECOMING TP
ISBN: 978-1-63215-231-2
$9.99

VOL. 2: CALL TO ADVENTURE TP
ISBN: 978-1-63215-446-0
$12.99

VOL. 3: ALLIES AND ENEMIES TP
ISBN: 978-1-63215-683-9
$12.99

VOL. 4: FAMILY HISTORY TP
ISBN: 978-1-63215-871-0
$12.99

VOL. 5: BELLY OF THE BEAST TP
ISBN: 978-1-53430-218-1
$12.99

VOL. 6: FATHERHOOD TP
ISBN: 978-1-53430-498-7
$14.99

Daniel Warren Johnson Mike Spicer
EXTREMITY
WARRIOR

VOL. 1: ARTIST TP
ISBN: 978-1-5343-0242-6
$16.99

VOL. 2: WARRIOR TP
ISBN: 978-1-5343-0649-3
$16.99

VOLUME 6: INVASION
KIRKMAN
AZACETA
OUTCAST

VOL. 1: A DARKNESS SURROUNDS HIM TP
ISBN: 978-1-63215-053-0
$9.99

VOL. 2: A VAST AND UNENDING RUIN TP
ISBN: 978-1-63215-448-4
$14.99

VOL. 3: THIS LITTLE LIGHT TP
ISBN: 978-1-63215-693-8
$14.99

VOL. 4: UNDER DEVIL'S WING TP
ISBN: 978-1-5343-0050-7
$14.99

VOL. 5: THE NEW PATH TP
ISBN: 978-1-5343-0249-5
$16.99

VOL. 6: INVASION TP
ISBN: 978-1-5343-0751-3
$16.99

REDNECK
The Eyes Upon You

VOL. 1: DEEP IN THE HEART TP
ISBN: 978-1-5343-0331-7
$16.99

VOL. 2: THE EYES UPON YOU TP
ISBN: 978-1-5343-0665-3
$16.99